Michael Bond wa~~~~
wards his parents moved to Reading, seventeen ~~~~ ~~~~,
Fortunately they took the pram with them, but it did leave
their son with a taste for foreign travel.

Brought up in a home where books were part of the furniture, he discovered at an early age the first of the three 'R's.
School gave him the third – arithmetic – but, apart from a
hearty dislike of team games and Latin verbs, not a lot else.

Service with the RAF and the army during the Second
World War ensured he had all the foreign travel he needed for
a while. It also introduced him to the second 'R' when, suffering from a surfeit of sand-dunes in Egypt, he wrote a short
story which he sent to a magazine called *London Opinion*.
Acceptance not only proved that miracles sometimes happen,
but provided the key to a door which, equally miraculously in
his view, has remained open ever since.

MICHAEL BOND

BEARS &
FOREBEARS

A Life So Far

HarperCollins*Publishers*

HarperCollins*Publishers*
77–85 Fulham Palace Road,
Hammersmith, London W6 8JB

This paperback edition 199?
1 3 5 7 9 8 6 4 2

First published in Great Britain by
HarperCollins*Publishers* 199?

Copyright © Michael Bond 1996

The Author asserts the moral right to
be identified as the author of this work

ISBN 0 00 638771 3

Set in Goudy by
Rowland Phototypesetting Limited
Bury St Edmunds, Suffolk

Printed and bound in Great Britain by
Caledonian International Book Manufacturing Ltd, Glasgow

For my parents. A thank you.

CONTENTS

'Autobiography is history.'

Gore Vidal (1925–)

CHAPTER 1

Boys Will Be Boys

Boys do not grow up gradually. They move forward
in spurts like the hands of clocks on railway stations.

Cyril Connolly (1903–74)

I was born on Wednesday, 13 January 1926, at 2 Edinburgh Terrace,
one of a row of cottages lining the bank of the Kennet and Avon Canal
in Newbury, Berkshire; a market town situated some sixty miles west of
London, known locally for its cattle market and famous nationally for
its racecourse.

I weighed over eleven pounds at birth. My mother must have decided
enough was enough for I remained an only child, and I can't say I blame
her. When I began to grow she took to standing me in bowls of Tidman's
Sea Salt every evening in case I went bandy with the weight. It seems
to have done the trick because in an early photograph taken of me sitting
on a cushion, they look reasonably straight.

Some years later I came across the photograph and began to worry
about the round object lying between my legs, wondering if some vital
part of me had become detached. If it had, then it was probably lost for
ever; mother was a great tidier-up. But I exchanged notes with a friend
and we decided that all was well – there was nothing much to choose
between us.

According to the census figures, in the ten years between 1911 and
1921 the population of Newbury had increased by a mere 188 – from
12,107 to 12,295. An average of 18.8 births per annum didn't say much
for the fertility rate of stockbreeders and racehorse trainers, until one
recalls that the Great War to end all wars had taken place during that
time and there was a large minus figure to be deducted.

Any new editions ought to have been welcomed, but apart from an entry in the local paper, my arrival on the scene went largely unreported. *The Times* of London was concerned with more momentous matters: the theft of a motor car and its contents from some unspecified garage; the fate of a bus conductor who was appearing at Mansion House charged with allowing an excess of passengers to board an omnibus en route to East Ham – 'the weather was bad and the people swarmed on before I 'ad time to count them. I only did it to oblige!'; the adverse trade balance; something they called 'weather probabilities' – cloudy, unsettled weather was due to set in later in the week; and the fact that during the previous twenty-four hours the weight of atmospheric dirt deposited on South Kensington measured 6 lb per million cubic yards. Nothing changes!

On the day I was born the January sales were in full swing. It was possible to buy a carved walnut Queen Anne bedstead at Waring & Gillow for £8.10 (usual price £10.15), not to mention a fine old house standing in 53 acres of Devonshire countryside for £3,000.

A fortnight later John Logie Baird transmitted a postcard-size image of a ventriloquist doll's head, and at midnight on 3 May, the first general strike in Britain's history was declared. A detachment of Grenadier Guards was sent to escort food lorries from the docks to their Hyde Park depot, and an armoured car was seen in London's Oxford Street. Winston Churchill appointed himself editor of the newly formed *British Gazette* and demanded unconditional surrender from what he termed 'the enemy'. In no time at all it became a class war, with white-collar workers manning transport in order to get their colleagues to work. Nine days later it was all over.

It was also the year when Warner Brothers demonstrated on Broadway the first film which had its own sound.

'I remember, I remember, the house where I was born,
The little window where the sun came peeping in at morn.'

Well I don't, actually. Six weeks after I was born the population of Newbury was further depleted when my father, a Post Office sorting clerk, was transferred to Reading. It must have been a great family upheaval, for Reading was seventeen miles nearer London with a population of over 90,000, and in present-day terms it would have been a bit like being sent abroad.

My first bedroom window looked out from 21 Gloucester Road on to Belmont Road, one of many long, straight streets of identical terrace houses built towards the end of the nineteenth century. In New York they would have been called W. 23rd or something similar, but in Reading they had rather grand names like Connaught, Norfolk and Cranbury.

Our house was the penultimate one in a row and it boasted a back entrance to the garden which was reached via a zig-zagging narrow pathway with a high fence on either side. My father considered it a mixed blessing as he had to keep it creosoted which took up a lot of his time, especially when I was helping. When I eventually started school I sometimes used it as a short cut home, although I wasn't very keen because of all the cobwebs and the fear that I might meet a bogeyman round the next corner.

The far end of Belmont Road formed a T-junction with the main Oxford Road where there was a hospital and a public house called the New Inn, and where open-topped trams rattled their way to and fro into and out of town. My window faced north, so it didn't see much sun, and as our house lay at the bottom of a steep hill, neither did the one in my parents' room at the back.

Other rattling noises could be heard from time to time. They came from a railway goods yard which lay between the Oxford Road and the River Thames. The nightly bangs and crashes from wagons being shunted to and fro as train sets were assembled seemed endless. I used to lie awake trying to work out the length of each train by counting the bangs.

In the morning I woke to the sound of clinking milk bottles from a dairy a few doors along the street, and washed in cold water from a jug which stood alongside a bowl in the bathroom. The bowl was supported in a metal frame and when the plug was removed the water emptied into a bucket underneath.

After using the toilet I would run downstairs as fast as I could. I had to reach the bottom before the cistern stopped flushing, otherwise the world would come to an end. Small children's minds are full of secret fears.

I also remember my bedroom for being the place where Doctor Marshall removed my tonsils and adenoids. When I came round after the operation there they were, laid out in a bowl for my inspection. The smell of ether has stayed with me too, and goes with the kind of flowered wallpaper you still come across from time to time in old French hotels.

In that same room I discovered the truth about Father Christmas. Unlike Shirley Temple, who had the blinkers removed from her eyes one December when she was taken to see Santa at a store in Los Angeles and *he* asked for *her* autograph, I heard mine enter the room. He had a pipe and he smoked Three Nuns tobacco, as did my father, which even to my small mind seemed an unlikely coincidence. The sound of my mother hissing 'Hurry up, Norrie!' confirmed my worst suspicions.

In some ways I felt relieved. I hadn't much liked the Father Christmas I'd been taken to meet at McIlroy's store in Reading, nor could I picture him coming down our chimney. All the same, I felt betrayed. Until that moment I had always taken everything my parents told me as gospel, although in the morning as I delved into the pillowcase and unwrapped my first Rupert Annual, a box of Lott's Bricks – so clean and white and shiny they looked good enough to eat – my first Hornby clockwork train set, a wooden fort – which was exciting to put together, but didn't actually do anything – and countless other toys, I didn't let on I knew. From then on it was a game that two could play, a battle of who could stay awake the longest on Christmas Eve. But my father must have twigged, for it never happened again.

I don't remember what my parents gave each other. Mother was very keen on Yardley 4711 and wouldn't have given a thank you for Chanel No. 5. My father was always happy with smoker's requisites: a tobacco pouch, or a new pipe – a Barling probably, for he always rated them very highly. When it came to unwrapping the parcels he was usually in trouble for taking his time undoing the knots rather than cutting them, but his training with the Post Office had instilled in him a respect for string.

One of my earliest memories is of being rushed out into the garden in order to see the world's biggest airship pass over. The R101 was 770 feet long and had been built at a cost of £600,000. It looked menacing, like something from another world. The people on board said it was so quiet that even at a height of 2000 feet they could hear the sound of car horns on the ground below.

Had they been flying over Gloucester Road a few years earlier they might have heard a large explosion coming from number twenty-one.

It was my father's addiction to his pipe, coupled with a certain absent-mindedness, that very nearly brought about my early demise. Soon after we moved to Reading my mother went out shopping one morning, leaving him with strict instructions to make sure the oven was warmed up ready for lunch. At the appointed time he turned on the gas and, having searched in vain for some matches, pottered off to look for a box. He was gone for some time and when he returned his first thought was to light his pipe. He had a habit of putting spent matches back into the box, so it took him a while to find a fresh one.

I think I can dimly remember the explosion, but perhaps it's simply that I heard the story repeated so many times it began to seem as though I did. It must have been fairly sizeable, for the kitchen dresser fell on top of me, breaking most of my parents' wedding china in the process. I was in my pram at the time and fortunately the hood was up, so I escaped unharmed, but my father wasn't allowed in the kitchen for a long time afterwards – which probably suited him.

Such excitements apart, life was very tranquil in those pre-war days.

When Jerome K. Jerome wrote *Three Men in a Boat* he didn't think much of my new home town, dismissing it in a mere two or three lines: 'We came in sight of Reading about eleven. The river is dirty and dismal here. One does not linger in the neighbourhood of Reading.' Along with Harris, George, and Montmorency the dog, he accepted a tow from some friends in a steam launch and they made good their escape as fast as possible, although he had to admit that a little way upstream the River Thames became very lovely, as indeed it still does once you get beyond Pangbourne.

That was in 1889.

Prior to then, Reading had been noted mainly as a centre of the cloth trade and for being the birthplace of Archbishop Laud. It was where John of Gaunt had been married, and Henry I lay buried in the Cluniac Abbey he had founded in 1121, later to be consecrated by Thomas à Becket. In the same abbey a monk is reputed to have written an early hit tune which he called 'Summer is a Comen In'.

The town I grew up in during the late twenties and thirties was by then famous for its beer, bulbs and biscuits: H. & G. Simonds beer, Suttons Royal Seed Establishment and Huntley & Palmers biscuits. The latter had been set up in 1841 to manufacture that 'hard dry bread, made to be carried to sea', as Doctor Johnson once described it.

Reading also had a football team in the third division; two theatres, the County and the Palace; three cinemas, the Vaudeville, the Central Picture Playhouse and the Caversham Electric; and a gaol which was famous for having once housed Oscar Wilde, who in cell 33 wrote a ballad about his experiences.

In 1929 a fourth cinema, the Pavilion, was opened. There you could *see and hear* Al Jolson in the first 'talkie' to play in Reading, *The Singing Fool*. It proved so popular it was retained for a further week. As an added attraction there was Norman Tilley at the mighty organ.

There was motorized transport, of course, but I don't remember ever seeing a car parked on the street, and the only van which sticks in my mind was one which had THE BLIND MAN painted on the side. I used to worry about him being unable to see where he was going. Words on shops and vans intrigued me from an early age and I believed my father when he told me the letters 'MPS' outside a chemist's shop meant 'Member of Parliament Sometimes'. 'Est.' I translated as 'Estuarated', although I had no idea what it meant.

Practically everything was delivered to the house by horse-drawn vehicles. The horses usually wore nose-bags and you could hear chewing noises coming from deep inside, accompanied by the warm, sweet smell of hay. As soon as they had gone on their way there would be a rush to collect manure for the garden.

The rag-and-bone man, who looked all rag and bones himself, paid regular visits, as did the knife grinder. Freshly baked bread arrived in a horse-drawn van, vegetables came on an open cart. Milk was delivered in churns on a hand cart and it was a high spot of the day to be allowed to take a jug into the street so that a pint could be poured from a measure which had a brass plate on the side. There were no refrigerators; it was kept cool under a piece of wet muslin on a marble slab in the pantry, and in the summer it went off very quickly. For the same reason, pork was only eaten when there was an R in the month.

Everything else came from old Mrs Robins' corner shop at the end of Gloucester Road. Mrs Robins bought cheap and sold dear. Tea was measured out in cones made of old newspaper given to her by the customers; any spare leaves were promptly swept back into the plywood tea chest, and when that was empty it, too, would be sold. Butter was cut into small pats with a wooden spatula. Things were marked up out of all proportion, including the chocolate pyramids which I always coveted, and lemonade powder, which also came in a paper cone. There is nothing so expensive as being poor.

One day I was sent to Mrs Robins to pick up some groceries, which meant her leaving the front of the shop unattended, and while I was waiting I happened to notice a small, half-eaten block of Cabury's Dairy Milk chocolate lying on top of a tin of biscuits. It was beginning to go soft in the rays of the afternoon sun and it didn't take me long to convince myself that I would be doing her a good turn if I moved it for her. Given that one good turn deserves another, I slipped it into my pocket. I immediately regretted what I had done, but by then it was too late for I could hear footsteps approaching.

That night I suffered agonies of remorse, made even worse when the thought struck me that it might have been *poisoned chocolate* left out to catch the mice which we all suspected inhabited her shop.

It taught me a lesson. Over the years, like millions of others, I have had no compunction about using a firm's telephone to make personal calls, or helping myself to their notepaper, or indeed many of the other things which as an employee one justifies under the heading of 'perks' (until such time as one becomes an employer – when it goes under another name). But it was the only time in my life when I have knowingly stolen anything.

Strawberries appeared in early June, in time for racing at Ascot. They were around for Wimbledon, then disappeared again. There was no question of their being available at any other time of the year, but we enjoyed them all the more because of that.

Street games happened in strict rotation. Hoops made of iron or wood materialized as if by magic on a certain day; wooden tops appeared on another and the air would suddenly be filled with the sound of cracking whips. Conkers heralded the approach of winter, and nearer Christmas we would start on the lengthy process of making butterflies out of crepe paper, and paper-chains from strips of coloured paper and Stephen's gum mucilage. I don't remember our ever having a Christmas tree – my mother would have been impatient with the pine needles falling out and making a mess everywhere.

* * *

Not everything moved at such a leisurely pace. Reading had always been
an important railway junction, dating back to the days of the broad
gauge track when third-class passengers travelled in open trucks, and the
Great Western Railway prided itself on the service it provided. For many
years a succession of Castle Class engines broke the world speed record.
Ingenious ways of providing non-stop trains to the west were thought
up. The Cornish Riviera Express held the record for the longest non-stop
journey – 245.6 miles – by scooping up fresh supplies of water from
troughs placed midway between the rails.

It was the age of inventiveness, of striving for improvement and of
pride at providing the best possible service. In association with Imperial
Airways, who supplied the Westland Wessex monoplane and its crew,
the Great Western Air Service was formed, ferrying passengers between
Cardiff and Plymouth at a cost of three pounds ten shillings. The Post
Office played its part too, picking up letters in special bags suspended
from gantries at the side of the track as mail trains shot past. Inside the
train there would be travelling sorters ready to receive them. It was
possible to post a letter in Reading in the morning and know it would
be delivered to an address in London that same afternoon.

People used to visit Reading station just to see the Cheltenham Flyer
or the Cornish Riviera Express pass through. Obeying the shouts to stand
well clear of the platform edge, one gazed in awe as they thundered past,
savouring a brief glimpse of the driver peering out of his cab, or the
fireman slaving away on the footplate. Superior beings from another
world; how one envied them, and how important one felt if either one
of them actually waved.

In the quiet which followed, we would listen to the wheel-tappers at
work with their hammers on any train which happened to be standing
idle, making sure the metal rang true. Then we would go and watch
other, smaller engines take on water.

The nearest equivalent closer to home happened periodically when
the roads were being resurfaced. Gangs of men would suddenly appear
and the air would be filled with shouts and the smell of tar. And then
a steamroller would arrive, rumbling and clanking up and down the road,
hissing and spitting like some story-book monster.

In summer the Wall's ice-cream man would appear on his tricycle at
the bottom of Belmont Road. It seemed to take for ever before the words

STOP ME AND BUY ONE could be clearly seen on the side of the cart, and I always lived in fear of him selling out before he reached Gloucester Road (although if he did he invariably pedalled back to the depot for fresh supplies). On a hot day the numbingly cold triangular Snofrute water ices were the most popular and at 1*d* a time well worth waiting for, although towards the end they tended to disintegrate rapidly, tasting of the cardboard they were wrapped in.

On Sunday afternoons in winter the muffin man came round the streets carrying a large wooden tray on his head and ringing a hand bell. I often wondered if he had a flat head under his cap, but he never removed it, preferring to reach up over the top of the tray when he served his customers. We toasted the muffins and ate them sitting in front of a roaring fire with the curtains drawn. It was something else we looked forward to and no grate was complete without a long brass toasting fork among the fire-irons.

I can't say I was ever really aware of our being badly off, although at times it must have been hard for my parents to make ends meet, for the country was on the verge of bankruptcy. Luckily people's needs were fairly simple in those days and one wasn't bombarded on all sides by advertisements for 'the better life'.

Everything was paid for in cash and my father still managed to send a postal order home to his parents every week. I have never been envious of other people's good fortune, but I do remember when I was small being invited to the birthday party of someone in my class at school. I was picked up in a car and whisked off to a large house on Caversham Heights, just outside Reading, and there – during a game of hide and seek – I went into a large bedroom and saw laid out on the carpet an electric train set of unbelievable luxury. It had points and buffers and a station and tunnels and several engines. When I got back home and looked at my own clockwork Hornby outfit with its two sections of straight line it seemed very tame by comparison.

I sought consolation in my Meccano set, which I think gave me more pleasure than anything else I was ever given. It was more than a toy; it taught me to use my hands and my imagination.

In 1931 an all-party government was formed and the pound was devalued by 30 per cent. Panic on the Stock Exchange forced it to close down for two days, and Britain came off the gold standard. There were riots in London and Glasgow, and for two days the Atlantic Fleet was prevented from sailing by a strike of 12,000 naval ratings.

All this, of course, passed over my head, although one wet day when my mother was taking me out shopping in the pushchair – probably because she was trying to save the tram fare into Reading – she suddenly stopped and burst into tears because both her shoes were leaking and falling apart. Then she turned round and we went back home. I was forbidden to tell my father what had happened, and I don't think I ever did, for he would have been mortified on her behalf.

Although it's probably all in the mind, the seasons themselves seemed more clearly defined in those days. The winters were colder and never passed without snow at some point. Ponds froze over and there was skating. There was ice on the *inside* of the bedroom windows at night. In the morning there would be beautiful, fern-like patterns on the glass. Stone hot-water bottles and warming pans were still practical objects of everyday necessity, not antiques. The former were lethal if you turned over in your sleep and accidentally touched one, and in the wrong hands a copper warming pan filled with hot coals from the fire could set light to a bed in about five seconds flat, as happened on more than one occasion when I pleaded to be allowed a go.

In the fashion of the day, all the woodwork of the house in which I grew up was painted a dark brown. It might even have been furnished by the same Waring & Gillow who advertised in *The Times*, although it more likely came from Camp Hopson in Newbury, where my mother had worked for a short while before getting married at the age of nineteen. She used to tease my father by telling him that she could have married into money because one of the directors was keen on her, and I daresay it was true, because she was very pretty at that age.

In the front room downstairs – only used on special occasions – there was a three-piece suite which included a sofa, one end of which could be let down to make a bed. Each item sported a snow-white antimacassar – a precaution against the hair oils of the time.

There was an aspidistra in the window, and a glass-fronted cabinet kept locked at certain times of the year when it housed a bottle of Bourgogne's South African Burgundy; prescribed by Doctor Marshall when mother felt she needed building up (she avoided doctors most of her life in case they 'found something wrong' with her). It came in a dark flask-shaped bottle, and it was the only time I ever saw anything approaching table wine in the house. I think she was put off the genuine article by my father, who firmly believed, as did many who served in France during the First World War, that the raised punt in the bottom of the bottle was a fiendish trick on the part of the French so that they could get away with putting in less liquid.

Drink went to my mother's elbows, or so she always said, so a bottle was made to last several weeks. What it must have been like by the time she reached the end I hate to think, although she always swore it did her good and I daresay it tasted suitably medicinal by then.

Doctor Marshall was a great believer in burgundy and I suspect prescribed it to himself quite regularly. He remained our family physician until the time came when we moved away from the area. When he wasn't out visiting, he occupied a very gloomy surgery and he probably took to drink at an early age. What in my innocence I'd assumed to be a smell of ether which went with his profession was more likely to have been whisky or gin. All the same, he was a kindly man, who gazed benevolently, if at times rather hazily, over the top of his glasses as he tended to his patients' needs – in my case measles, mumps, chicken pox, and a series of broken arms. I never saw a Mrs Marshall.

I acquired a reputation when I was small for being a good little boy, largely because I kept myself to myself and didn't say very much, especially at meal times when small children were often told they 'should be seen and not heard'. All the same, I used to think a lot, and it irritated me when people took me at face value. It isn't that one necessarily wants to be thought of as bad, simply that *wicked* sounds much more interesting.

From an early age, having my virtues extolled in front of others invariably made me want to prove how really bad I could be when I tried. Which was probably why, one tea-time when I was on display at my Auntie Ethel's, I came to throw my feeding bottle across the dining-room. Auntie Ethel, who lived at Woolton Hill on the far side of Newbury, was one of my mother's three older half-sisters, and because it was my first visit I don't doubt everyone was laying it on a bit thick.

Shock waves rose from all sides as the bottle hit the sideboard, scattering photograph frames and china ornaments far and wide. Al Capone probably did far worse things when he was small, but I doubt if he would have done them in Auntie Ethel's house – not before he'd got his first sub-machine-gun anyway. My cousin, Eric, who was older than me and liked a good giggle, was in trouble for laughing, but his sister, Betty, who was older still, had the good sense to keep quiet.

However, I'd proved my point and we weren't invited back for a long time afterwards.

One morning, soon after I learned to walk, I followed my mother to the front door as she opened it to the baker. For some reason best known to myself I was carrying a house brick. The story goes that he leaned over and patted me on the head, remarking what a clever little boy I was, able to lift such a large brick all by myself. At which point I promptly let go of it.

It landed on his foot and produced a very satisfactory reaction. My mother stood up for me. Knowing her, she probably said he shouldn't have had his foot in the way and that it served him right.

Shortly after that we changed our baker – or he changed us.

I was even less popular with my paternal grandfather, largely on account of having waded through some wet concrete, part of a garden path which he had spent the entire weekend preparing and laying as a kind of belated moving-in present. It was a work of art. There were steps and a rustic archway, which in time would be covered with Paul Scarlet roses.

I had probably been out rescuing snails. There were lots of them in the garden and I used to like following their trails before the blackbirds got them. I imagine that had I been born in France I would have made good use of them.

The chemical industry had yet to discover pesticides, so most insects roamed freely and there was much more wildlife than there is today. In the winter there would be the nightly routine of baiting mousetraps, and in the summer out would come the rolls of sticky flypaper. That always seemed a dreadful way to go.

As with the baker, grandfather's visits, never very frequent, ceased altogether and I don't recall seeing him again before he died. Nor do I recall ever meeting my paternal step-grandmother, who apparently made it very clear when she became grandfather's wife number two that she didn't approve of his existing offspring and wanted nothing to do with them.

After he died there was a family row over the will. My father, who was a very upright man, retired from the scene in disgust, leaving his two elder brothers and a sister to sort things out between them. My mother would have taken his side, for she was very protective, and once she had made up her mind about something there was no changing it. But it must have been how we came to inherit a four-poster bed which filled my parents' bedroom until the evening Doctor Marshall took a fancy to it.

He had been summoned to lance a particularly virulent boil on my father's posterior, but instead of reaching for his scalpel he took one look at the bed and made an offer for it on the spot. My father, who by then was dying for him to get on with things so that he would be able to sit down again in comfort, accepted it. Afterwards he was in great trouble with my mother for letting it go so cheaply, but looking back on the episode I suspect she was secretly pleased to see the back of it – she would have considered it a great dust-collector and more trouble than it was worth.

Dust was anathema to her and everything in the house was kept highly polished; the brass cover on the doorstep with Brasso, the red-tiled kitchen floor and the linoleum with Mansion polish; the stove was regularly black-leaded. Despite the hard times, we even had a Mrs Blake who used to come and 'do' for us, but she was much more interested in gossiping and didn't last very long. Like many of her kind, she was a 'specialist' and always cleaned the same things.

The chimney sweep paid twice-yearly visits and another childhood treat was to be sent outside to give a warning shout when the end of his brush appeared out of the top of the chimney pot.

Clothes were pressed with flat-irons heated on the gas stove, as were curling tongs when my mother's hair needed doing. The working temperature of the latter was always checked first on a piece of paper, and the smell of singed newsprint is something else which brings instant recall.

Gas was used for lighting as well as cooking, and that in turn meant incandescent 'mantles' which glowed white hot and disintegrated at the slightest touch – with the end of a pencil, for example – so when I went to bed in winter it was usually by candlelight or a Price's nightlight standing in a saucer of water.

The bath water was heated by a geyser which had seen better days and it was my father's job to light it on Friday nights. My mother and I used to wait at the bottom of the stairs until he gave the all clear. As a treat I was often allowed a Reckitts bath cube.

Although television had been invented, in practical terms it was still a thing of the future. The BBC as an organization didn't come into being until 1922 and to many people the word 'wireless' still meant a crystal set. If you went into a room and saw someone wearing headphones you had to be careful not to bang the door in case the cat's whisker became detached. Our crystal set came from Gamages and, when it did work, it was a case of taking it in turns.

The main source of music was provided by a wind-up gramophone, endlessly churning out 'Selections from the Desert Song', Ernest Luff's 'Oh, for the Wings of a Dove', Peter Dawson singing 'Boots' and a record of 'The Laughing Policeman'.

Such entertainments as we had were mostly live. When the circus came to town posters began appearing on hoardings weeks ahead, so that by the time it arrived on a special train the excitement had built up and all the town would turn out to see the elephants leading the big parade through the streets. If you were lucky, you might even catch a glimpse of the lions pacing up and down in their mobile cages. Crowds followed on behind to watch the big top being erected, which was a whole show in itself – like a ballet. Sometimes there would be a visit from the Russian Cossack Riders, and at Christmas there would be the pantomime.

My early childhood ambitions, which for a long time had centred on being an engine driver when I grew up, fluctuated from lion taming, or walking the high wire, to riding bare-back brandishing a scimitar.

I was almost four years old when the R101 flew over and before I was five it was to crash into a hill near Beauvais in France while on its way to India. There was an awesome explosion as the five and a half million cubic feet of hydrogen needed to keep it aloft ignited, reducing the airship to a twisted mass of red-hot metal in a matter of seconds. My mother must have been greatly relieved two or three years later when electricity finally came to our house. She hadn't trusted gas since my father blew up the kitchen and the R101 disaster would have confirmed her worst fears.

The big debate centred on whether or not to have two power points, one in the downstairs hall and another on the upstairs landing, but as it would be a long while before we had any appliances the problem was largely academic.

In any case by then my mind was on other things.

Her name was Sheila and if old photographs are anything to go by we seemed to spend most of our time chatting across the garden fence. One picture shows her looking at me over the top, her silver blonde hair glowing in what little we ever saw of the evening sun, hanging on to my every word. From the rapt expression on her face I was obviously on to a good thing. It was only a matter of time and playing my cards right.

However, impatience got the better of me and in the end I dealt myself a losing hand.

One day when my parents were out I invited her round to see my Hornby train set. Without a murmur, and with an innocence I've rarely encountered since, she followed me into the toy cupboard. Once inside I shut the door, and obeying what must have been very primitive instincts indeed, for I had no real idea *why* I was doing it (It's the truth, your honour!), I began to remove my trousers.

In my haste, I had left the door slightly ajar and in the dim light filtering through the gap even Sheila sensed that all was not well. Far from following my example with whatever was to hand about her own person, she began to cry and no amount of bribing with offers of free lollipops until the end of time, or unlimited goes with my train set, would make her stop.

It was the end of a beautiful friendship, and never again were we allowed to talk to each other over the garden fence.

Nowadays her mother would probably have rushed for the nearest HELP!-line and mine would have been in urgent need of a good lawyer!

My next adventure was with a girl called Patsy.

Even at the tender age of eight, Patsy had already built up quite a reputation in the neighbourhood. My mother used to say things like, 'You don't want to play with *that* girl . . . she's no better than she should be.' But since I had no yardstick by which to judge her, and since she struck me as being rather nice, I did want to play with her.

My big chance came one morning when she invited me up to her bedroom. We leaned out of the window for a while, exchanging such pleasantries as I could muster in those days, then she disappeared.

When I looked round I found to my surprise that she had taken her knickers off and was sitting on her potty doing what was known in polite circles as 'big jobs', although I think at the time she called it something else. She seemed pleased with the result and when she stood up you could see why. It was all curiously disturbing. Until then, going to the lavatory had always been a bit of a chore; I hadn't realized you could actually get pleasure from it. When she invited me to have a go, I needed no second bidding.

Unfortunately, just as I had settled down and reached the point of no return, the door opened and her mother came into the room. By this time Patsy was fully dressed and sitting demurely on her bed, leaving me to take the can, for want of a better phrase.

Yet another beautiful friendship bit the dust, and by now my own reputation in the district was worse than Patsy's. I no longer had to worry about being classified as a good little boy and I must say I felt rather hard done by.

It was an early lesson in two basic facts: not only is life unfair, but some people – especially Capricorns – are never satisfied.

CHAPTER 2

Family Pursuits

It's no good telling me that there are bad aunts and good aunts. At the core they are all alike. Sooner or later, out pops the cloven hoof.

P. G. Wodehouse (1881 – 1975)

When I was three, my maternal grandmother was admitted to the Royal Berkshire Hospital. Shortly before she died I was taken to see her, isolated behind a lot of glass, rather like a framed photograph. Because of my age I wasn't allowed into the room, and no one ever told me what was wrong – the dreaded word cancer was never mentioned – so all I really remember of her is that she looked very white and ill.

Auntie Ethel, who had also come to pay her last respects, took me back with her to Newbury until it was all over. She must have forgiven me my earlier debacle with the feeding bottle, but it wasn't long before I blotted my copybook again, this time with an old glass-fronted longcase clock operated by means of a massive brass encased weight.

Winding it was a weekly ritual carried out by my Uncle Frank, and I used to watch enthralled as he opened the glass door in order to raise the weight by means of a chain. I was dying to have a go myself and the opportunity arose sooner than expected. I had only been there a few days when I found myself left on my own for a while, with strict instructions not to leave the house or answer the door, come what may. I had no intention of doing either. I knew exactly what I had in mind.

As soon as the coast was clear, I had the clock door open in a flash. There was a lovely clicking noise from the ratchet as I pulled on the chain and the weight began to rise. In fact it was such a lovely noise I couldn't resist giving one more tug for luck. I'm still not sure which was worse, the chain coming away in my hand, the crash as the weight fell into the well of the clock, or the silence that followed.

The time between Auntie Ethel arriving back home and her realizing the clock had stopped seemed like an eternity, especially as I had deprived myself of the only means to measure it, but it could only have been a matter of seconds. I wasn't actually sent to bed without any supper that night, but I remember wishing I had been. Conversation was minimal and the little there was took place as though I didn't exist.

Uncle Frank owned a garage and for various reasons tended to keep a low profile when he was at home, mainly because it worked overtime when he was out and about. He was a handsome man, who even to my untutored eye looked very rakish when he was dressed in his chauffeur's uniform. During the season various well-born local ladies engaged him to drive them to the races, and he kept a large Vauxhall with leather upholstery and a roomy interior permanently at the ready.

He was a man of many parts. When he wasn't out philandering he liked reading in bed – although I have no idea what his tastes were – and he had designed a small clip-on electric heater to keep his arm warm while he was holding the book. He showed it to me one day and I felt very privileged. He also played the violin, and with his son, Eric, kept several pigs in a state of brick-built splendour. They were fed according to a strict formula laid down by Griffins pork butchers in Newbury. I can still smell the twice-daily buckets of meal, and taste the sausages, too. Griffins were reputed to make the best for miles around, and I suspect Albert Roux is right when he says that meat from contented animals tastes the best.

Uncle Frank was always very kind and let me work the hand-operated petrol pump for customers. I think it was partly because I was interested in things mechanical and used to spend hours playing with the tools in his workshop, but also because when he went out and about during the day he often took me with him to act as an alibi. Sometimes, when he was paying one of his 'calls', I would be left alone in the car for ages. But I never minded because it meant I could sit behind the wheel and pretend I was driving. Also it was nice to be with an uncle for a change. Most of my aunts had been widowed in the First World War. Afterwards I used to be quizzed by Auntie Ethel, who would be out for blood because she'd had to keep the lunch hot, but I had learned to keep mum.

Perhaps not surprisingly, my own extra-curricular activities had suffered a severe setback at the hands of Sheila and Patsy and it put me off girls for quite a while. About seven years to be exact.

I daresay it was partly to take my mind off the whole thing, and at the same time teach me one or two things about the facts of life, that my parents bought me a fox terrier puppy. He came from a local pet shop and I called him Binkie after a character in one of my magazines.

If he taught me anything at all about sex it was how not to go about it. From an early age, Binkie's idea of bliss was to rape any likely looking object which was unfortunate enough to come into his line of sight. Had the indefatigable Barbara Woodhouse, doyenne of canine obedience classes, been around at the time she would have taken a very dim view of him, as did most of our visitors. They usually sat with their hands firmly clasped over their knees and, if they happened to drop anything, avoided bending over to pick it up until Binkie was safely out of the room or having his lunch. Mrs Woodhouse's cries of SIT! would either have fallen on deaf ears or they would have produced a quite undesirable result on the rug.

Demonstrating by example how to behave in public wasn't what he was best at, but in most other respects he was a lovely dog and he was to remain my constant friend and companion all through my school days.

After I went into the forces he had to be put down on account of his increasingly bad temper following a major fight with a much larger dog he fancied. He was a fearless creature, but for once he came off worst and was badly bitten. Subsequently, he developed a habit of turning on people when they came up behind him; it was a case of the biter not wishing to be bit.

Putting him down was probably my mother's doing. She always saw things in terms of extreme black and white. There were never any shades of grey in between. In her eyes a playful nip would have constituted a major assault, something that might well lead to rabies. 'Better safe than sorry.'

If she ventured out after dark, which she rarely did, it was always 'pitch black' outside. The sun, when it shone, was invariably 'blazing down'. Hot drinks became 'stone cold' if they were left standing a second too long (unlike humans, who became blue). If it rained, then it rained 'cats and dogs', and if a light wasn't turned off it had been left 'full on'.

She was impatient with red tape and often tore things up, or conveniently 'lost' them if they didn't meet with her approval; much to my father's alarm, for he was a born civil servant who simply had to read the small print. He was such a dedicated reader of small print that in later life when he needed to have his eyes tested he always insisted on reading the whole sight board from top to bottom, no matter how many times the optician pointed in desperation to individual lines of letters. If there had been a copyright notice he would have read that too.

Early photographs of my parents taken soon after they were married suggest that butter wouldn't have melted in my mother's mouth. It was hard to picture that when she was small she once took a pony upstairs into her bedroom. Unable to get it back down again, there it remained for several hours, restlessly clumping around on the bare boards of her bedroom while my grandfather, who had arrived home unexpectedly, tried to conduct a business meeting on the floor below, pretending nothing untoward was happening overhead.

She was a great believer in old-fashioned remedies for aches and pains, and, looking back, there was a lot to be said for them; at least they were all tried and tested and none of them had any side effects.

Bottles of smelling salts dotted the house in case anyone had an attack of the vapours. Vick Brand Anti-Vapour Rub was regularly applied to the chest, calves' foot jelly was thought to speed recovery after an illness and there was always a large jar of it in the larder. Iodine was kept at the ready and during most of my early childhood my knees were stained a light shade of oak. Before going to school in the morning I was given Andrews' Liver Salts, which I drank as a treat, like lemonade. It always sounded much better than it tasted, as did the nightly spoonful of a sticky brown substance called Virol, which looked as though it ought to taste of chocolate, but didn't. The state of one's bowels was considered very important in those days and on Sunday evening, following a copious lunch, a dose of California Syrup of Figs prepared me for the week ahead. Grown-ups took Carter's Little Liver Pills.

Sunday was the gastronomic high spot of the week. My mother had the reputation of being a good cook. Beef with Yorkshire pudding and roast potatoes alternated with mutton and onion sauce. Beef was my favourite because it meant toast and fresh dripping in front of the fire for several nights to come; the rich, dark brown bit beneath the crust was best and it made a change from bread and milk. Roast veal was considered a treat; chicken a luxury reserved for special occasions, like birthdays and Christmas. In season, peas were always fresh from the pod and cooked with a sprig of mint, but for the rest of the year they were dried and had to be soaked overnight in a muslin bag which came in the packet.

During the week we had the remains of the meat made up into Cornish pasties or shepherd's pie, or else we had faggots from the local pork butcher.

Wisely, my mother also did the carving and the 'dishing up' as she called it, for my father wasn't a very practical man and would have tried her patience sorely by taking too long over it. Everything had to be served 'piping hot' and eaten before it had a chance to get cold.

In early spring, after Sunday lunch, we would go out into the country to gather bluebells, and in the late summer there would be blackberries to pick. My father always took his walking stick so that he could use the crook to reach the branches at the back – the tantalizing ones with the finest berries. Those of us who had gone on ahead would wait impatiently for him to catch up, but he was deaf to our cries and wouldn't be hurried.

Covered in insect bites and nettle rash, we would arrive back home hungry for tea, when there would be fish- or meat-paste sandwiches and home-made fruit or seed cake, followed by trifle – alternate layers of sponge cake and tinned fruit, with a dash or two of sherry; the whole held together by the addition of jelly, followed by another layer of Bird's custard topped with a layer of cream and decorated overall by a sprinkling of chopped nuts.

Or else there would be bananas mashed up with a fork, sprinkled with caster sugar and served with cream off the top of the milk. When the war came and bananas disappeared, people tried mashing up boiled turnips mixed with banana essence, but it was a poor substitute.

Sometimes we would round things off with an orange. Afterwards the segments of peel would be turned inside out and my father would take out his pocket knife and make incisions to form teeth. We all had a good laugh when we looked in the mirror. He was also very good at peeling apples, slowly and meticulously, so that the peel ended up in one long curly strip.

The one thing mother excelled at was making pastry. People always spoke highly of her pastry. She wasn't a great one for tarts, although nothing was wasted and any left-overs received a liberal coating of jam before they were popped into the oven.

Pies were her great speciality. The first rhubarb of the season started it off. Later, when the rhubarb began to fade, it would be eked out with apple, and gradually the latter took over completely, acting as a standby until it was blackberry time. During the winter it was steak-and-kidney or chicken-and-ham pie. No matter what they contained, they were always delicious.

She never used a pair of scales in her life and couldn't be bothered with recipe books. Years later, when I became interested in such things, I often asked about her pastry, but I never got a wholly satisfactory answer. It was always, 'Oh, you take some flour, butter and sugar and some milk and you mix it together . . .' That bit I knew – it was the magic ingredient 'X' which seemed to be missing whenever I had a go.

The tastes and smells of childhood stay with you all your life; mint sauce with roast lamb, apple sauce with pork, home-made green tomato chutney, the remains of the cake-mix scooped out of a bowl on the end of a finger, the mouth-watering waft of air when the time came for the oven door to be opened, the smell of oilcloth on a kitchen table and the feel of it, always shiny to the touch. As with Proust and his *madeleines*, such things evoke instant memories.

I don't recall there being any such smell or tastes at Auntie Emm's, second in the league of my mother's half-sisters with whom I was occasionally sent to stay.

Emily Stevens' husband, George, had been killed on the last day of the First World War, leaving her with three boys to raise. The job completed to her satisfaction, she lived by herself in a cold house on Wash Common just outside Newbury and was rarely without a cigarette in her mouth. She had a gravelly voice and coughed a lot, so she was only called on in an emergency.

When she wasn't giving me lectures on how to behave, she used to take me for long walks on the common. It was called Wash Common because during the Civil War it had been the site of a famous battle and blood was said to have run down the hill into the town. She used to try and get me to identify various bits of plant life on the way, something I was never very good at, and her continual grumbling when I got it wrong probably put me off botany for life.

One evening she took me to see an old friend of hers who she said was very clever, and I was warned in no uncertain terms to be on my best behaviour. He turned out a be a dry and dusty man, and the walls of his house were almost entirely lined with books, like a public library. I was suitably impressed, although I didn't actually like him very much.

He was also a sportsman of some renown, or he had been when he was at university, and almost immediately he started quizzing me on the subject, clearly anxious to score points. Apart from being able to identify test cricketers from my collection of Player's cigarette cards, my knowledge of sport rated even lower than that of plant life. Clutching at straws, I declared an interest in running, implying by my tone of voice that I was pretty much a dab hand at it.

'Short or long distance?'

'Both,' I said, falling headlong into the trap.

'That's very interesting. So how long does it take you to run a hundred yards?'

Not wishing to let Auntie Emm down I essayed a wild guess.

'Ten seconds!' he repeated gravely. 'That's pretty good. And how about the mile? Don't tell me you can do that in four minutes.'

Out of the corner of my eye I could see Auntie Emm's face growing blacker by the second.

'Oh, less than that,' I said recklessly.

We left earlier than I'd expected and we were hardly outside the front door when Auntie Emm started laying in to me, vowing that I would never be invited to stay with her again.

I wasn't too sorry. Auntie Emm meant well, but she had never really got over the loss of her husband and felt the world had treated her badly. Besides, she always insisted on standing over me when I was having a bath and when she bent down the ash used to fall off the end of her cigarette, leaving me even dirtier than when I first got in.

My father would have answered her friend's questions like a shot. He was a great follower of sport all his life and he would have had the facts at his fingertips.

On summer evenings we played endless games of cricket together in a nearby park. He did all the bowling and running for the ball, while I batted. He was a very kind and patient man who knew that the most important thing you can give a small child is your time. It was a belief which must often have been sorely taxed when he arrived home tired from work and I stood over him, bat in hand, anxious to get going, watching him eat every mouthful of his high tea. How he must have prayed at times for rain to stop play while he was upstairs changing into his other 'togs', as he called them.

He had a large stock of such phrases. 'Things are a bit humpty' wasn't good news. 'That's put the kybosh on it', meant plans had fallen through. 'A1 at Lloyds' was high praise indeed, and to say that something was 'all Sir Garnett' meant all was well. For years I thought it was *cigar net* and I pictured some vast cylindrical safety net in the sky protecting us all. 'Napoo', often preceded by, 'Between, you, me and the gatepost,' was old army slang meaning something was a wash-out.

Extremely law-abiding and a stickler for protocol, he was never less than properly dressed. Until they went out of fashion, he wore spats over his shoes, and even when he went for a paddle in the sea he usually kept his hat on in case he met someone he knew. On the other side of the coin, if he felt he had been crossed or taken advantage of, he would dig his heels in and woe betide anyone who got in his way.

When I was about eight, he was given the job of carrying out an early form of time-and-motion study on country postmen's rounds. It meant his leaving for work very early in the morning, so a knocker-up used to be sent to the house. In the end, the neighbours complained, for he was a member of the 'one up – the lot up' brigade. My father reverted to tapping his head before he went to bed: six taps for when he needed to wake at six a.m. It always seemed to do the trick, although it didn't work for the half-hours.

It must have been hard going, for he insisted on using a standard-issue Post Office bicycle. With its 28-inch wheels, its oil lamps and hard leather saddle, it wasn't exactly light-weight, but in the event the job didn't last more than a few months. Setting off to work one morning he managed to get both wheels caught in some tramlines. Buster Keaton would have cycled all the way to the depot, hotly pursued by a tramcar – there would have been horrifying near-misses at junctions, with vehicles going in all directions – but my father simply fell off after a few yards and broke his collarbone, so that was that. He was probably trying to raise his hat to someone he knew.

One winter a mysterious parcel arrived unexpectedly and there was great excitement when my father announced that he had sent away for a kit of parts to build a real wireless, one we could all listen to through a loudspeaker. Although he had been in the Royal Corps of Signals during the First World War, he didn't have a practical turn of mind, so it took some weeks and eventually outside help had to be called in.

My mother didn't exactly say, 'I told you so!', but clearly she would have preferred dealing with S. Bodmin Dyer 'The Gramophone Specialist' who advertised in the local paper.

An aerial was duly erected in the garden, together with a large insulated double-pole switch just inside the window so that if there was a thunderstorm the wireless could be isolated and any lightning would pass down a copper pipe hammered into the ground. Whenever there was a storm during the night my mother used to get dressed in case *she* was struck. As a double precaution she often sat under the stairs until it went away.

When we were finally able to join the Twiddleknob Family – characters in a popular strip cartoon of the time – it was sheer magic. There was Children's Hour with 'Uncle Mac', who, when he wasn't reading out birthday messages telling lucky children that if they looked behind the sofa they might find something to their advantage, played Larry the Lamb in S. G. Hulme Beaman's wonderful world of Toytown, or introduced exciting plays by L. du Garde Peach and Franklyn Kelsey. 'Romany' kept everyone enthralled as he took his two children and his dog for make-believe walks in the country, communicating on the way his intense love of the outdoors. There were talks by the Zoo Man, and on affairs of the day by Commander Stephen King Hall, who always signed off with the subversive words, 'Be good, but not so frightfully good . . .' Far from grumbling about repeats, one couldn't wait to hear each and every one of them all over again. Above all, none of the broadcasters or presenters shouted at you or talked down.

The simple fact of hearing music issue from the loudspeaker seemed wonderful too. There were bands led by conductors with strange-sounding

foreign names, like Herman Darewski who was relayed from the Winter
Gardens at Blackpool. Debroy Somers and his Savoy Hotel Orpheans
came from the heart of London. J. H. Squire and his Celeste Octet
introduced the odd jazz item, and Jack Payne conducted the resident
BBC Band. What more could anyone wish for?

Not that it was always easy. You couldn't take a wireless set for granted.
Every few days accumulators had to be taken to be recharged. The
120-volt high tension batteries lasted longer, but when one did fail we
had to go without altogether until we could afford a replacement.

Luckily, I was brought up in a household where books were part of
the furniture of life, so there was always something on hand; *The Swiss
Family Robinson*, *Riders of the Purple Sage*, *Biggles*, *What Katy Did*, *Bulldog
Drummond* . . . I devoured them all, over and over again – especially *The
Swiss Family Robinson*. I enjoyed the practical bits, like making Wellington boots out of an old pair of socks covered with rubber solution from
a convenient tree and when I came to write about Paddington there
were echoes of the mother's duffle bag in his suitcase with its secret
compartment.

Summer holidays were taken on the Isle of Wight. Armed with suit-
cases and a bucket and spade, dressed-up for the occasion, we would set
off for Reading West station. I would be posted at the town end of the
wooden platform to watch for the tell-tale smoke which would mean
the train had left the main station and it was time to stand by.

And as the guard blew his whistle and the driver gave an answering
toot, we would settle back in carriages decorated with maps and sepia
photographs of southern England. Stopping occasionally at wayside
stations to take on other passengers, changing at Basingstoke, until
finally, as the train emerged from the end of a long tunnel beneath the
South Downs, we would reach Portsmouth Harbour and board a paddle
steamer to take us across to the island.

The first year we went I was sick with excitement and I felt very sorry
for myself. I didn't realize how lucky I was. Until Billy Butlin came along
with his idea for Summer Camps and his policy of 'a week's holiday for
a week's pay', millions of people never set eyes on the sea.

The second year I caught religion in a big way. Glancing out of the
carriage window as we neared the harbour, I saw a bird floating head
down in the water and for a long time afterwards included a plea for

dead birds the world over in my prayers. Had they been answered Alfred Hitchcock would have had a field day.

When the Fleet was in, the Solent would be packed with naval craft, and sometimes if you were lucky you saw one of the great ocean-going liners heading for Southampton. There were excitements all the way.

It was the equivalent of 'going abroad' – a possibility which, even if she had been able to afford it, wouldn't have occurred to my mother in her wildest dreams. She didn't hold with such things. Civilization as she pictured it ended at Dover. She did her overseas travelling vicariously, listening to the tales my father told of his time in France during the war. As far as she was concerned the rats he described as climbing over sleeping Tommies at night probably did the same thing in hotels now the war was over. It stood to reason. They had to go somewhere.

At Ryde we caught another train at the end of the pier which took us on to Sandown. The whole journey was a holiday in itself and Paddington would have considered it very good value indeed.

Once there he would have loved the smell of the ozone and the cry of the seagulls, the excitement of erecting deck chairs, the feel of the ribbed wet sand on his paws and the sucking effect as the tide went out. He would have enjoyed drawing in the sand with the end of a stick and filling his bucket with water. Like me, he would have needed to eat his seaside rock as soon as possible in order to make sure the word SANDOWN went all the way through, and afterwards he, too, would have wished he hadn't. He would have been very keen on the coloured sands from Alum Bay, and the charabancs with their 'Mystery Tours' of the island, and the seashells, and fishing in rock pools and ice-cream cornets, and the joy of making endless sandcastles with battlements topped by a Union Jack on a stick or a windmill which made a lovely whirring sound when the wind blew, and a moat which ran down to the sea so that it filled when the tide came in.

He would have enjoyed the donkey rides and the Punch and Judy show – although he might well have given Mr Punch some very hard stares. Mr Punch always made me feel uneasy too when he lost his temper.

I don't remember my father ever making any concession to being on the beach other than taking off his shoes and socks and rolling up the bottoms of his grey flannel trousers. In all the photographs taken by my mother on her Box Brownie, he is wearing a jacket and tie and smoking the inevitable pipe.

A guide-book of the time mentions that Sandown Bay was often described as being 'like the Bay of Naples'. The editor did admit that in his view it bore only the remotest resemblance, and certainly Mr and Mrs Gate, who ran the boarding house where we used to stay, could hardly have been mistaken for typical Neapolitans.

Their bungalow was situated on top of some cliffs overlooking the bay and they ran what, across the water in Portsmouth, would have been called a 'tight ship'. There were notices everywhere listing things that were not allowed and guests were expected to be out all day, come rain or shine. Mrs Gate certainly wouldn't have tolerated any modern 'hanky-panky' after lights out; small children were bad enough, and meal times were a bit of a strain, with everyone being on their best behaviour and saying how nice it all was.

Something had to give, and after several years, having studied *Holiday Haunts* (a wonderfully fat book which was published every year by the Great Western Railway, price 6d) it was decided to give Weymouth a try instead. But it wasn't the same and really only memorable because my father was nearly arrested for begging.

Out for a stroll one day we encountered a 'blind' man playing a violin and, somewhat unusually, for she tended to concentrate her viewfinder on family activities, my mother decided to take a picture of him.

Having handed her the camera, my father dutifully stationed himself nearby, holding the canvas case at the ready for when she had finished.

Enter another man and his wife, the woman fumbling in her bag. Without looking up, she deposited some coins in my father's camera case. As usual, he was too busy raising his hat to realize what had happened.

Afterwards there was a nasty scene, with my mother telling my father off for not noticing what was going on, the man berating his wife for not watching what she was doing, and the 'blind' violinist, who had miraculously recovered his sight, accusing my father of trying to steal his hard-earned takings and threatening to call the police.

I nearly saw my first talking picture at the Regal cinema in Newbury. The film was *Sunny Side Up*, with Janet Gaynor and Charles Farrell. I was once again staying with Auntie Ethel and she obviously considered it a bit of a coup – one up on Reading – for she invited a whole crowd of friends and relations along too. But her triumph was short-lived because the projector broke down and after a long wait she left in a huff with the rest of us following on behind. I remember being secretly pleased on Reading's behalf.

My mother's third half-sister emigrated to Alberta, Canada, after the First World War, having become Mrs Dick Langford when she married a Canadian soldier who in peace-time was a ranger in the National Park service, so she was a non-starter in the rather desultory race to have me to stay. But in any case, far and away my own favourite was Auntie Norah.

Auntie Norah had a husband in America, a Chinese back-scratcher and a Bell cream-maker, which I was allowed to operate as a treat when funds permitted. She also smoked a lot, but she did it through a long cigarette holder, rather in the manner of the then current advertisements for de Reszke cigarettes, and she used an ashtray in a way which made it seem much more glamorous than Auntie Emm's method of hoping for the best. Smoking and glamour went together in those days and it was the done thing to keep cigarettes in a silver case: Virginia one side, Turkish on the other.

Norah Battie's husband, Jack, didn't appear in the flesh until much later. Uncle Jack was a rolling stone and he remained one until the day he died of pneumonia at the age of eighty-three in Brighton, the town where he was born. He spent most of his life fleeing from one thing or another, but perhaps most of all from the thought of settling down.

After leaving school he entered into service with the Duke and Duchess of Sutherland, but an accident involving a coal scuttle and what became a kit of parts for a valuable Chinese porcelain vase soon put an end to it. Joining the merchant navy, he received his first taste of life in the waterfront cafés of Antwerp. His appetite whetted, he made his way to Canada, and followed that with journeys between Colombia and Bristol on a banana boat.

In 1915, seeing a poster of a man with a waxed moustache pointing a stern finger in his direction and uttering the immortal words, 'Your Country Needs You!', he joined the army.

Arriving on the Western Front just in time for the battle of Arras, it wasn't long before he discovered why Kitchener needed him so badly. Having had several pieces of shrapnel removed from his right leg and shoulder back in 'Blighty', he was given five days' leave and then returned to his unit. Wounded once again following hand-to-hand trench fighting during a surprise attack, he owed his life to a German medical orderly who found him lying in a shell hole. Resisting attempts by fellow countrymen to shoot Uncle Jack there and then, the orderly managed to carry him back behind the German lines. And there, apart from two unsuccessful attempts to escape, he remained until Armistice Day.

After the war a doctor told him he should consider taking a long sea voyage to help him get over it all. Taking the doctor at his word, Uncle Jack spent the next fifty years afloat.

His life was one long series of adventures. During Prohibition, when his ship, the *Leviathan*, was laid up in New York harbour for repairs, he got a temporary job as a barman at a club called the Riviera, which was run by a racketeer named Ben Marden. Falling for the charms of a girl who was a frequent visitor, he discovered all too late that she was already bespoken by the boss.

A man of few words, Mr Marden didn't waste many of them on Uncle Jack. 'I thought of having you cleaned, but I'm kinda partial to veterans and seamen. Still, I ain't keeping her for you to play around with,' was his succinct summing-up of the situation. 'So get the **** outa here.' Within the hour Uncle Jack was on a bus from Fort Lee heading west.

He ended up as a chief steward on the San Francisco to Sydney run via Honolulu, which was largely patronized by rich American filmstars. He grew affluent on the tips and perks that went with the job, but he was also a big spender and knew that you couldn't take it with you. It was always a case of easy come, easy go.

Auntie Norah and Uncle Jack had two children, Roger and Jean, both a few years older than me, and both in my eyes as glamorous as their mother. Jean taught me how to ride her bicycle by the simple expedient of letting go of the handlebars one day when I was trying it out for size at the top of a hill, and Roger used me as a captive audience when he was learning to play the mouth organ and practising his conjuring tricks. I felt as though I had been made an honorary member of the Magic Circle.

I was nine when I got my own first bicycle; a Hercules. It was a Sunday and I couldn't wait to take it out. After lunch, handlebars and saddle adjusted, tyres pumped up, I set off for a ride in the country. After I had gone three or four miles, I became aware of increasing pain in my stomach. It had been niggling away all that morning, but knowing it might result in my being kept indoors I had kept quiet about it. The ride back was agony and I reached home more dead than alive.

Doctor Marshall arrived on his bicycle, and without removing his clips diagnosed appendicitis. Rather than waste time looking for a telephone box, he tore off down Belmont Road to Battle Hospital. By this prompt action he undoubtedly saved my life, for by the time the ambulance arrived my appendix had already burst, which was often fatal in those days. I woke to find a large incision in my stomach, held together by an assortment of clips and stitches between which several large drainage tubes emerged.

I wasn't allowed to ride my bicycle for a long while. Instead, I spent the time endlessly taking it to pieces and putting it back together again, counting the ball-bearings until the day when I could.

At least I was excused games. I was never very keen on team games. If someone passed me the ball, my first instinct was to get rid of it as soon as possible. I lacked the killer instinct, so when teams were being picked I was usually among those who were left out, which suited me well.

When I was at last able to take to the road, my father and I enjoyed many happy days out together. He was a fund of knowledge on exactly how long it should take to cycle from pillar-box A in some remote country village, up hill and down dale to pillar-box B, and he used to time our rides with a gold hunting-cased watch which he kept at the ready in his waistcoat pocket, nodding approvingly if we arrived on schedule and confirmed his original estimate. He was very proud of the watch, which had been given to him by his colleagues when he left Newbury, and when he opened the front of the case it was so highly polished inside you could see your face in it.

My remaining grandfather still lived in Newbury, but he came to see us regularly and he always gave me sixpence. When he retired it was decided that he should come and live with us permanently. I thought the sixpences would stop, but they became a weekly ritual instead.

From the room next to my bedroom in Gloucester Road I used to watch out for him after lunch on Saturdays. As soon as I caught sight of him emerging from the New Inn to begin weaving his way up Belmont Road I was out of the front door and running so fast my feet hardly touched the ground, or so it seemed to those watching. I don't know what we talked about as we walked slowly up the road together. He was just lovely to be with and I always felt very safe holding his hand. I felt he needed me too, for he always seemed less steady on his feet at the weekend.

He would give me my sixpence and often a parcel of bloaters to carry. Later that afternoon we would have them for high tea, which would include an assortment of his favourite cakes: Lardy Cake, mouth-wateringly crisp on the outside and gooey within (but it had to be fresh), or slices of Navvy's Wedding Cake, so called because it was made with all the bit and pieces left over at the end of the week. My own favourite was Fuller's Walnut Cake accompanied by a glass or two of 'Tizer – the appetizer', which was all the rage.

Grandfather always wore a cap and was never without a carnation in his buttonhole. He also had a waxed moustache and smelled of the bay rum which he used on his hair. As with Doctor Marshall, I'm not sure the smell was necessarily always what I took it to be at the time.

A printer by trade, he suffered from poor eyesight, but until the day he died he always bought his glasses from Woolworth's – sixpence each lens and sixpence for the frame. If he could read the price on the display they were fine.

He was a great tease and used to send me out in the garden with a salt cellar, promising me a reward if I could put some on a sparrow's tail. I never managed it, but I got my reward just the same.

He once persuaded me to take a drum to pieces in order to see where the sound came from. I was very upset when I realized the truth, for it had been one of my best Christmas presents that year, but looking back on it I suspect he may simply have been wanting a bit of peace and quiet, for he liked his afternoon nap.

The following summer we gave Southsea a try for our holidays, taking grandfather with us. There wasn't much of a beach, but by then I was growing out of making sandcastles, and there was a canoe lake, a minia-ture railway, and two piers, both with amusement arcades. South Parade Pier was my favourite because it went further out to sea and had the better amusement arcade. By standing on tiptoe I could just see inside a machine called 'What the Butler Saw', but it was very flickery and no matter how fast I turned the handle nothing interesting happened. There were machines with monkeys on a pole, and others with cranes that somehow never quite managed to grasp the slippery prizes in their equally slippery jaws, delivering sweets instead. There were endless ways of losing a penny at the flick of a lever.

It was on South Parade Pier that I got my first autograph. Egged on by my grandfather, who was a military band addict and loved nothing better than sitting in a deck chair in front of the bandstand, I waylaid the Director of Music of the Band of the Royal Marines. I don't think anyone had dared do it before and there was a moment's hesitation during which I felt my stomach turn to water, because I knew he was a stickler for being on time and I was making him late. But I returned triumphant; my grandfather was very pleased with me and I thought the conductor was the best one I had ever seen.

And it was on the promenade at Southsea, not far from the pier, that one morning I witnessed one of the few family rows.

I had almost succeeded in persuading my father to take me up in an aeroplane – a five-shilling return flight from Portsmouth to the Isle of Wight. The thought appalled my grandfather and he dug his heels in, threatening to leave home if we did any such thing. 'If God had meant us to fly, He would have given us wings,' was the line he took.

He thought the world of me and used to say things like: 'I don't know where he'll end up.' Clearly, as far as he was concerned if I went up it was likely to be in the Solent, so that was that.

It's nice when other people have confidence in you, and he instilled in me a conviction that it's possible to do most things in life if you really want to and are prepared to work hard.

Despite my dislike of team games, I did support Reading football team for a while. Their ground was nearby and Grandfather sometimes took me there for a treat.

Charley Barley was my hero. Reading had bought him from Arsenal (there is no record of how much they paid). I daresay that by first division standards he was past his prime, and he was never a great goal scorer, only managing one during the time he spent with the 'Gunners'. But once he got possession of the ball he could out-dribble most other players

– *all* other players as far as I was concerned – and while he was at Reading he added another sixteen. In my book he could do no wrong and history records that in 1935 when Reading played his old club in an FA Cup match: 'Barley always made an industrious, not to say vigorous, rover.' You can't say fairer than that!

Then one day I met him. He was pushing his bicycle up Cranbury Road which ended in a steep hill near our house. As I overtook him, I plucked up the courage to stop for a brief chat. I remember being surprised that he seemed to find the hill hard going. In the end, after we had run out of things to say, I went on ahead.

Shortly afterwards Charley Barley announced his retirement. Determined to cheer him on to the last, I persuaded grandfather to take me to his benefit match, but he wasn't playing. It soured my view of professional football and I have never been to a game since.

In January 1936, King George V died and, along with the rest of the nation, we followed events on the radio, awaiting the moment when Edward, Prince of Wales, would be crowned King.

Then, one evening a few weeks later, my father arrived home from work in a state of shock. He could hardly wait to get inside the door.

It seemed that late the previous night a train containing a very inebriated Prince had pulled into Reading station. Incensed at being delayed, he opened the window of his carriage and began roundly abusing everyone in sight. A couple of postmen, who happened to be waiting on the platform for a mail train, heard him turn to a travelling companion and say he was never going to be King of this b . . . . y country. (Although he repeated the story many times, my father could never bring himself to use the word 'bloody', although he always added the 'y' to make sure the meaning was absolutely clear.)

At first people pooh-poohed the whole thing, for although the rest of the world knew what was going on, a voluntary press censorship ensured that most of Britain was kept in the dark about the Prince's infatuation with a twice-divorced American.

As the story unfolded during the weeks and months which followed, the radio began to replace the fire as the focal point in people's living-rooms. But there was much else to hear besides.

In that same year, Rudyard Kipling died and Dame Laura Knight became the first woman to be appointed to the Royal Academy. The first cross-Channel train link between Dover and Dunkirk was established and Fred Perry won the Wimbledon singles title for the third year in succession.

In Germany, Hitler launched the Volkswagen 'People's' car. A few weeks later he ordered his troops into the Rhineland.

In England two new planes, the Spitfire and the Wellington bomber flew for the first time, and the liner *Queen Mary* set sail across the Atlantic on her maiden voyage, receiving a tumultuous welcome in New York as she won the Blue Riband.

Nearer home, Mussolini was using mustard gas on the defenceless Abyssinians, and in Berlin, Heinrich Himmler was put in charge of the Third Reich's police force. The following year he was to open a concentration camp at Buchenwald, built to house enemies of the state. At the same time he took control of already existing camps at Dachau, Sachsenhausen and Lichtenburg.

A game called Monopoly was sweeping America, whilst back in Germany the black athlete, Jesse Owens, was the star of the Berlin Olympic Games, winning both the 100 and 200 metres, the former at 0.3 seconds outside my own record-breaking time of ten seconds. Hitler must have been even more mortified than Auntie Emm.

That October in London's East End, 100,000 people built barricades in an attempt to prevent a march by 7,000 of Oswald Mosley's Blackshirts.

And then, on 11 December 1936, the country heard the voice of the Duke of Windsor, uncrowned King of Great Britain and the Empire, announce his abdication. That same evening he boarded a destroyer at Portsmouth and left England for France and Mrs Simpson. It was perhaps the first crack in what until then had seemed an impregnable institution known as the House of Windsor.

In 1937 Uncle Jack received American citizenship papers and sent for Auntie Norah and his family. It was all very sudden and I felt sad to see them go.

But before that happened another reminder that nothing is for ever and was waiting just around the corner.

Christmas was hardly over when my grandfather was taken ill and once again I was sent to stay with Auntie Ethel, travelling by myself in a guard's van, with strict instructions not to speak to any strange men.

Grandfather died on 2 January 1937. For a long time afterwards my most treasured possession was a printing block he had made for me which spelled my name. The type was held between two small pieces of hardwood tightly bound together with string. I could never resist taking things to pieces, and inevitably the time came when I cut it open. As with the drum, I soon wished I hadn't. I tried putting it back together again, but it was never quite the same, for it needed the expert's hand. I was very sad to have done that to someone who had such faith in my abilities: I felt I had let him down.

CHAPTER 3

A Little Learning

'*Quel malheur!*' murmured Monsieur Charpentier.
Rap!
'Woo-hooooh!'
Really, it was quite a surprising occurrence in the
Remove Form Room at Greyfriars.
The rap of the ruler on Billy Bunter's fat knuckles
sounded almost like a pistol-shot, and the yell that
followed fairly woke the echoes.

Frank Richards (1876–1961)

One day, all unwittingly, my father did me a very good turn. He introduced me to a weekly boys' magazine called the *Magnet*. We were out
for a walk with Binkie one morning when he happened to notice it
being advertised on a hoarding outside a newsagent's shop. It had been
his boyhood reading and he suggested I might like to give it a try. At
first I resisted the idea. Like most boys of my age I lived for the present:
anything which smacked of being 'old hat' was beyond the pale. Also,
my school days were far from being the happiest days of my life. The
thought of reading about someone else's problems didn't exactly thrill
me. In the end I compromised and for the sake of peace and quiet agreed
to give it a go for a couple of weeks.

Until then, comics had come and gone. I had never been totally loyal
to any one in particular. I wasn't very keen on the *Boy's Own Paper*,
which was always telling its readers to take a cold bath if they were
troubled by their thoughts, ignoring the fact that some people actually
get pleasure from them, and going on about how to excel in games,
which I knew I never would, so I tended to go for whichever magazine

happened to have the best free gift; one week *Hotspur*, another week the *Wizard*.

I was deeply addicted to catalogues; Halford's I knew by heart, along with the Hornby *Book of Trains* and the *Hobbies Annual*, which always came with free plans of things to make tucked inside.

The *Magnet* turned out to be totally different to anything I had come across before and I was hooked from the word go. Best of all, it made me laugh out loud.

Set in a fictitious public school called Greyfriars, the stories centred around the adventures of Harry Wharton & Co., of the fourth form, who together made up a group known as the Famous Five. But out of a whole host of characters, the undoubted hero, the reason why most people bought the magazine, was an unlikely specimen called Billy Bunter. Alone amongst the other boys, who all wore grey flannel bags under their blazers, Bunter got away with trousers which had an unbelievably hideous pattern of enormous black and white squares. When he adorned the cover of the *Magnet*, as he usually did, it could be spotted a mile away and one's feeling of anticipation quickened, knowing he would be getting into another of his scrapes, and wondering how on earth he would get out of it.

Otherwise known as the Fat Owl of the Remove, Bunter was the epitome of all a schoolboy shouldn't be; grossly overweight, for ever borrowing money on the expectation of fictitious postal orders he knew would never arrive; lazy, obtuse, cunning, lying his way into and out of trouble, unloved and unlovable, he had nothing to recommend him. He was an anti-hero if ever there was one. But when he slipped an exercise book inside the seat of his trousers before receiving a justifiably severe caning from Mr Quelch, the angular master of the Remove, his readers squirmed with him. If we laughed it was with the uneasy feeling that there, but for the grace of God, go I.

Unlike the editor of the *Boy's Own Paper*, who must have been responsible for filling many an Englishman's mind with guilt complexes, Frank Richards, who wrote the stories, created an evergreen world full of wholly believable characters, whose reactions and phraseology were so totally predictable it gave one a warm feeling of security and strengthened one's belief that all was for the best in the best of all possible worlds.

I used to read it from beginning to end – often under the bedclothes at night with the aid of a torch – from the top left-hand corner of the front cover through to the bottom right-hand corner of the back, with its advertisements for stamps and guitars and Webley air pistols, billiard tables, cricket bats (willow blades, rubber handle, treble spring; worth 10s.6d – only 5s.6d!), and other accessories; not to mention lotions guaranteed to rid you of spots, and offers to cure blushing or increase your height by 2–5 inches in less than twelve days. Someone once told me they had sent away for the last named and received a block of wood through the post! The Trade Descriptions Act didn't exist in those days.

I was so steeped in the *Magnet* I felt I could have written the whole thing myself.

Although I didn't realize it at the time, it was a wonderful grounding in the business of writing. It taught me the importance of always giving value for money, of the need to capture the reader's attention with the opening paragraph and at the end leave him feeling satisfied, yet wanting more. It taught me the value of plotting and of the natural rhythm of good story-telling. Above all, it taught me that if you have well-developed, well-rounded characters and put them into believable situations, the story will develop of its own accord. If the author doesn't believe in his characters no one else is going to.

The name Frank Richards adorned the cover of the *Magnet*, but it was only one of twenty-eight pen names used by Charles Hamilton, who died in 1961 at the age of eighty-six. Bunter, by then, had reached the technical age of seventy-six. In the *Guinness Book of Records* Charles Hamilton is credited with having written over 100,000,000 words. The *Magnet* and its companion journal, the *Gem*, which was about another school called Rookwood, accounted for 80,000 words a week, mostly churned out on an old upright Remington. The pleasure he gave during his lifetime is immeasurable.

Fee-paying public boarding schools are a peculiarly British institution and there doesn't seem to be the equivalent of the *Magnet* in other countries. A curious fact about Charles Hamilton is that although he spent a lifetime writing about public schools he never went to one himself, but then neither did the vast majority of his readers. In fact, he was educated at 'a school for young gentlemen in Ealing', near to where he was born.

Apart from a relatively small elite who have their names put down at birth, schooling is often a case of pot luck; a matter of one's family living in a certain place at a certain time.

It was pot luck, plus the fact that my mother was much taken with the rich purple colour of the blazer, that led to my receiving a Catholic education, although we were, if anything, lapsed C. of E. In any event, the time came when I exchanged my plain belt with its snake motif buckle for a superior version with coloured stripes.

Other than the difficulty I'd had in going to sleep during compulsory rest periods, and playing the triangle from time to time, I remember absolutely nothing about my primary school beyond the smell of unwashed blankets. I used to pull mine over my head to keep out the afternoon light and to prevent the teacher finding out I was still awake.

My new school, on the other hand, gave me an invaluable grounding in the fact that life is basically unfair. One of the great advantages of English schools is that they prepare you for the worst. It's rather like serving a prison sentence before you commit the crime. The Irish Brothers who ran it were strict disciplinarians, compensating for their enforced celibacy with the aid of thick inch-wide rubber straps, kept at the ready beneath their long black gowns. They were whipped out like six-shooters on the slightest pretext. Some masters were worse than others; some, one quickly realized, positively relished the task and one steered clear of them as far as possible, hiding behind corners until they had passed. In the classroom, pupils became adept at dodging pieces of chalk and wood-backed blackboard cleaners which the Brothers occasionally threw at their charges out of sheer frustration. It was a case of the quick and the dead.

Caning was the headmaster's prerogative; a perk of the job. There was a certain ritual attached to it; the long wait in the corridor outside his room beforehand, the slow flexing of the bamboo cane and the testing of it on his gown. The latter sometimes gave rise to a small dust cloud. But since caning was always administered on the hands, I never had a chance to emulate Billy Bunter and place an exercise book inside my trousers.

Ear tweaking was another painful punishment, and although I never actually saw anyone's lobe come away in a master's hand, it always looked as though it must do and often felt as though it had. Checking it out at the time was considered a sign of weakness, so it was with a sense of relief that one discovered during break that it was still there. The human body can withstand an extraordinary amount of abuse.

There was a school 'library' in a glass-fronted cabinet and an up-to-date science lab, but the doors to both were kept firmly locked unless parents of prospective pupils were in the offing.

One thing we did have in common with Greyfriars was a French master who was the spitting image of Frank Richards' Monsieur Charpentier.

'Mossoo', as he was nicknamed in the stories, was the epitome of all the Monsieur Duponts and Monsieur Blancs in school textbooks current at the time; short and stout, excitable, with a pencil moustache and a permanently worried air.

Although I don't recall our 'Mossoo' ever murmuring *'Quel malheur'*, he did inadvertently teach us our first French swearword. In the nature of things it was the one word none of us ever forgot, proving that in the end repetition is still one of the best methods of learning.

It was John Allaway who relayed the news. He arrived at school one day all excited because the previous evening he'd met the French master coming out of a pork butchers in the Oxford Road where we normally bought our faggots. He was carrying a packet of sausages and as they passed each other it slipped from his hand, landing, as ill luck would have it, in the middle of a pile of dog mess on the pavement. At which point there had been a loud cry of *Merde*!

We couldn't wait for the next French lesson. As soon as it began a forest of hands shot up.

'Please, Sir. What does *merde* mean?'

'Is it French for sausages?'

'Please, Sir, I can't find it in my dictionary.'

'Is it masculine or feminine?'

Poor man. We ragged him mercilessly. Some days the noise level was so high it brought the headmaster running. 'Mossoo' stuck it for the rest of the term and then left.

He was followed by a Miss Campion, who wore glasses and was a bit of a dragon, or so we thought. But at the end of her first term she appeared looking radiant in a hat and flowered dress and announced she wanted to show us her fiancé. *Sensation! Murmur! Murmur!* John Allaway was convinced it was another taboo French word. The truth was something of a let-down; it was a man, very English and clearly embarrassed at being shown off in front of the class. That was the last we ever saw of Miss Campion. One of the Brothers took over and somehow French lessons were never the same again.

John Allaway, taking his mind off magazines like *Razzle* and *Stocking Parade* for a change, tried pushing his luck once too often and fell foul of the English teacher, Brother Ambrose – or 'Hambone' as we called him – a master notorious for his incredibly short temper. Brother Ambrose bustled into the room one day clutching a pile of exercise books which he distributed around the class and then invited Allaway to stand and read aloud from an essay he'd written on gardening. All was quiet until he got to the fatal bit.

'. . . Some people put manure on their rhubarb. We prefer custard on ours!'

Brother Ambrose led the gales of laughter which rocked the classroom, then he held up his hand for silence.

'Come here, boy!'

Allaway approached the platform.

'Hold out your hand.'

Out came the rubber strap.

To say that my days at school were among the least happy of my life wouldn't be entirely true; there were moments of enormous fun and times when I laughed so much I thought I would burst with the pain, but on the whole I don't look back on them with any great pleasure. Being a day boy at a boarding school, and a Catholic one at that, left me feeling a bit of an outsider. Bullying was rife and largely unchecked. It went in waves and was, I suppose, a form of ethnic cleansing. When I knew it was going to happen to me I used to hide in the shrubbery until the bell rang.

But there was no escape. 'They' would be lying in wait at break time, all set for goings-on behind the bicycle shed: tortures, debagging, or the throwing of bits of school uniform into the 'coffee pot' – a well-shaped brick-built enclosure of unknown depth where the gardener kept his manure. You considered yourself lucky if you got away with simply being dumped in after your uniform. The sense of relief when it was someone else's turn was immeasurable, although I'm glad to say I never took advantage of the fact and joined in.

Children can be very beastly to each other and inflict untold miseries when they feel like it.

An act of beastliness on my part, although I didn't realize the full meaning or extent of it at the time, happened one day when a boy called Edmund Pierce and I were invited to spend the day with Neville Cohen, a newcomer to the school, whose father ran a chemist's shop.

It turned into a case of two's company, three's a crowd, and after a while there was an argument over something totally trivial.

Anxious to wound, and instinctively aware that there are times when a single word can strike home and inflict more damage than a whole stream of invective, I chanted 'Jewboy!' at Neville Cohen.

In my defence it was an age when boys' stories were peppered with derogatory expressions like wops, wogs, chinks, dagos, frogs, yanks, limeys, yids and the like, but it was no excuse: I had meant to hurt, but not to cause great pain.

He went white, as though he had been struck, and rushed indoors to tell his father, who took immediate action. Locking his shop to customers, he came out into the garden and gave me a short, sharp lecture, one he had clearly delivered many times before and which came from the heart. Then he forbade me ever to speak to his son or to visit their house again.

I tried to apologize, but he wouldn't listen. All he would say was that he hoped one day I would realize what I had done, and of course, over the years I did.

Whenever I see pictures of the Holocaust, of Nazi concentration camps, or indeed any form of intolerance, racial or otherwise, I think of Neville Cohen, and of his father, burning with rage and sorrow on his son's behalf.

And, as with my moment of weakness in old Mrs Robins' shop, I would have given anything to turn back the clock. Of course I couldn't, but both taught me a lasting lesson.

There were days when I did everything I could to avoid going to school. Slivers of soap covered with sugar was one method. Swallowed whole before breakfast, they usually produced the desired effect long before it was time to leave home. Another ploy, much less successful because it required a degree of accuracy, entailed hitting my knee with a sharp stone in an effort to draw blood without inflicting too much pain. My route to school took me along Parkside Road, which in those days was unmade, so there was no shortage of stones. I usually ended up arriving late, but with badly bruised knees.

One day on the spur of the moment I sought refuge from my tormentors by inventing a short piece of prose which, although it lacked meaning, sounded impressive. It did the trick, stopping them in their tracks, and I subsequently used it from time to time in moments of dire emergency.

Eventually it came to the attention of Brother Ambrose, and he signalled me out front and bade me do my party piece. It was, I suppose, a public performance of my first unaided literary work.

'The verbosity of your impudence is atrocious and if you do not immediately resume your former attitude I shall be bound to administer adequate punishment.'

I normally recited it as fast as I could, relying on speed to divert attention from the actual words, but on this occasion I enunciated everything as clearly as possible.

'Now, boy!' barked Brother Ambrose, an unholy gleam in his eye, 'Perhaps you will kindly explain to the rest of the class precisely what you mean by that.'

I floundered unhappily for some moments before retiring from the platform, my reputation and sole means of defence in tatters.

Worse still, from that moment on I was a marked man. The low profile I had worked so hard to achieve over the months had been penetrated. I was made to exchange my desk in the back row for one at the front, and for several terms I had to endure the verbal barbs of Brother Ambrose, who let no opportunity of calling on me to explain things pass him by, and who once – for a reason I never fathomed – leapt on me in a paroxysm of rage and gave me such a battering about the head it reduced the rest of the class to total silence.

As I lay in a heap on the floor, I hoped I would get a mastoid like my cousin Eric. Then the police would come and Brother Ambrose would get his just deserts.

'Hard luck, Bondy!' everyone said afterwards, and I knew they meant it.

Not all the masters were like Brother Ambrose. Some were kindness itself and one longed for crumbs from their table. Because I rode a bicycle, one of them occasionally sent me into Reading to pick up a parcel from a shop which was run by the parents of Tim, a boy in my class who was later to become my 'best friend'.

'Just ask for the usual – they'll know.'

The parcel was always tightly wrapped ready for collection and the brother would be waiting for me when I got back, having proudly accomplished my mission.

It wasn't until years later that I realized the shop, which was part of a mineral water factory, was also an off-licence.

The Brothers' celibacy must have washed off on their charges, for apart from an entry in an early diary – 'Went newting with Jesse: *super!*' – girls, for all practical purposes, might not have existed. Girls spelt TROUBLE.

Not that I was entirely uninterested. For a brief period I spent several nights sitting up late at my bedroom window in the hope of seeing a naked woman at large. I'd happened to overhear a conversation between my mother and Mrs Blake, the one who 'did' for us. According to Mrs Blake there was a lady in Belmont Road – 'no better than she should be' – who had developed a habit of taking off all her clothes and running around the streets naked whenever there was a full moon. But either I had misread the lunar symbols in my diary or she waited until the very early hours, for she never materialized.

When she was eventually pointed out to me in broad daylight I couldn't see what all the fuss was about.

For a long time I had to content myself with daily visits to Woolworth's. Propping my bicycle up outside the store, I did the rounds, checking on all the items they had for sale until I could have done an inventory in my sleep. At the same time I seized the opportunity to gaze furtively at the statuesque girls behind the counter.

They seemed too remote for words; the real-life equivalent of the sort of beings one saw staring out of the pages of film magazines, and as far as I was concerned equally unattainable. I would have run a mile if one of them had actually spoken to me. Instead, I used to go back home and lie on my bed with my eyes closed, darting in my mind from one to the other as I tried to place them in order of preference. I took the advice of the editor of *Boys' Own Paper* and had a lot of cold baths as well.

It wasn't until long afterwards that I realized they were standing on raised platforms behind the counter so that they could see over the top, but by all accounts a lot of film stars needed building up too.

The time came when we said goodbye to 21 Gloucester Road and moved to a larger house on a new estate not far from my school. It was semi-detached, with bay windows and woodwork varnished in imitation graining, a much-sought-after embellishment for which Haddocks, the builders, had acquired a reputation. A 'Haddock-built house' had a certain cachet.

They came in three sizes, the only noticeable difference between them, apart from the price, being the shape of the bay windows in the biggest two, or the lack of any at all in the smallest. But from a social point of view it was the equivalent of the Indian caste system; the occupants of the three different classes rarely mingled, or even spoke to each other. The largest houses were on the highest ground, convenient for the Corporation bus stop and with space for a garage; the smallest were on low ground near the main railway line and the winter floods. Number 7 Winser Drive was on the middle ground, and with the English propensity for naming their houses, we called ours 'Viewlands'.

Binkie was pleased to have a bigger garden, not to mention endless possibilities for country walks along the Kennet and Avon Canal, where I would fish for minnows (but to my secret relief never actually caught any other than by using a net – although to a minnow the means is probably academic).

To celebrate the move, I acquired three guinea-pigs. I called them Pip, Squeak and Wilfred, after some strip cartoon characters whose adventures were chronicled in a daily newspaper. As a means of learning the facts of life they proved even more of a let-down than Binkie, adding confusion where previously none had existed; at least with Binkie one knew exactly where one stood. One of them, I never discovered which – and they certainly weren't letting on – produced a litter of young. I tried to get my money back from Edmund Pierce, who'd sold them to me having professed expert knowledge on the sexing of guinea-pigs, but he was having none of it.

I suppose I could have borrowed a book on the subject from the public library and looked up the relevant diagrams for myself, but as a source of reading material it was low on my mother's list. 'You never know where they've been,' was her attitude. She much preferred her subscription with

Boots, the Cash Chemists, who before the war ran a lending library. It struck me that the same stricture might well apply to their books, but at least they had antiseptics close to hand.

My mother visited Boots once a week and always came back armed with the week's reading, mostly English detective fiction – she didn't approve of American crime novels, pronouncing them too violent. So at a relatively early age I became steeped in the more civilized Home Counties style of murder, as related by the likes of Freeman Wills Crofts, John Rhode and Agatha Christie.

When those were exhausted, photography took over for a while. After a lot of agonizing I bought myself a second-hand Kodak 'Autographic' camera from a shop called Oddments in the Oxford Road. It was owned by a young Arthur Negus, who was to achieve fame on television in the *Antiques Road Show*. It cost me 7s.6d, and when I got it home and examined it more closely I decided I'd been sold a pup, for behind the lens there were some pieces of interleaved material which looked as though they were cracked.

I plucked up courage, and once again tried getting my money back, but like Edmund Pierce before him, Arthur Negus wasn't having any of it either.

Back home, I found that by moving a lever I could make a hole in the centre of the cracked metal plates grow larger or smaller. With the discovery of the variable aperture came a whole new world. From that moment on, instead of putting titles under my photographs, I put things like '1/100th sec. at f4.5 – weather cloudy'. I did my own developing and printing, using pie dishes which I borrowed from my mother. It didn't seem to affect her pastry and the excitement of seeing pictures appear where none had been before has never dulled.

Fretwork was another hobby, especially around Christmas time when there were presents to be made. The dining-room table bore numerous nicks around the edge where I had been in too much of a hurry to use the clamp-on metal cutting table provided with my Hobbies outfit. And when I wasn't out taking pictures or making pipe-racks, I was busy with a soldering iron, building amplifiers and radio sets.

Words like 'electronics' and 'miniaturization' had yet to be coined. 'Tranny' meant a transformer, not a transistor radio or a photographic transparency. I used to play around with bits of wire and valves and large coils with 'Hear What the Wild Waves are Saying' printed on the side. The thrill of getting a wireless set to oscillate almost equalled that of seeing a photograph appear on a sheet of bromide paper, and I can still remember the distinctive smell of ebonite when it was being cut with a hacksaw. All the while, over and over again, I played my one gramophone record: 'I Like Mountain Music'. It was my 'test record' for every new amplifier I built – the equivalent of the BBC's 'Teddy Bears' Picnic'.

Recently, when I was telling my grand-daughter, Robyn, about it – bemoaning the fact that when I was small I only had the one tune to listen to – she said: 'Why didn't you turn the record over, Papa?'

In 1933, on a screen which had grown from postcard-size to around six inches by four, a performing seal was shown making its way across the marbled entrance hall of Broadcasting House – probably on its way to the canteen.

In 1935 the first ten Penguin paperback books were published. They included *A Farewell to Arms*, by Ernest Hemingway, Eric Linklater's *Poet's Pub* and Mary Webb's *Gone to Earth*. Although one didn't realize it at the time, it was the start of a revolution in the book trade.

Around that time my father had a telephone installed. It was an object of some veneration, not to say fear on my mother's part. Until then bad news had always arrived by telegram. The sight of a telegraph boy propping his bicycle up outside a house sent a feeling of dread through many a household during the First World War, and it continued to do so for years afterwards.

I can't remember who made the first incoming call, but it was as though the house had been struck by lightning. My mother had palpitations, clutching her breast and saying: 'Who on earth can *that* be?' in accusing tones.

She never lost her fear of the telephone. If it rang after six o'clock in the evening the cry was: 'Who on earth can it be at this time of night?'

The obvious solution was to pick up the receiver and find out, but that was usually left to my father.

Anywhere outside Reading counted as a trunk call, which meant the whole house went quiet and conversations were kept to a minimum.

In November 1936, after spending several years experimenting with rival systems, the BBC committed itself to a daily television service from Alexandra Palace using a high definition system developed by EMI Limited.

That same year you could buy a brand new Ford 'Popular' car for £115.

In time the one would provide the masses with a window on the world, and the second a means of viewing it at first hand.

Films were still the most popular form of public entertainment. Along with Tim, my newly acquired 'best friend', who lived just around the corner from our new house, I became an addict. We went as often as possible – whenever we could afford it.

Cinemas provided a wonderful escape from reality. Going to the 'flicks' became a way of life. By the end of the thirties Reading had no less than nine cinemas and for 1s.9d you entered a world of velvet-covered seats, textured walls with concealed lighting, rich curtaining, and ceilings with tiny lights which twinkled overhead during the intervals like stars in the night sky and made even the usherettes look glamorous.

Above all, it was a world of happy endings. Life seldom lived up to the Hollywood of those days. Apart from cigarettes, it was the only narcotic available to the man in the street and it came with all the extras: double features, The March of Time, 'shorts' with the Three Stooges or the Ritz Brothers, a Pete Smith Speciality, plus a cartoon, next week's trailers and the inevitable newsreel. Numbered seats didn't exist, and if you felt so inclined, which I often did, you could stay put and see the whole programme through again. During the interval there would be a rush to find better seats. The newly built Odeon next door to the Palace Theatre boasted a display box outside which showed moving 'stills' from the current feature films; inside it had an organ which rose up through the floor and made the whole building shake when it was being played. Constantly changing coloured lights inside the organ added to the effect. On Sunday evenings the Odeon bridged the gap between the silver screen and the music hall by staging live band shows: Billy Cotton, Ambrose, Geraldo, Jack Jackson, Jack Hylton, Joe Loss – I saw them all.

Film Pictorial and the *Melody Maker* kept me up to date on all the latest gossip.

Because of the different distribution systems at the time, films were around for much longer. First-run cinemas in the centre of town took their pick, after the London run of course, and long queues would form.

Afterwards they would go on to the second-run establishments, like the Rex, the Granby and the Regal, all of which changed their programmes twice a week, so there was never a shortage of things to see.

Each of the cinemas had its own particular smell. After being taken in a school party to see *David Copperfield* I stayed clear of the Granby for a long time. There was a very peculiar odour – probably because there had been a lot of other school parties that week. I sat through it wondering if in some way it was meant to add colour to the film – an early 'Smell-O-Vision'. It put me off Dickens as well.

All the same, it had an extraordinary cast list: Basil Rathbone, Maureen O'Sullivan, Lionel Barrymore, Roland Young, Frank Lawton, Lewis Stone, Elsa Lanchester and many more ... Freddie Bartholomew was in the title role, and W. C. Fields played Mr Micawber. He replaced Charles Laughton, who had resigned after two days of shooting. At the time, rumour had it that on the rushes Laughton looked as though he had designs on the child star!

'A' films were a problem because we weren't allowed in without an adult, so either we waylaid someone in the queue and got them to pretend we were with them – in which case we got in half-price – or one of us pretended to be an adult and paid the full whack.

One day I borrowed a pair of my father's long trousers and by standing on tiptoe at the box office, managed to get in to see an 'adults only' double bill of Boris Karloff's legendary *Frankenstein* and *Dracula* with Bella Lugosi. (Both had an H certificate, which meant *no one under sixteen* was allowed in!) But I wasn't that shocked. Having dabbled in wireless, there was little you could do with terminals that I didn't know about, and after my many efforts trying to avoid going to school I was used to the sight of blood.

It was the Golden Age of Hollywood. The stars were like gods and goddesses, and, although the reality was somewhat different, it was an age of putting people on pedestals, not knocking them down. For all its faults, Hollywood knew what people wanted and gave it to them. It fixed its sights on the vast and growing middle classes; its only competitor, the music hall, had always catered for the so-called working classes. In their wisdom, the Hollywood moguls knew instinctively that mystery lends its own enchantment. Remove it and film stars become just like anyone else. Once that happens there is no going back; something our own royal family has since found out to its cost. As General de Gaulle once wisely said in another context: 'Authority doesn't work without prestige and prestige doesn't work without distance.'

Above all, from the very first shot and the opening music, you knew where you stood with the studio system.

It was MGM for the big musicals; Paramount had the Marx Brothers, Bing Crosby, Bob Hope and Dorothy Lamour; Warner Brothers specialized in gangster movies; and with Universal you knew that if there was a hotel scene Franklin Pangborn would be behind the reception desk playing the flustered manager and you could settle back, ready to enjoy a good laugh at his expense.

Along with millions of others I fell in love many times over. Claudette Colbert one week, Barbara Stanwyck the next, believing that if only we could meet it would be love at first sight for them too; a belief which was carefully fostered by the studios.

I watched Deanna Durbin receive her first screen kiss. The film was called *Nice Girl?* and Robert Stack was the lucky man. Making allowances for her undoubted podginess and her unfortunate habit of holding up the action by bursting into song on the slightest pretext, I had been in love with her myself for quite a while, so I had mixed feelings.

That there were others who felt the same way shouldn't really have come as a surprise, for soon after she made her debut in *Three Smart Girls* I sent off for her picture, and much to my disappointment when it arrived some weeks later her signature had been printed. It destroyed something rather precious and I resolved that if I ever became famous I would always make sure that anything I signed would be genuine.

I didn't care much for Judy Garland, or Fred Astaire for that matter. It wasn't until many years later that I began to appreciate how great they were. I suppose it took me a while to shake off the inbuilt British suspicion of anyone who is exceptionally good at something. Instead, I revelled in the Andy Hardy films; Mr Moto, played by the wonderful Peter Lorre; Charlie Chan, first with Warner Oland and later with Sidney Toler; and the sort of backstage musicals that Jack Oakie and Alice Faye always seemed to be in.

Perhaps we were easily pleased, but films, and indeed most forms of creative work, are like wine: you need to drink a great deal of the bad and the mediocre before you learn to recognize and appreciate the good.

Gradually, over a period of time, I began to concentrate more and more on the credit lists and learned to recognize the work of particular directors and cameramen.

Despite the competition, music hall was still popular and all the stars of the day visited the Palace Theatre: Max Miller, Ronald Frankau, Larry Adler – who inspired me to swap my ocarina and my Jews Harp for a Hohner mouth organ – not to mention the great illusionists of the day like Maskelyne, who could fill an entire bill. As with the cinemas, I loved the red plush and the atmosphere; the advertisements that were projected on to the safety curtain during the interval, the electric signs on each side of the stage that changed to show the number of the act, and above all the live orchestra. I laughed at jokes I didn't really understand, hoped that Phyllis Dixey would reveal all behind her ostrich feathers – but she never did, and if she had I'm not sure I would have recognized what it was I was supposed not to see – marvelled at the acrobats and the jugglers, and watched open-mouthed as girls were sawn in two and elephants disappeared before my very eyes.

Afterwards, not appreciating the fact that all these people had honed their acts to perfection over the years through sheer hard work, often forced to die a thousand deaths in front of notoriously hard to please first-night audiences at places like the Glasgow Empire, I tried to emulate them. But the jokes never sounded quite as funny and I never did make middle C on my harmonica. My mother made herself scarce when she spotted me with a saw, and Binkie positively refused to disappear when I waved my wand.

One evening at the Palace Theatre the curtain rose prematurely after a quick scene change and revealed a stagehand who had been caught unawares. I decided that was what I wanted to be when I grew up – a scene shifter. Without learning any lines he not only received a round of applause from the audience, but there were cries of 'More! More!' from the back.

My parents greeted the news with a distinct lack of enthusiasm. School fees were costing them money they could probably ill afford on top of their mortgage, and it must have seemed a poor return for their investment in my future.

So instead of treading the boards, I lowered my sights and embarked on my *big enterprise*, the one which in the end took up most of my spare time. I began constructing a marionette theatre, complete with revolving stage, lighting equipment and sound. It began life in a small way in a corner of the garden shed, but as it expanded it gradually forced my long-suffering father to remove his tools to a coal shed nearby.

The job completed, in a burst of enthusiasm he challenged me to a race down the garden path.

Head down, I set off between the two sheds as fast as I could go. It wasn't until I drew near the fence at the bottom of the garden that I realized I was on my own. Looking back over my shoulder, I saw my father lying on the ground clutching his head. Closer inspection revealed a bump the size of a duck's egg. After a couple of yards – enough to get up speed – he had run slap-bang into the shed!

The great thing about the theatre was that it combined all my interests: carpentry, electricity and photography. Scenery and props had to be made, puppets constructed and made to work. There were scripts to be written and programmes to be designed and printed out on a home-made copier, the plans for which I had got out of one of my annuals.

In the beginning the fun was all in the building, but gradually I began to realize there would be no room for an audience, so I transferred the entire thing to the loft, glossing over any problems I might encounter in trying to attract an audience, particularly my own mother, who didn't like heights and Tim, who wouldn't have got through the opening.

School was very much an intrusion into all these activities and I couldn't wait for lessons to finish so that I could get on with things and put on my first show.

However, it was 1939 and it wasn't to be; there were other intrusions on the horizon. Newsreels, which the previous year had shown pictures of Mr Chamberlain returning from Germany waving his piece of paper and saying 'Peace in our time', were becoming steadily more gloomy.

That March, Hitler entered Prague, occupying 'foreign' territory for the first time, whilst in England the Government announced they were doubling the strength of the Territorial Army and introducing conscription for the over-twenties. The unthinkable – another war with Germany – was becoming a distinct possibility. The consensus of opinion was that if it did happen it would all be over very quickly. The thought that it might last long enough for me to become personally involved never entered my mind.

One morning I arrived at school rather earlier than usual and found my form room occupied by several extremely large boys smoking cigars. Several of my form mates produced cigarettes and we all sat down to welcome our new friends, who turned out to be refugees from Holland. Such *entente* as we had managed to establish vanished in a flash when Brother Ambrose came into the room and caught us at it.

His response was less than *cordiale*. Quelch-like, out came the strap. Drawing the line at tackling the Dutch boys, who were bigger than he was and pretended they didn't understand what he was saying anyway, 'adequate punishment was duly administered'. One could hardly blame Brother Ambrose on that occasion, although I did think he might have done more to conceal the nicotine stains on his own fingers when he confiscated our cigarettes.

On 31 August the Government began the massive evacuation of over 1.5 million children from the cities. Neither the children nor their parents knew where they were going, only that 'both would be told later'. Labels round their necks, gas masks slung over their shoulders, and each carrying a small case containing toothbrush, comb, handkerchief, spare clothing and enough food for the day the children departed; for many it was to be their first sight of the country and all that went with it; the cows, the sheep, the green fields. For their parents, given the knowledge that they might never see each other again, it was an unbelievably heart-rending occasion.

At 5.45 a.m. the next day Hitler invaded Poland. At 10.00 a.m. the BBC was given two hours to close down its television station so as to prevent the signal being used as a navigational aid by German aircraft. The last programme to be transmitted was a Mickey Mouse cartoon.

CHAPTER 4

Decision Time

Youth would be an ideal state if it came a little later in life.

Lord Asquith (1852–1928)

On Sunday, 3 September 1939, having listened to Neville Chamberlain's voice on the wireless declare '. . . this country is now at war with Germany. We are ready,' my father and I went out into the garden in order to make sure we were. The sun was shining and we filled a sandbag with earth, one of several which had been issued to us. Carrying it back to the house together, it proved much heavier than we had expected and, not knowing quite what to do with it, we stood it by the back door. It seemed rather futile, but at least it was a gesture.

Deciding to leave the others until after lunch, we went indoors to await developments. Anticipating the worst, I had already persuaded my parents to let me cover the windows with a criss-cross pattern of sticky tape to prevent damage by flying glass. An air-raid siren sounded and we gazed up at the sky wondering if bombs were about to fall (I had seen newsreels of the Spanish Civil War being waged), but nothing happened.

Elsewhere, all over the country, people were doing much the same thing, although on a grander scale. Cinemas and theatres were closed down and sports gatherings involving large crowds were prohibited. The Coronation Chair had already been taken to an unknown destination for safekeeping, along with works of art and other treasures from the major museums.

BBC Radio began dispersing its orchestras and other departments. Sleepy country towns like Evesham suddenly found themselves invaded by strange men with beards who spoke with a foreign accent, and in some instances, when they enquired the way to 'ze secret radio station', found themselves being arrested as spies.

Members of the variety department, having opened their sealed envelopes marked 'Top Secret', found themselves heading for Bristol. For several days it seemed as though only Sandy MacPherson was left to hold the fort, interminably playing old favourites on his organ.

Pending the issue of identity cards, people were advised to wear labels bearing their full name and address around their necks. Signposts and station names were removed in order to confuse the enemy. It certainly worked as far as the general public was concerned. A strict black-out was enforced; cars were allowed one headlight provided it had a hole which was no more than two inches wide. Buses, their windows covered with adhesive netting, ran with interior lights turned off, and the occupants of railway carriages made do with a blue glow. On foot, the populace at large had to grope their way round. In the early days of the war more people were killed or injured in London as a result of the black-out than by bombs. Along with the vast majority of the population, I stayed indoors listening to the radio.

It was the end of my seaside holidays as a child. Beaches along the south coast were closed and barbed wire appeared where once there had been sandcastles. In the cities, railings were removed from parks and other public places as the drive for scrap metal began.

In readiness for the onslaught, mortuaries were stacked with piles of cardboard coffins, but for a while the only bombs to go off were those left by the IRA in Piccadilly Circus and Charing Cross, and at Victoria Station, where a man was killed.

The black-out was strictly enforced. Air-raid wardens patrolled the streets to make sure the regulations were obeyed. People were advised to eat plenty of carrots to improve their night vision. I remember a man living a few doors away who was very pleased with himself because he had drilled a hole in the front of his pipe and inserted a piece of red glass so that it would glow when he was out at night. It was hard to tell whether he was coming or going.

Another casualty, which brought home to me the seriousness of the situation, was the *Magnet*; an early victim of paper rationing.

The war put an end to my theatre project. At night the 'house lights' could be clearly seen through gaps in the roof tiles; one thing Haddocks, the builders, hadn't bargained on. While other theatres gradually began to reopen, mine was to stay closed for ever.

Sandy MacPherson added songs like 'Run, Rabbit, Run' and 'We're Going to Hang Out Our Washing on the Siegfried Line' to his repertoire. He was joined by Mr Middleton, 'the radio gardener', who every Sunday afternoon exhorted us to grow more vegetables as part of the Dig for Victory campaign. Over breakfast the fruity, down-to-earth tones of Dr Charles Hill, the 'radio doctor' – later to become Director-General of the BBC – lectured us on the state of our bowels, advising us all to eat more prunes.

Life settled down into an uneasy calm before the storm. It was the start of what became known as the 'Phoney War' – what the French called the '*drôle de guerre*' – although for those at sea it was anything but phoney.

The day war was declared a German U-boat sank the liner *Athenia* off the Hebrides with the loss of 112 lives. Even so, the Air Minister, Kingsley Wood, rejected a plan to bomb the Black Forest on the grounds that it was private property. Hitler must have rubbed his hands with joy and wonder.

By the middle of October, 156,000 tons of British shipping had fallen victim to the U-boats, including the battleship *Royal Oak*, which was torpedoed while it was at anchor in its home base at Scapa Flow.

The following year, when the liner *Andorra Star* was sunk by a German U-Boat, the hotel and restaurant industry would mourn the loss of some 1,500 of its Italian and German members, including many top chefs. Classed as 'enemy aliens', the ship had been transporting them to Canada for the duration.

On the other side of the coin, an estimated twenty U-boats had been sunk and before the year ended the pocket battleship *Graf Spee* had been scuttled after being trapped in the River Plate by British warships.

That December, King George VI ended his Christmas Day broadcast to the nation by reading some lines from a poem by a little-known author.

> I said to man who stood at the gate of the
> year: 'Give me a light that I may tread safely into the

> unknown.' And he replied: 'Go out into the darkness
> and put your hand into the hand of God. That shall be
> to you better than light and safer than a known way.'

It struck exactly the right note and afterwards people flocked to buy copies of Minnie Louise Haskin's poems. A hasty reprint sold 43,000 copies and ensured her an entry in *Who's Who*.

It must have had a powerful effect for it remains one of the few poems I can still remember.

The beginning of 1940 was so cold the Thames froze over for the first time since 1888. There was a shortage of coal, and butter, bacon, sugar and meat were all rationed. It was even colder for many people in Europe as Germany began the mass deportation of Jews from occupied countries under the direction of Adolf Eichmann.

When spring finally arrived in England that year the pheasant shooting season was extended by a month for fear the birds, deprived of their natural food, would endanger the crops.

I left school at the age of fourteen, more restless than wise. I was conscious that in many ways I had fallen short of everyone's hopes and expectations, including those of my parents, and certainly my grandfather had he still been alive. Deep down I nursed a feeling that one day I would do something to make up for it, but I had no idea what.

The only tangible thing I had to show for my time there was an Ingersoll wristwatch; the first prize for coming in last in the slow bicycle race the previous summer. I remember cursing myself for not having pedalled a little faster and arrived first, for it meant going up in front of the assembled pupils and parents to collect it.

One of my last school reports, which I now wish I had kept, said: 'Bond suffers from a distorted sense of humour.'

I got a job as an office boy in a solicitor's office. Every morning I had to carry piles of metal deed boxes up from the strongroom in the basement in case they were needed. Then I operated the telephone switchboard, licked stamps, copied the day's letters on to a kind of crepe paper from a roll which was kept moist in a large earthenware jar, and generally made myself useful.

Sometimes, to save postage, I was allowed to deliver local letters by hand. I always looked forward to that because it meant an hour of freedom, wandering round the town – to Simonds with its smell of malt and hops on days when beer was being brewed, past the Cadena Café with its whiff of roasting coffee. I could call in at W. H. Smith's and scan the shelves, hoping to find a book I could buy – which wasn't easy, publishers were pegged to a ration of paper based on the amount they had used before the war. On one such visit, in desperation I purchased a book by a Dr C. E. M. Joad. Cyril Joad was head of philosophy and psychology at London University's Birkbeck College, and he achieved instant stardom when he became a resident member of a radio programme called *The Brains Trust*, which in its time achieved record audience figures of up to twelve million. He was a man with an extraordinary breadth of knowledge on practically every subject under the sun and he was a born communicator. In a sense you could say that through his book I went back to school again, but this time it was on my terms and I kept it to myself.

Important legal documents were transcribed in longhand on to parchment by a man who worked in a solicitor's office in another part of Reading. Whenever I delivered anything, he was always the worse for drink, but he had the facility for writing in copperplate at high speed and never making a mistake. He did that all his life and probably never dreamed, if he dreamed at all within his alcoholic haze, that one day a great many of his efforts would be cut up into small pieces when parchment lampshades became the fashion.

Occasionally in my wanderings I was able to get hold of cardboard sleeves for my growing collection of gramophone records: Count Basie, Mugsie Spanier, Tommy Dorsey, Louis Armstrong, Benny Goodman, the Quintet of the Hot Club de France with Stephane Grapelli and Django Reinhardt, Artie Shaw, Lionel Hampton, Gene Krupa and hosts of others. Cardboard sleeves were in short supply and in the end they disappeared altogether.

I was also able to keep an eye open for other things, like queues forming outside a tobacconist or a chemist, indicating that a supply of cigarettes or razor-blades had arrived. The news always spread like wildfire and you had to be quick off the mark. Shop assistants became adept at recognizing people who tried to go round a second time.

There were two girls working in the office, Miss Bryant and Miss Jordan, and there was a certain amount of rivalry between them. Miss

Bryant was the older of the two and she was always smartly dressed in a two-piece suit, with never a hair out of place. I went in awe of her, grateful for any 'good morning' crumbs which fell from her table when she sailed past in a cloud of perfume. She always typed the important letters and had a man friend whom no one ever saw. Some evenings she had to leave promptly because they were going out together, and woe betide anyone who brought her work at the last moment. When that happened we all suffered.

Miss Jordan wore frocks which billowed up when she was in a hurry. She had a boyfriend who married her soon after I arrived, so that pleasure was shortlived.

During the lunch hour, when everybody else went out and I was left in charge, I used to read through the divorce files over my sandwiches, hoping I might find something juicy, but I never did – only a lot of sadness and bad feeling. Sometimes I unscrewed the front of the telephone switchboard and looked inside. I always got pleasure from the smell of the wiring and the elegant way it was arranged.

I also taught myself to type, using Miss Jordan's machine – I wouldn't have dared use Miss Bryant's, she always knew when it had been touched – and got pleasure out of copying old house plans and property maps on to blue tracing paper, which was also part of my job.

At the end of the day I carried the deed boxes back downstairs again.

For all of these things I was paid the princely sum of ten shillings a week.

Deprived of our seaside holidays, Tim and I took up cycling in a big way. I changed my old upright Hercules for a Raleigh with dropped handlebars and a three-speed derailleur gear. Together we pedalled our way round the countryside armed with flasks clipped to our dropped handlebars, and panniers stuffed to capacity with groundsheets and other camping equipment. Sometimes, we got as far as Malvern, a hundred miles away.

Tim had some aunts in Malvern Wells and it was there one day that I spotted a familiar bearded figure in knickerbockers coming out of the theatre. As a dare, I asked for his autograph, hoping to add it to my collection of two. (The other one I'd acquired was that of J. H. Squire, of the eponymous Celeste Octet.) But George Bernard Shaw wasn't in a very good mood that morning and he chased me away with his walking stick. It marked the end of my collection, for I never dared ask anyone again.

We also had several encounters with Tim's Uncle Percy, who accompanied us over the Malvern Hills on his bicycle and made us laugh so much there were times when we had to take refuge in a ditch.

Unfortunately, he combined a weakness for the horses with a less than keen eye when it came to judging their competitive spirit on the track, and the next time we visited Malvern he was 'away on holiday'. It didn't occur to either of us to wonder why he had gone away by himself or even to ask where he'd gone, but when it happened a second time we began putting two and two together and came up with what I fear was the right answer. Uncle Percy was once again doing time.

There was also an Auntie Kit, who insisted on making a pot of tea whenever we went to see her so that she could read our fortunes in the leaves. She was always suitably primed about our current goings-on beforehand, so there were never any great surprises in store, and before we left for home she invariably said she could see a long journey ahead of us.

I don't think any of the people we met were real uncles and aunts, it was simply a title one automatically bestowed on one's elders.

By the middle of 1940 the phoney war was over. BBC newsreaders, who until then had remained anonymous voices, started giving their names before each bulletin in order to establish their identity. Following complaints in the House of Commons that the team of five all sounded remarkably alike, a Yorkshire actor named Wilfred Pickles was brought in and became the first national newsreader with a regional accent. He caused a minor sensation at the end of the day when he wished his listeners 'good neet'. Several years later it was established that the German Secret Service had, in fact, been training voice-alikes in readiness for a possible invasion.

Wilfred Pickles' voice came over loud and clear on our new HMV radiogram, which actually plugged into the mains. Gone for ever were the accumulators and the high-tension batteries. The cabinet alone was a work of art and a cause for comment whenever we had visitors. My father thought it had a very good tone and he particularly liked the bass notes.

On it we listened to news of the Battle of Britain and afterwards heard

Churchill tell the nation that 'Never in the field of human conflict was so much owed by so many to so few.'

Later that same year, when the blitz was under way and Hitler was planning his invasion of the British Isles, he made his famous speech: 'We shall defend our island, whatever the cost may be. We shall fight on the beaches, we shall fight on the landing grounds, we shall fight in the fields, in the streets, and in the hills . . . we shall never surrender.' It is hard to convey now the effect his words had on the nation, but the sound of his voice can still bring tears to the eyes.

In between my expeditions with Tim, I used to cycle regularly from Reading to the other side of Newbury – a distance of some twenty miles or so – ostensibly to stay with some newly discovered aunts, but mainly because I had become rather keen on the grand-daughter of one of them.

Auntie Annie and Auntie Gee ran a dog kennels near Greenham Common. Both their husbands had been killed in the First World War.

Auntie Annie Church, Pamela's grandmother, was a tall, aristocratic lady who had lived in the old flour mill at Newbury, close to where I was born. She was very patriotic and at the end of the day always switched the radio on so that we could all stand to attention for the national anthem.

Auntie Gee had been married to a man who was captain of the Newbury fire brigade in the days when the engines were horse-drawn. She owned a pekinese dog which was always yapping, but since she had been stone deaf from an early age, and relied on lip-reading, it seldom bothered her. When the penny did drop she would yell blue murder and frighten all the other dogs, for unbeknown to herself she had a very braying voice when roused and they must have thought they were about to be attacked by a wild animal.

The kennels had been built by Uncle Ernest, one of Auntie Annie's two sons. They were ahead of their time, a model of all that any dog might require. Warm, weatherproof, easy to keep clean, each with a separate run; Uncle Frank's pigs would have felt at home there.

Uncle Ernest was a romantic figure in my eyes, for he had lost a leg as a fighter pilot in the First World War. The end of a polished wooden propeller adorned one of the walls of the house and alongside it there was a picture of him standing in front of a Sopwith Camel.

He further endeared himself to me when he was admitted to the Royal

Berkshire Hospital in Reading with suspected appendicitis and proved such a difficult patient the staff took his false leg away from him. My father happened to visit him later that day and was persuaded on some pretext or other to retrieve it from a cupboard. Uncle Ernest then promptly made good his escape through a window, leaving my father to explain to the authorities what had happened. It was the kind of thing Bulldog Drummond would have done, although that was no consolation to my father at the time.

Over the years the kennels had been further added to and extended by a local handyman who was adept at joining together old gypsy caravans and portable summerhouses, of which Auntie Annie seemed to have a never-ending supply. The net result was a veritable maze of buildings which spread higgledy-piggledy around the garden, in and out of the raspberry canes and vegetables, until they ended up near a little brick-built outhouse which contained a family two-seater toilet – the cause of much nudging and knowing winks whenever there were guests.

For some reason one of the sections – a portable bungalow – housed someone called Auntie Maude, who slept in a bed which was propped up on some unopened chests of linen and silver brought from the old mill. At the time it never occurred to me to ask about the relationship or why she lived there. It wasn't until after she died that I discovered she was my cousin Roger's grandmother, and only recently did I learn that, like me, Roger had been born at 2 Edinburgh Terrace. How that came about is hard to say. The mysteries of adulthood so often remain unquestioned by children, and now all those who might have shed some light on the subject have long since taken their secrets with them to the grave.

The same local handyman was also responsible for installing various heating systems in the main house, so that the kitchen, where most of the pipes ultimately converged, resembled the interior of a submarine. When he left to go into the army he took with him in his head the master plans, rendering many of the systems unusable except by the very brave or the incurably foolhardy.

Auntie Annie's great forte as a kennel owner was her willingness to cater for her clients' every whim, for which, of course, their owners paid extra. As a result, apart from the dogs in the outside kennels, there were dogs in every room of the house; some chained to the walls, others free to roam about at will. It was impossible to go to the toilet without literally having one's every movement watched over. Some dogs had been there for years, treating it as a home from home. Binkie was invited to stay one weekend, but he proved to be a subversive influence and wasn't asked again.

My father accompanied me once on his bicycle in order to help with the accounts and do the tax returns, but after spending a day crouched over shoe-boxes full of old bills and receipts he emerged shaking his head and looking very pale. On the way home he admitted he wished he hadn't seen them.

Occasionally Auntie Annie would suffer a heart attack, usually in the garden, where she would collapse on to a bench outside the kitchen. Pam would stride past, grim-faced in her jodhpurs, muttering, 'The old girl's a goner this time,' as she went in search of the smelling salts.

But Auntie Annie always recovered. When she was in her eighties she fell out of a train as it was leaving Newbury station and broke her leg. She sued the railway and for a while conducted her affairs via an old-fashioned hand telephone with a separate earpiece, until one day the local operator, unable to contain herself any longer as she listened in to a particularly juicy piece of local gossip, interjected some comments and not only cooked her own goose but deprived the Post Office of a good deal of revenue.

Auntie Annie and Auntie Gee were keen cinema-goers. They were particularly partial to Nelson Eddy and Jeanette MacDonald (the Singing Capon and the Iron Butterfly as their detractors called them), and visits to the Regal Cinema in Newbury became something of a nightmare. Because her right leg was in plaster, Auntie Annie had to occupy a seat at the end of a row so that she could leave it sticking out into the aisle. Auntie Gee sat beside her, armed with a torch which she shone on Auntie Annie's lips whenever the exigencies of the plot became too much for her to follow and she needed an explanation.

Pamela used to curl up beside me, both of us doing our best to pretend we weren't with them, but knowing all would be revealed once the lights went up.

Unlike pigs, dogs require exercising, and during that period Pamela and I grew adept at taking as many as a dozen at a time for walkies, each one on the end of a long rope – one of Uncle Ernest's less happy ideas. It only needed one dog to take it into its head to start a fight and the rest would all shoot off in different directions at the same time, some to join in, others seizing the opportunity to settle long-standing scores of their own, the rest out of sheer panic. As an exercise in arm-stretching it was even more effective than carrying deed boxes.

In between times I used to sublimate my passion for Pamela by helping her clean the family silver in an old-fashioned hand-operated machine with revolving brushes. If I was in very good odour I was allowed to trim the wicks on the many oil lamps dotted around the house, making it shady and mysterious at night when they were all aglow. My passion remained unrequited, but the silver positively sparkled of an evening as we sat round the dinner table listening to Auntie Annie hold forth.

One of the very nice things about Auntie Annie was that she didn't mind telling stories against herself. One Christmas Day she was out paying a visit to an old friend and her route took her up a long hill past what was then Newbury Workhouse. As always, the way she was dressed owed nothing to current fashion. As she drew near the gates a tramp emerged, took one look at her and called out: 'If you 'urry up, Mum, you'll be just in time for Christmas dinner.' The fact that he had meant it in earnest only added to her laughter.

After a year spent working in the solicitor's office I decided to ask for a rise. I remember standing outside the chief clerk's office trying to pluck up the courage to knock – plucking up courage was something one had to do a lot of in those days. I kept going through the motions and missing.

When I finally made contact it sounded as though I was trying to batter the door down. After I'd explained what I had in mind he pondered the matter for a while and then reluctantly offered me an extra two-and-sixpence a week on the strict understanding that I mustn't expect it to be an annual occurrence.

One day we stopped work half an hour early in order to celebrate the retirement at the age of sixty-five of one of the clerks. Mr Jackson had been with the firm all his life and had never married, probably because he had never been able to afford to. We had tea and cakes and he was given a gold watch. Afterwards he said goodbye and that was the last we saw of him.

I resolved there and then that the law was not for me. Somehow or other life had to have more to offer than endless torts and codicils. The thought of arriving in this world and then departing, leaving scarcely a ripple behind, appalled me, but I still had no very clear idea of what I wanted to do.

CHAPTER 5

Growing Pains

But did thee feel the earth move?

Ernest Hemingway (1899–1961)

One day in desperation I answered an advertisement in a local paper. It said, quite simply, 'Wanted: Someone interested in radio.'

To my great surprise I received a reply on BBC headed notepaper from an address only a few doors away from where I was working.

I turned up for an interview, answered a few simple questions about Ohms Law, and from that moment on my life changed dramatically.

I think Frank Howe, the Engineer-in-Charge, was impressed that I had even heard of Ohms Law. When, without any hesitation, I recited its three variations: 'E over I equals R, E over R equals I, and E equals IR', followed by a brief demonstration of my dexterity with a soldering iron, I was in.

Life with the BBC was very different to anything I had known before. It was more cosmopolitan for a start. It was also more demanding.

If the internal phone wasn't answered on the first ping the voice at the other end would say, 'What kept you?' To this day, I still make a dive for the telephone whenever it rings.

A person's function in life was immediately apparent by his or her initials, much as it is today. At the very top was the DG (Director-General). I started life at the other end of the alphabet as a YT(t), which meant 'Youth in Training (transmitters)'. When anyone asked me what I did, I always said vaguely that I was with the BBC, which sounded much more important. In any case, the existence of a transmitter in Reading was all very hush-hush and we weren't supposed to talk about it.

In the beginning the BBC engineering division had been mostly staffed by ex-naval personnel and there was a great tradition of spit and polish. The large, high-powered transmitters were run like a ship, with the discipline to match. By their very nature most of them were on high ground out in the wilds, miles from anywhere, more often than not permanently snowbound in winter. Some had a reputation for being places of punishment where people who had blotted their copybook as were sent.

The transmitter where I found myself was nothing like that. It was one of a chain of low-powered synchronized units which had been set up across the country to carry the National programme. The theory behind it was two-fold: at the first warning of enemy aircraft approaching they could be switched off locally without affecting the others, and then be brought back on the air again when it was all clear. Secondly, in the event of an invasion, they could operate independently and be used to relay important announcements. For the same reason, we all had to learn the morse code so that we could maintain communication in an emergency. The goal was 20 wpm, but once again my interest in radio stood me in good stead. With the aid of what was known as a 'bug' key (operated with a sideways rather than an up and down movement) I was able to reach much higher speeds. As with riding a bicycle, it was a case of once learned never forgotten.

Our transmitter was in the centre of Reading and it occupied the top floor of a five-storey building on the bottom floor of which there was a British Restaurant – a wartime innovation where people could buy a nourishing meal for a few shillings. Because we did shift work we had our own Belling hotplate and over the months I grew adept at making omelettes out of dried egg, one packet of which was available every month. Later on I branched out into mock scrambled eggs, using a double boiler and cooking the mixture as slowly as possible, until it tasted almost like the real thing.

My culinary prowess began to be remarked upon, until one day I used an electric kettle for boiling a cabbage and then forgot to tip the water away afterwards. The following shift used it for making tea and for several weeks afterwards my name was mud.

The BBC were facing staff problems because of the war and soon after I joined they began recruiting women in the engineering department. Which was how it came about that I found myself working alongside – and as things turned out, sometimes on top of – Mrs Chambers, who was a WO, or Woman Operator, and had 'been on a course'.

It was an encounter for which my previous experiences with Patsy and Sheila had left me ill-prepared.

Mrs Chambers was some twenty years older than me and certainly wasn't in need of any operational training. By virtue of her age and seniority, it was part of her job to take me in hand and teach me all she knew, a task which she set about with enthusiasm despite a tendency at times to stray from the set curriculum.

She had blonde hair, a warm and generous mouth, and a superior line in thighs which she displayed to all and sundry whenever the opportunity arose. Looking back, I now realize what I didn't appreciate at the time; Mrs Chambers was partial to anything in trousers.

She had firm but full breasts which rattled like a drum if she shook herself violently (it had something to do with a post-natal problem with dried milk). One evening I accidentally bumped into one of them when I was passing her some coffee.

I apologized. 'That's quite all right,' said Mrs Chambers, looking at me with sudden interest.

Somehow I failed to withdraw my hand from the back of her chair as I sat down beside her. The temperature in the room soared as we watched a programme meter for a while, then she leaned back against my hand and I felt my throat go dry.

'I didn't', she said at long last, running her tongue round her already moist lips, 'think you were like that!'

Until that moment I can't say that I had thought I was either.

'Oh, I don't know,' I replied, assuming my man-of-the-world voice. It came out higher-pitched than I had intended, and Noël Coward might have done rather better with the dialogue, but then he'd probably had more practice.

Drunk with success, I slid my hand along the back of the chair and touched her shoulder. The next moment my other hand was seized in a vice-like grip and I felt it being steered gently but firmly in the direction of her bosom. I'd never actually touched one before and I wasn't quite sure what to do, so I gave it a tentative squeeze.

The hairs on the back of my neck weren't the only things beginning to rise and I hid my embarrassment beneath a copy of the *Radio Times*, hoping against hope that she wouldn't ask me to fetch her another coffee for a moment or two. But I needn't have worried. Liquid replenishment was low on Mrs Chambers' list of priorities. Breasts heaving up and down like an ocean swell, she closed her eyes and let out a deep sigh of ecstasy.

'Tomorrow evening,' she whispered, 'we'll go for a nice walk in the Forbury Gardens. *After* dark!'

I nearly fell off my chair with excitement. The Forbury Gardens, one of George Palmer's many gifts to the town commemorating his success in the world of biscuits, had become a notorious local nightspot. Stories were rife about the goings-on there. One told of a girl who'd had one of her nipples bitten off by an over-sexed GI; another was about a Pole who had taken a nun there only to discover on further investigation that 'she' was a 'he', and a German spy at that!

I didn't sleep very well that night, and the following morning I went round to tell Tim all about it. But all he kept saying was, '*How* old did you say she is?' and 'Tell it to me again.'

In the event, the Forbury Gardens turned out to be a bit of a damp squib. It was cold and nearly all the benches were already occupied by foreign soldiery with the objects of their affections. Worse still, if the hairs on the back of my neck were still doing their stuff, the rest of me – or that part of me which was all-important – certainly wasn't.

'Never mind,' Mrs Chambers gave it a proprietorial pat. 'These things happen. Besides, tomorrow's another day. Tomorrow I shall take you to my caravan and *we'll make real love!*'

Until then I had never been quite sure what 'making love' really meant. I'd heard other words used to describe what I *thought* it meant, but I wasn't at all sure where the dividing line came between advanced osculation and 'the other thing'. But Mrs Chambers managed to imbue her words with such depth of feeling there was no doubt as to what *she* meant by it.

I slept even less well that night, and the following morning, having briefed Tim on the latest turn of events, I set off towards the railway station, conscious of his envious gaze following my progress along the road.

'Tell me what it's like,' he called.

I waved goodbye.

Mrs Chambers' caravan was situated on an egg farm some forty miles from Reading, and before we embarked on the last leg of the journey she led me on a short excursion up Guildford High Street.

'I'll get something for lunch,' she announced, 'while you do some shopping. Unless,' she added meaningly, 'you're in the Boy Scouts already.' I began to wish she would stop talking in riddles and come straight out with it.

She did the next best thing. She gave me a playful push in the direction of a chemist's shop and blew me a conspiratorial kiss which didn't go unnoticed by those inside.

The shop turned out to be crowded and I hung around for a while peering at combs and hairbrushes, trying to avoid looking too conspicuous as I searched in vain for other items.

Glancing out of the window, I caught sight of Mrs Chambers. Having completed her own shopping in record time, she was tapping her wrist-watch impatiently. In desperation I made a hurried purchase.

'Jolly good,' she said approvingly as I joined her on the pavement. 'That wasn't too painful was it?'

'Er . . . no,' I said, clutching the tube of toothpaste in my pocket. I glanced round in the hope of seeing another chemist with fewer people inside, but it was too late. Mrs Chambers propelled me in the direction of the bus stop.

The egg farm, or the little of it I took in, wasn't quite as I had imagined it. Somehow there were fewer chickens and more caravans than I'd pictured.

As we went through the gates, Mrs Chambers quickened her pace. 'We mustn't hang about,' she hissed. 'The owner of the site may be around and he's a bit funny about these things. Besides, he knows my husband.'

I beat her to the caravan by a short head.

The inside of the van was also a bit of a let-down; really little more than a bed on wheels. It was also very hot and stuffy; a combination which was having as devastating an effect on my ardour as had the cold the previous night.

Mrs Chambers bolted the door, then drew the curtains. 'We don't want any peeping Toms do we?' Emptying her shopping on the bed she turned to me. 'Would you like to eat before or after?' she enquired. Then she gave a giggle. 'Or both!'

'Before,' I said hastily, bringing delaying tactics into play.

It struck me that the curtains were a bit on the thin side; they certainly didn't have much effect on the ambient light level. After dark in the Forbury Gardens was one thing. Daylight in a caravan was something else again.

Somewhere or other there is probably a world record for dismantling the inside of a house on wheels and setting it up again as a dining-room, complete with sink and stove. If there is I can only say Mrs Chambers would have beaten it lying down; a position she lost no time in adopting the moment she'd finished tackling her second record-breaking effort – that of downing a ham salad whilst at the same time getting undressed.

'Time for afters!' she called, as she caught sight of me slowly toying with the remains of some Russian salad.

I tried not to look at the recumbent figure on the bed. 'I . . . er . . . I think perhaps I'll do the washing-up first,' I announced.

Mrs Chambers sat up and stared at me. Catching sight of the expression on her face, I turned my back and began to undress, folding my trousers with painstaking care.

'Oh, dear,' she said, as I turned to face her. 'We *are* at half-mast aren't we?'

I nodded miserably, grateful that the word 'mast' had been used at all in the circumstances.

'Never mind.' With a mixture of surprise and alarm I watched as Mrs Chambers reached for a pillow and placed it expertly beneath her posterior. 'Give me the you know whats. I'll soon make you feel better.'

It was the moment of truth. 'I . . . er . . . yes . . . well, that's another thing,' I began. 'You see . . . I didn't . . . I mean . . .'

Mrs Chambers heaved a deep sigh. Ever resourceful, she replaced the pillow with a towel. 'All right,' she said. 'We'll do it the other way. But hurry up, we haven't got all day.'

I eyed her doubtfully. I wasn't too sure about the first way yet, let alone any possible variations.

Until that moment the only naked lady I'd encountered was my Auntie Lou, and she must have been eighty at the time.

I'm not sure if she was a real aunt or one of those people one was always told to call 'aunt', but from time to time she came to stay with us in Gloucester Road. All I know is that apart from being very old she was totally blind, or so I had always been told, and she tended to spend most of the time in her room.

One morning she called me in and having felt in her purse gave me a coin.

'Now that *is* a florin, dear,' she said. 'Not a half-crown?'

I assured her that it was indeed a florin and went back to my own room only to discover to my horror that in my excitement I had made a mistake and it was a half-crown after all.

Caught on the horns of a dilemma, I spent some moments agonizing over whether to suffer the embarrassment of admitting that I couldn't tell one from the other, or pretend I hadn't noticed. In the end I decided to return it lest I be accused of stealing from the blind.

When I got back to her room Aunt Lou was out of bed and standing naked in front of the dressing-table mirror. She had her back to the door and I remember being surprised at how white and young her body looked – not a wrinkle to be seen – and also by the fact that her hair, which I had only ever previously seen worn in a tight bun, hung down her back, reaching almost to the floor – or so it seemed. I didn't stop to measure it, but for a long time afterwards I often wondered what she was doing in front of the mirror, and whether she was quite as blind as she made out, but that only added to my mortification.

Mortification was my prime emotion as I returned Mrs Chambers' gaze that day. Minus her clothes she was much larger than I had expected. Perhaps it was the way she was lying, but it felt a bit like setting out to conquer Mount Everest having left one's crampons behind.

I lingered for a while near the lower slopes. Through a gap in the curtains I could see the world outside going about its business. People were hurrying to and fro. Any one of them might have been the owner of the site making his rounds, or even Mr Chambers himself. I became even more limp at the thought.

'Perhaps,' I said brightly. 'You'd like a cup of coffee first?'

The journey home was not a happy one. The earlier *joie de vivre* had been replaced by a silence you could have cut with a knife. The train from Guildford was crowded with soldiery and, ignoring me completely,

Mrs Chambers flirted madly with an oafish, khaki-clad individual sitting opposite. Unaware of the undercurrents, he clearly thought he was on to a good thing, which he could well have been had the journey been any longer. I felt waves of jealousy, which was what was intended.

During that period I found myself working with someone called Tommy Dresser who supplemented his income by writing short stories for the *London Evening News*. From time to time a cheque would arrive in the post and he would take us all out for a drink on the strength of it. I used to look at him and wonder how he managed it. He wasn't at all my idea of how a writer should look. He made it sound as though the act of creation was easy; a matter of tossing something off when the fancy took him, which perhaps he did, although I doubt it.

I decided I wanted to do something creative too, but not having 'lived' as he had (he'd spent some years in the merchant navy) I felt it needed to be something other than writing. I decided to try my hand at drawing a cartoon and, after a lot of thought and lying awake at night, came up with one showing a man with two heads sitting behind a desk. The caption read: 'I always say, Smithers, that two heads are better than one.'

I sent it off to *Punch* – there was nothing like starting at the top. It was returned fairly promptly accompanied by a rejection slip, across the top of which someone had written 'Sorry–try again', which meant my enthusiasm wasn't entirely dampened.

I kept the whole thing secret. The only person I did tell was Mrs Chambers, but she treated the notion of my doing *anything* creative with such contempt it made me all the more determined to prove myself.

If the earth beneath her caravan hadn't moved that day on the outskirts of Guildford, and it has to be admitted that Mrs Chambers herself had hardly hit number one on the Richter scale, then it was to make up for it in the not too distant future; 10 February 1943 to be precise.

The afternoon was dull and drizzly, and because it was pay day there were four of us in the transmitter room – two more than usual.

Hearing the roar of a plane approaching fast and low, one of the group rushed to the window.

We heard a shout of: 'Christ! It's a Dornier!'

Before anyone had a chance to say, 'Pull the other one', there was a violent explosion and we were all thrown to the floor. I remember bracing myself for the long fall to come, convinced it was the end, for the building was so old and dried out if you climbed through the window on to the roof, which we sometimes did on a nice day, you could actually prise the bricks apart with your fingers.

From that moment on everything seemed to take place in slow motion. Having barely recovered from the first shock, we were about to pick ourselves up when there was a second explosion, closer still this time, then a third – seemingly right on top of us – followed by a fourth. It all took place over a period of a few seconds, but at the time it seemed an eternity.

Afterwards we learned that the pilot of a lone German bomber on his way back to Germany, happening to pass over Reading, must have decided to gain extra speed by reducing his load whilst at the same time striking a blow for the Fatherland. Having dropped his string of bombs right across the centre of the town, the crew began machine-gunning any stray pedestrians as they scuttled for home.

At the time, the worst part was waiting for the floor to collapse, which seemed inevitable. But miraculously it didn't. Because of the speed at which the plane was travelling and the angle of trajectory, the third bomb had literally blown away the bottom half of the building we were in, leaving us suspended between those on either side.

As the roar of the plane died away and everything went deathly quiet, I decided there and then that whatever way I was ultimately destined to go it wouldn't be in an air raid. It felt as though it couldn't have been closer. But it wasn't until I managed to clamber down the shattered staircase and reach what had once been ground level that I realized quite how lucky we had been. The whole of the restaurant and all those who had been inside were now in the basement, buried beneath tons of rubble. I came across a girl lying at the foot of the stairs with both her legs blown off and I can still see the look of mute despair in her eyes as she gazed up at me. I couldn't think of anything to say. As I clambered over the rubble I caught sight of a movement and a hand emerged from between some bricks clutching a set of false teeth. It's strange the things one wants to save at such moments.

We did what we could until help arrived, but it was all too little.

Fortunately it was a Wednesday and early-closing day in the town, otherwise the death toll would have been much higher. In the event, forty-one people died and as many again were seriously injured.

I was late home that evening and everyone assumed I had been among those killed. They stared at me as though I were a ghost, and it wasn't until I looked in a mirror that I realized the mess I was in. It took several days to get rid of all the dust. On the bus everyone had avoided sitting next to me. I suppose they took me for a singularly unwashed workman, or perhaps they were just being terribly British.

Nowadays I would probably have been offered counselling, but in reality it was no worse than similar happenings taking place almost every day in other parts of the country, and who would have counselled the counsellors? Instead, I became embroiled over the next few weeks in an argument with the BBC accounts department on the subject of my pay, which had disappeared into thin air. Had the pay packet actually been in my hand at the time? In which case it was technically my responsibility. Or had it still been in the hand of the Engineer-in-Charge? In which case I would be entitled to receive a replacement. In the end I was given the benefit of the doubt.

A new site was quickly found. A team of high-powered engineers arrived, and within a few days we were on the air again.

Mrs Chambers took double advantage of the event and applied for a transfer to London, but not before she exacted her revenge.

Turning the knife in the wound before leaving, she told me with great glee of her philanderings on the bank of the Thames with one of the engineers and – with every word underlined – how wonderful it had been.

I discovered what it was like to have a broken heart and for a while I was inconsolable. Broken romances are life's rejection slips, but I didn't even have the benefit of one to carry around with me. I wrote, but my letters were returned unanswered.

Then one day, out of the blue, she invited me to lunch in London with her husband. We dined in the brasserie at the old Lyons Corner House near Charing Cross Station, several rungs up the ladder from the usual run of Corner Houses.

After the 'Nippies' in black dresses with white starched pinafores and bonnets, their order pads hanging at the ready, the hordes of elderly waiters who had seen it all before and the equally elderly orchestra playing in the background, seemed like High Society indeed.

It was an uncomfortable meal; one that Mr Chambers had clearly been through many times before – he probably had a table permanently booked – for his wife was obviously making some sort of point. But he seemed to take it all in good part.

Afterwards he returned to his office in the City and Mrs Chambers took me back to a rather bleak semi-detached somewhere in South London. There she gave me my cards and a parting gift in the form of an old radio set, which didn't work but which she said I could keep if I managed to repair it. The cabinet was so large I wasn't even able to wave goodbye as I staggered out into the street.

I couldn't afford a taxi, and the conductor of the first bus I stopped wouldn't let me on, so I had to carry it to the nearest underground station. Somehow or other I managed to get it back to Reading.

I never did repair it, but I kept it for a number of years and in the end took the radio to pieces for the parts and used the cabinet as a place to put tools in. Which, come to think of it, was really rather apt, for that's what Mrs Chambers was – a place to put tools in ... if you were lucky!

It had been a salutary experience and one I had no wish to repeat, although in later years, talking about such things with others I came to the conclusion that if people are totally honest a great many 'first times' leave a lot to be desired. Fear of failure is the very opposite of being an aphrodisiac. All the same, it would have been nice to have known that at the time.

CHAPTER 6

Chocks Away!

If God had meant us to fly He would have given us wings.

My grandfather

On 13 April 1943, at the age of seventeen and a quarter, I volunteered for the RAF. When I got back home and told my mother she had palpitations. It was something she always suffered from when the rhythm of her life was disturbed.

Looking back on it, and mindful of the then current stories that the average life-expectancy of a rear-gunner was around three weeks, I can understand her reaction. I suppose I should have talked it over with my parents first, but it didn't occur to me that there was anything to discuss. I had been brought up in a family that always did its duty in times of national emergency and in my case, like my mother's budgerigar, Joey, I was anxious to spread my wings.

After we moved house, Mother had a series of budgerigars of various colours, green, grey and blue, which she tried to teach to talk. Conversation was not what most of them were best at, and it needed a certain amount of goodwill on the part of the listener to accept that they were actually saying their name. They were all called Joey and were known as 'little artfuls' – an expression she used later on in life to describe people like the Kray Brothers.

The big breakthrough came with the arrival of Joey IV. Once he got going he hardly ever stopped talking, especially when the radio was on, *especially* when it was something everyone wanted to listen to, like ITMA. He thrived on noise and when he wasn't talking or scattering empty seed shucks around the room he used to ring a bell in his cage to let everyone know he was still there. My mother always insisted that he sat under it whenever the air-raid siren went, using it as a makeshift tin hat. If it was pointed out that he was still doing it long after the 'all clear' had sounded, she would say darkly: 'I expect he knows something we don't.'

Iodized nibbles and groundsel did little to ease the racket, and sometimes in desperation she used to let him out of his cage. Bearing out my grandfather's theory about God giving wings to those who were meant to fly, he would treat my father's bald head like a helicopter landing pad, albeit one which also did duty as a comfort station. My mother kept a supply of cotton wool balls in a biscuit tin so that she could clean up afterwards. It was always done in a trice; a kind of reflex swooping action. My father, tired after a day at the office, often with a spell of Home Guard duty thrown in as well, usually had his nose buried in the paper and remained blissfully unaware of what was going on.

Sometimes, on a voyage of exploration, Joey would spy one of the few remaining hairs on the top of my father's head and he developed a technique of wrapping it round his beak and then giving a sharp tug. Whether he was collecting hairs in order to satisfy some latent nest-building instinct, or whether he simply liked making people jump, we never knew, but if it was the latter he had struck a rich seam, for it made my father leap into the air shouting, 'Strike me pink!' Often, it was the high spot of evenings at home.

I suppose the truth is I'm not really a bird lover. They have sharp beaks, beady eyes, and are infinitely quicker off the mark than I am. The spectre of psittacosis following a sudden lunge is never far away. It seemed another good reason for joining the RAF.

With a teenager's lack of finer feelings I consoled my mother with the news that I was going to be a fighter pilot, not a rear-gunner. Secretly, I rather fancied myself being allowed to walk around with the top button of my uniform undone. In any case, there were still nine months to go before I could be officially called upon to serve.

It was around that time that she began sitting in front of a mirror pulling out grey hairs with the aid of a pair of tweezers, despite others telling her that for every one she removed seven more would grow.

In the meantime I became a part-time messenger in the fire brigade, which at least gave me the benefit of a proper military gas mask and a working knowledge of where all the water hydrants in the area were situated.

At the request of the RAF, I also visited the dentist for the first time and not surprisingly had to have several teeth filled. Even so, I got off considerably lighter than my father. When I was small he had all his removed in two goes. It's hard to picture now, but dentists weren't geared to saving teeth in those days.

However, before that happened a more serious diversion arrived on the scene in the shape of a girl I called then, and still think of as, 'N.K.' (It was the BBC influence – everyone had to have initials.) She was tall and slim, and with her high cheekbones she reminded me of Claudette Colbert.

I was deputed to show her around and generally look after her. She called me 'T.M.B.' (my forename name being Thomas), and for a while we enjoyed a beautiful and totally platonic friendship. We did lots of 'first things' together. I went to my first symphony concert and visited my first London theatre. Over endless cups of coffee in our favourite coffee shop we set the world to rights. We exchanged locker keys at work and left each other books to read. I added to my list of authors and together we discovered Eric Linklater, Somerset Maugham, Graham Greene, Alexander Woollcott, P. G. Wodehouse, Freud, Stephen Leacock, and many others.

Sometimes, if we were on different shifts, she would use her meagre rations to bake me a treacle tart which she would leave for me, and once, while out for a walk in the country, we came across an enormous mushroom, which provided us with a variety of meals for several days.

One day she bought me a record of Frank Sinatra singing 'All or Nothing at All'. Perhaps she was trying to tell me something . . . perhaps there is no such thing as a purely platonic relationship . . . but I know she was very special and the time we spent together was totally unique and carefree and unforgettable.

I wanted it to last for ever, but that November – six months earlier than expected – I was summoned to report for duty. In theory, it was so that I could attend a pre-service mathematics course at Cambridge.

I said goodbye to all my friends at the BBC and they gave me an album containing Tchaikovsky's Fifth Symphony, played by the Philadelphia Symphony Orchestra. It was the first album I had ever owned.

On my last evening, N.K. and I went to a pub together and over a glass of beer she asked me how I felt about her, but no one had ever asked me that before and I was too shy to tell her she was the nicest person I had ever met.

The next morning I said goodbye to Binkie and then to my mother, who was convinced she would never see me again. In a way she was right, for emotionally at least that was when I left home.

My father, who was with the Post Office Planning Division in London by then, insisted on accompanying me, taking a later train to do so. It put me in a bit of a quandary because N.K. had promised to meet me on Paddington station.

She was wearing a light blue trilby hat and looking very pretty. My father raised his hat to her and I said goodbye to him. I expect he knew that although, God willing, I would always come back, life as we had known it together had come to an end. He must have felt very empty. Much more so than I did at the time – it's always worse for the ones who are left behind. For me, the sadness comes now when I think about it. It's a dreadful scourge being British at times like that; unable to say all the things one ought to say. No doubt had we been born Italian we would have embraced each other and probably shed a few tears.

As it was, N.K. and I took the underground train to Baker Street where we had our last coffee together before I saw her on a train to Northwood Hills. As I recall, the carriages still had the words 'Live in Metroland' stencilled on the side, which made it sound very romantic and far away, instead of a mere ten miles or so.

She gave me a pocket-size fluffy toy cat called Bismarck and then we, too, said goodbye, although we were to write to each other every day for a long time.

Feeling a bit like an evacuee, with my minimal basic requirements packed into an attaché case, I slowly made my way up Baker Street to the Air Crew Reception Centre at Abbey Lodge, a block of flats that had been requisitioned for the period of hostilities.

Later that day, having been inducted, numbered (1895711), inoculated, kitted out, reduced to the lowest common denominator by the resident barber – a man who must have made a good living on the side by accepting pieces of silver from naïve fools like myself who thought it was going to make a difference to the amount of hair he removed –

shouted at by people the likes of whom I hadn't previously thought existed, arms aching through scrubbing wooden floors already worn thin by previous intakes – 'it 'elps make the jabs circulate' – we set off in ragged fashion towards Regent's Park Zoo in order to be fed and watered in what had once been the restaurant.

Clearly singled out for early promotion, I brought up the rear of the column holding a red oil lamp. Halfway there the light went out and I was shouted at once again for swinging it about.

Queueing up at the counter with my plate, I eyed some grey, lumpy-looking mashed potato and asked a WAAF wielding an ice-cream scoop if she would mind my having only one portion rather than two. She told me that I would get what I was 'fucking given', and I retired to the nearest table in a state of shock. I had never before heard a woman swear, and as I sat gazing out of the window, it struck me that the regular inmates of the zoo – the few creatures deemed harmless enough to escape evacuation or being put down – were faring rather better than I was. At least their keepers treated them with a modicum of respect.

As an only child, who until that moment had always been perfectly happy with his own company, I realized for the first time the intense loneliness one can feel in a crowd of complete strangers, many of whom seemed completely unable to pass the time of day without using at least one four-letter word. I was glad of Bismarck's company.

The next day, along with the rest of the intake, I took what to me seemed an incredibly easy exam and for once I was the one scribbling away while those around me sucked the end of their pencils. Much to my astonishment, when the results came through I was told I wasn't going to Cambridge after all. Along with a number of others, I was being posted straight to Scarborough. There were those who thought the whole thing was a trick to get people in under age. I suppose it might have been, but at the time I didn't mind. Having been assessed as PNB (pilot/navigator/bomb-aimer) material, I was anxious to get cracking.

Scarborough meant doing press-ups on a cold, wet beach in mid-winter, watched over by unhappy looking seagulls who had seen it all before and were noticeably keeping their own stomachs well clear of the sand; learning to swim on my back by numbers in an equally freezing pool, which before the war had been condemned and was now in an even worse state of repair – the smell of wet rot was stronger than that of chlorine; drilling, marching, being given an enthusiasm for mathematics by an elderly master from Eton who had been called up as an instructor, and who turned what until then had been an extremely dull subject into one which had elegance and precision and above all was not to be feared.

We were stationed in the Grand Hotel overlooking the bay and the scrubbing of floorboards was once again the order of the day. Old sweats told us to pee in our boots to make the leather soft; some did, some didn't. It was one of those theories that's hard to prove or disprove, although I suspect those who suggested it derived a certain amount of vicarious pleasure when they saw the theory being put into practice.

The local amusement arcade echoed to the sound of the Mills Brothers singing 'Paper Doll'. Wills' Capstan cigarettes were 9d for ten. 'Active Service' packs of Brylcreem were one shilling, and beer was a shilling a pint.

The daily rate of pay for an aircrafthand second class was two shillings, plus sixpence a day War Pay. Trainee pilots received an extra two shillings a day. It didn't amount to much – a total of thirty-one shillings and sixpence a week all found – but nightlife was non-existent and there was always the NAAFI in the evenings.

Elsewhere that year a hotel in Norwich was fined £70 for hoarding jam and a Knightsbridge chef was given three months' hard labour for obtaining black-market pork. It became illegal to 'misuse or wilfully to destroy milk bottles or to retain them unreasonably'. And on 8 January 1944 it was revealed that a new type of propellerless plane had been invented; it was powered by something called a 'jet' engine.

Letters home mostly boiled down to requests for jars of peanut butter, which I ate in vast quantities, but despite that – and notwithstanding the large amount of beer I consumed (for a while I was an honorary member of what we called the 'Ten Pint Club') – when I was posted to Scone in Scotland to begin my flying training proper, I felt fitter than I ever had before.

Scone was a small aerodrome a few miles outside Perth. It had been requisitioned at the outbreak of war, and the owner had been made a Wing Commander for the duration – or so the story went.

At long last the great day, the day for which I'd been waiting, had arrived.

Clad in wool-lined flying boots, sheepskin flying jacket and leather-trimmed goggles, I swung the prop of a Tiger Moth, jumped clear as the engine sprang into life, then climbed on to the lower wing and into the cockpit. Fastening the safety belt, I responded confidently to a thumbs-up signal from my instructor as we prepared for take-off.

The great thing, of course, was that I knew a lot about flying. My interest had been triggered one day in 1936, when I heard a strange noise in the sky over our house and rushed outside just in time to see a 'Flying Flea' pass over. It was a strange, skeletal object, completely open to the elements and powered by an 1100cc Anzani motorcycle engine. Designed by one Henri Mignet, a French cycle repairer, it could be built at home for under a hundred pounds and had a short but happy life before being declared unsafe and banned: much to my father's relief. I had been doing my best to persuade him to invest in a kit and it had seemed to me that he was wavering, reduced to making feeble excuses like, 'Where shall we land?', glancing meaningly at our pocket-size steeply sloping lawn. Statistically, landing the 'Flying Flea' was rarely much of a problem. It had a distressing tendency to turn upside down of its own accord during flight, at which point it would drop like a stone.

Nevertheless, the sight of it had excited my imagination, sowing the seeds of a desire to indulge in powered flight as soon as I possibly could; a desire which had been further whetted by Uncle Ernest.

Uncle Ernest never did have his appendix out, but as a gesture of thanks to my father for rescuing his wooden leg he showed us round the Miles aircraft factory at Reading, where he was then working. At his invitation, I touched the fuselage of a Magister aircraft in the making and came away with my fingers smelling strongly of dope. It was like a drug; the equivalent of today's glue-sniffing.

From an early age my school exercise books had been liberally decorated with drawings of Sopwith Camels; I could reproduce them with my eyes shut. The Biggles books featured largely in my early reading and I had seen *Dawn Patrol* with Errol Flynn and Basil Rathbone several times. I rather fancied myself in the Errol Flynn part ... 'There's no chance for a flight to get through, but one man – flying low, hedgehopping – might make it.'

Until then, most of my practical flying had been done in a Reading Corporation double-decker bus. Whenever possible I used to bag the front seat on the top deck and practise coming in to land as we hurtled down Castle Hill towards the town. On bad days, when some idiot at a request stop brought it to a halt, I had to make my excuses to the other passengers over the intercom; either that or convert the whole operation into 'circuits and bumps'. But on good days it was non-stop all the way. The traffic lights at the bottom would be green, and I would execute a left turn at the end of the runway, taxiing gently to a halt outside Picton's fish-and-chip shop in St Mary's Butts. Being British, the other passengers never applauded when I left the flight deck, but I could tell they were impressed.

Or, to put it another way, until that moment I had never actually been up in the air before.

Clutching the side of the cockpit as we trundled along the grass runway, I recalled my grandfather's words on the promenade at Southsea all those years before. God had not given me wings and I think even He might have cast doubtful glances at the ones I was about to entrust my life to. A good peck from a passing bird would have gone straight through the canvas.

As we gathered speed, my instructor tapped me on the shoulder, probably intending to cheer me up with another of his ghastly thumbs-up signs. His eyes, or the little that could be seen of them through my already misted-up goggles, registered total disbelief as I leaned over the side of the cockpit in order to be sick. I don't think he'd ever seen it happen before.

Several barrel rolls and one or two loops later found me wishing I was dead. Each time the plane turned upside-down – that moment when you fall a few inches before the harness takes the strain – I opened my eyes and gazed at the ground below and felt tempted to undo the buckle. At least the parachute would get me down safely. Only the knowledge that after I hit *terra firma* I would undoubtedly be put on a charge kept me from doing it.

It was a depressing discovery: Joey would have choked on his iodized nibble. Errol Flynn would not have been pleased, and Basil Rathbone's lips would have been compressed beyond all medical aid. As for Biggles ... he would have been at a loss for words.

Even more dispiriting was the realization that the RAF were not particularly sympathetic to my problem.

Sent back to London – Viceroy Court in Prince Albert Road this time

– I spent the first morning undergoing more tests; playing various word games and assembling odd-shaped pieces of cardboard into unlikely shapes. I had been very good at designing mazes when I was small and my efforts convinced a resident psychologist that I was potential navigator material. He should have had his head examined! A few of the intake dropped by the wayside, but perhaps, without really intending to, I'd made my pieces into the shape of other countries.

That lunchtime, while waiting impatiently outside Viceroy Court to be marched off for a meal, and having exhausted several choruses of 'Why Are We Waiting?', a group at the rear struck up with 'She'll Be All Wet and Sticky When She Comes', sung to the tune of 'She'll Be Coming Round the Mountain'. Gradually more and more of us joined in. A strong complaint was lodged by the occupants of some neighbouring flats and for the next few days we were all confined to barracks.

On the evening of what I felt might be my last day of freedom for some time to come, with Bismarck for company I took off for what in normal times would have been the bright lights of the West End.

It was all right for Bismarck – he was black and like all cats he was used to the dark. As far as I could make out as I groped my way around Wardour Street and Leicester Square, the only light came from myriad cigarette ends glowing in shop doorways. Disembodied voices called out invitations, and occasionally a match would flare or there would be a momentary flash of torchlight.

Bismarck was still with me, lending immoral support as it were, when I eventually found myself climbing the dimly lit stone stairs of a building in Whitcomb Street. They seemed endless – flight after flight.

Eventually I found myself in a small flat on the top floor. It wasn't exactly the height of luxury, minimalist would have been a better description, but there was carpet on the floor, a bed, a dressing table and a welcoming coal fire. From a small kitchen the sound of clinking china started up; presumably meant as a warning to clients that in the event of trouble help was close at hand.

My companion and I warmed ourselves in front of the fire and afterwards I fared better than I had with Mrs Chambers.

It had been very much a case of taking 'pot luck' as the saying goes, but she was young and blonde and, much to my relief, understanding. I couldn't have wished for a better tutor.

My parents at the time of their marriage in 1923.

In the garden at 21 Gloucester Road, Reading.

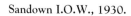

Sandown I.O.W., 1930.

Uncle Frank.

Auntie Ethel.

Auntie Emm.

Uncle Dick (in Rangers uniform) being presented to King George VI and Queen Elizabeth, Calgary, Canada, May 1939.

With Auntie Norah, Roger and Jean in Newbury in the early 1930s.

Uncle Jack tending to the needs of passengers en route to Honolulu.

Grandfather on the promenade at Southsea for the last time before the war.

Auntie Annie (left) with Auntie Ethel (right).

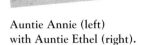

Binkie $^{1}\!/_{50}$th at f.11.

The next time I went down Whitcomb Street there was a hole in the ground where the building had been and I wondered if she had been there when the bomb fell. She, too, might have been taking pot luck.

In the fullness of time the hole was replaced by a multi-storey car park. Over the years I have occasionally left my car there, but never without picturing her and experiencing a feeling of regret that I never even asked her name. But then, she didn't ask mine.

From London I was sent to Manchester to join thousands of others awaiting shipment overseas to continue their training.

The current waiting period was around three months and with very little apart from endless fatigues to keep people occupied, the atmosphere at Heaton Park in the early spring of 1944 was one of distinct gloom; skiving had reached new heights. Anything was better than working in the cookhouse pan room. Cleaning never-ending piles of giant baking tins in lukewarm water was a depressing experience. The thought of having to eat out of them next day was the only thing that spurred us on to make a reasonable job of it.

I came across an ex-BBC engineer who was building a jukebox almost entirely out of wood – cogs and all. It must have lasted him throughout the war, which clearly was what he had in mind. He didn't seem disposed to talk to another ex-BBC man, probably for fear I might muscle in.

Another small group kept themselves busy planting bulbs in the CO's garden, hoping their posting would come through before the first shoots began to appear, at which stage they were destined to spell out unmentionable obscenities about his lovely lady wife.

Most of us had been leading a celibate life – training had left little time or energy for anything else – and at first it was difficult to adjust to having so much of both on our hands. Visits to the NAAFI were the high spot of the day. Anywhere one went in the forces there was always someone who could thump out a tune on the piano, consequently never wanting for a drink, usually provided by a budding Solomon swearing it would sound even better if the inside were christened with a pint of beer. (As with peeing in the boots, it was hard to tell whether it did or it didn't.)

But after a while that began to pall, so despite being forced to watch several sobering films on the perils of VD, followed by lectures from the MO warning us to steer clear of the local girls, not to mention rumours that the tea was always heavily laced with bromide, thoughts inevitably turned towards the opposite sex. We were much encouraged in this by a small group of older regulars who for some obscure reason were billeted in our Nissen hut. Every morning they regaled us with stories of their previous night's escapades, many of which seemed to start with chance encounters in cinemas sporting the double 'love seats' common in the north of England. One of the group, a tall individual with a very white face and a mop of curly black hair, had been nicknamed Pontius Pilate by his friends. He stayed in my mind because despite his angelic looks he was by far the most lecherous and foul-mouthed of them all.

Feeling that perhaps we were missing out on something, several of us enrolled at a dancing academy just outside the camp gates. The lessons sounded remarkably cheap. Once inside, it didn't take us long to discover the reason. They consisted of all the pupils forming a long crocodile, hands on the hips of the one in front, while 'Madame', having wound up the gramophone, led the way round the wooden floor, shouting instructions at the top of her voice.

The effect of forty or so airmen doing the rumba reminded me of my childhood and the clattering of goods wagons being shunted in the night. By the time the ripple reached the end of the line we were so out of synch the whole thing was a complete waste of time, so we caught a train into Manchester in order to lick our wounds over a drink.

I had scarcely had time to grab a stool in a well-known watering hole called the Long Bar, when a pint of beer appeared as if by magic in front of me.

'Girl at end said she'd like to buy you a drink,' said the barman, giving me a broad wink which, although knowing, seemed completely devoid of envy.

Peering along the counter, I saw why. Even though the owners of the bar were clearly trying to do their bit for the war effort by saving as much electricity as possible, the use of the word 'girl' was something of a misnomer; she made Mrs Chambers look like a fifth-former.

It was a 'spider and the fly' situation. I was desperate, but not that desperate, and made good my escape. Despite the MO's warning, I dare say she didn't have long to wait for a customer. Manchester at that time was full of lonely airmen.

I did meet a genuinely young and very beautiful Queen Alexandra's nurse one evening. I can't even remember her name or how the meeting came about, but eventually I found myself walking her back to her billet, which happened to be near the perimeter wall of Heaton Park. As we parted, I tentatively asked if I might kiss her goodnight.

Sweetly but firmly, she denied me the pleasure.

'It isn't', she said, 'very hygienic.'

Consoling myself with the thought that if she felt that way it most likely wouldn't have been very pleasurable either, we shook hands. She probably rushed inside to wash hers.

It being long past midnight, I joined a group of others who were attempting to scale the wall surrounding the park. Beery oaths filled the air as we gave each other bunk-ups. It was worse than Piccadilly Circus in the rush hour. As I landed on the other side, a patrol of waiting service police pounced.

There began a frantic chase through the woods, and being fitter than they were, we eventually gave them the slip. But I remember diving into bed with my clothes and boots still on, pretending to be asleep until the fuss died down. In the morning I had to get up early in order to wash and dry my sheets in case there was a barrack-room inspection.

I decided to give up the pursuit of wine, women and song, and devoted myself instead to the finer things of life; like wrestling at Belle View Park on Saturday afternoons.

Contemporaries of the 'girl' I had met on my first evening out usually occupied the front few rows, shouting out gratuitous advice to the contestants. Phrases like 'grab his balls' and 'give 'em a good twist' filled the air; advice which usually went down like a lead balloon with the one underneath, who would later get his own back by falling out of the ring on top of the ones who had been doing the most shouting, much to their screams of delight.

One day two of us went to the rescue of a woman in a back street who was being beaten up by her husband. Far from being grateful, she turned on us, and we were lucky to escape being beaten up ourselves. At least we seemed to have healed the rift, for the last we saw of them they were disappearing into a pub.

Compared with the kind of life I had led at home, I might have been on a different planet. My education was growing and broadening its base and it was jolly good value for money.

In a way I was sorry to leave Manchester. It had a wonderful public library, which I made use of whenever I could, and there were regular concerts by the Hallé Orchestra under Sir John Barbirolli.

But as I sat astride a gun barrel on the stern of the *Aquitania* at anchor in the calm waters of a Scottish firth, watching the sun go down over the hills before we set sail for America, I wasn't too distressed. For a while I even toyed with the romantic notion that perhaps I should have opted for the merchant navy in the first place. The ship felt so solid, so safe, so unsinkable; I could have been on the canoe lake at Southsea waiting for my number to be called.

It was the last time in my life I ever thought of a ship that way.

It was not a good time for crossing the Atlantic in a crowded troopship. The weather was foul and the German U-boat campaign was still being fought. For that reason the *Aquitania*, which had sufficient top speed to make travelling in a convoy unnecessary, altered course every six minutes – that being slightly less than the time it would take a U-boat to line up and score a direct hit with a torpedo – as it forced its way through the mountainous seas. The vast structure, which at first sight looked as though nothing could possibly upset its equilibrium, had been cut down to size by the elements. Despite its 40,000 tons it rolled about like a cork, creaking and groaning as though at any moment its rivets would pop. There were broken limbs, but I was beyond caring as I added chronic seasickness to my growing list of deficiencies.

Worse still, I had drawn the short straw.

Throwing rubbish overboard during the hours of daylight was strictly forbidden in case an enemy ship picked up the trail. Anyone caught doing it received the severest punishment. All rubbish, including the contents of swill bins – of which there were a great many, full of scraps floating in a sea of discarded tea – had to be tipped over the side each day at dawn. I was put in charge of one of the squads. Getting everything to the side of the ship, up ladders, along companionways, across decks in a howling gale, wasn't easy.

All the same, it gave less opportunity to dwell on one's fate than did my other fatigue: mounting guard in the bowels of the vessel, squatting gloomily alongside a watertight door, knowing that if we were torpedoed I might have to shut myself in on the wrong side and die a quick but horrible death alongside the rats – although, since I could still only swim the width of a pool on my back, even that seemed preferable to jumping over the side.

If ever a group deserved a reward for collective bravery it was the men of the merchant navy, one in four of whom died at sea.

It took all of five days to get my sea legs and by that time we were nearing New York. The harbour was alive with shipping; sirens sounded their greetings. There was a band playing on the dockside, and when we boarded a train at Grand Central Station – which was like no other station I had ever seen before – there were pretty girls to greet us and glossy magazines on every seat.

Heading north we went for a while alongside the Hudson River and I saw my first Mississippi-style paddle steamer, and there were cars painted in colours other than black. It was all heady stuff.

We were bound for yet another transit camp, at Moncton in New Brunswick, and when we arrived we were greeted by a sadistic British-hating sergeant who made us double with our full kit from the station to the camp. Once inside the main gates we were directed into a vast wooden drill hall, where the more enterprising got their own back.

In the absence of any command to halt, the leaders carried straight on. Hardly pausing for breath, they swarmed up the wall bars until they reached the roof, where they perched astride the enormous wooden rafters. There was nothing the sergeant could do about it then, but after the cheers and laughter had died down he made it very clear that our lives wouldn't be worth living for the rest of our stay there.

It was in Moncton, after an organized day out on the beach at a place called Shediac Bay, that I reported sick with sunstroke and found myself being put on a charge for damaging king's property. At the time it struck me as being very unfair, particularly as I hadn't wanted to go to Shediac Bay in the first place. Until then I had always regarded my skin as one of the few things left which no one else could lay claim to.

The sergeant must have been cast in the same mould as the renowned Colonel A. D. Wintle, who was reputed to have once barked at a wounded soldier: 'Stop dying immediately, and when you are out of bed get your hair cut!'

Life wasn't all bad. After war-time Britain we felt as though we were living in the land of plenty. If you went into a café and ordered bacon and eggs they asked how many eggs you wanted. In England they didn't even ask that in peace time! There was ice-cream the like of which I hadn't come across before, and for a while I had an off-duty job in a parlour making sundaes at a dollar an hour. When that folded, I got the same pay setting up pins in a bowling alley, although at times it felt more like danger money.

After about a month my posting came through. It was to Rivers, Manitoba, a small town on the prairies east of Winnipeg.

According to the sergeant who greeted us when we arrived, Winnipeg was 'the arsehole of Canada', and Rivers was two hundred miles up it. It was an early form of mass counselling and although I liked Winnipeg well enough, and the people there were very hospitable and kind, as far as Rivers was concerned, I saw no reason to disagree with his summing up during the whole of the time I was there.

For anyone prone to airsickness, a navigator's job in those pre-radar days was even worse than being a pilot. Dead-reckoning navigation entailed constant plotting of the aircraft's position, trying to draw straight lines on a chart whilst every movement of the plane was being transmitted via the pencil point. Sometimes when you hit an air pocket it hovered in mid-air an inch or so above the table, at other times the upward pressure was so great it broke. Astro-navigation, using a sextant to take bearings from the stars, was even more hazardous and nauseating.

Flying over the prairies had one big advantage: it was impossible to be lost for very long. The two railroad systems – the Canadian National and the Canadian Pacific – crossed in a dead straight line from east to west, and if the worst happened all the small towns had grain elevators with the name of the town painted in enormous letters across the top.

Several months and a good many flying hours later, having finally convinced those above that it was a mistake to entrust their expensive aircraft to a navigator whose sole ambition in life was to get back down to earth again as quickly as possible, I left Rivers for the last time one December morning and set off on my own for Halifax, Nova Scotia.

With no set time to be there and the train already several days late because of heavy snow, it was a good opportunity to see a bit more of Canada on the way. Ottawa was out of bounds to British troops, so I broke my journey in Montreal. Once again I came up against an anti-British barrier, this time in a services club of all places. I tried to take advantage of an offer of free hospitality, but having received what amounted to a lecture on the English always expecting something for nothing, I walked out into the snow and spent my last dollar on a bed in a dosshouse. I dare say the person delivering the lecture had good reason for doing so, but I suddenly felt very sorry for myself. It wasn't quite what Bismarck was used to either, and neither of us slept very well that night.

All in all, I wasn't sorry when I literally scrambled aboard a grossly overcrowded *Mauritania* as it was about to leave for England on a voyage which was, if anything, even worse than the outgoing one.

This time I found myself attached to the ship's police. We were carrying a large number of American troops. Gambling was rife and the stakes were high. I was issued with a truncheon and told to break up any games I saw taking place. I grew very adept at spotting crap games at thirty paces and doing an imitation of Nelson turning a blind eye. I suppose, had I been more sure of myself, I might have asked for a percentage of the house.

The weather was so bad and the boat so crowded that by the time we arrived off the Isle of Man we were reduced to eating K-rations for two days while we rode out the storm. K-rations were the US Army's solution to the problem of how to compress several days' worth of life-giving sustenance into the smallest possible size. They looked for all the world like tiny building blocks, and tasted much as one might have expected. They also had the added advantage of being practically indestructible and kept us quiet for hours on end.

Having eventually docked at Liverpool, we were taken to Blackpool for what was irreverently known as 'short-arm inspection'. Herded on to the end of a freezing cold pier, we queued to drop our trousers in front of a warmly clad MO seated behind an enormous spotlight. He appeared to be enjoying the whole thing for reasons that weren't entirely medical.

As I boarded a train for London, I spotted a sign saying 'Is Your Journey Really Necessary?' If it had said 'was', then I hadn't a lot to show for mine; the RAF must have written me off as a bad investment. But from a personal point of view the time had not been entirely wasted. I had chalked up a lot of firsts; things I would not otherwise have experienced.

Even when I had been hanging over the side of the *Aquitania* wanting to die, I had still marvelled at the incredible inky blue of the Atlantic at its deepest point.

The thrill of seeing New York from the sea for the very first time in the days when the harbour was alive with shipping was unrepeatable.

I had learned to play a reasonable hand of poker. In New Brunswick I had hitched a lift from Moncton to Saint John in a Model-T Ford, and while I was there I had heard my first live jazz filtering up through a grating in one street and negro spirituals coming out of a tiny church in another.

I had helped fight the annual forest fire, and at a camp concert that same evening I had listened to Cab Calloway sing 'Minnie the Moocher'. I had discovered a whole new world of authors – James Thurber, Dorothy Parker, Robert Benchley, the plays of Kaufman and Hart, S. J. Perelman, Raymond Chandler, Micky Spillane and Erle Stanley Gardner; my kitbag was stuffed with their books.

There is a lot to be said for having to pack all your worldly goods inside a kitbag. It shows you where your priorities lie. A strange paradox of service life was the feeling of freedom one had. Once you lay down roots and acquire possessions, life begins to close in.

Travelling by train across half a continent was an experience I wouldn't have missed. Puffing our way through forests so vast you entered them over breakfast and were still inside at dinner that night. Occasionally stopping at places so remote one wondered how on the earth people living there had become involved in a war being waged thousands of miles away, in many cases leaving home never to return. Riding along tracks laid on sleepers which had been cut from the very trees that had been felled to create a path in the first place, yet never a clearing without there being a Coca-Cola sign nailed to a tree.

Through the window I had seen men at work, riding the logs as the rushing waters carried them downstream to the great sawmills in the towns, and I had sat listening to trappers' tales as they boarded the train at nowhere in particular in order to travel goodness knows where.

In the observation car I had talked with a man who punctuated every sentence with a 'boing' as he hit a spittoon on the far side, not once but time after time, and at night I had fallen asleep to the mournful wail of a North American train whistle, which is like no other sound on this earth.

Once, in the early morning, as we stopped in some remote station I reached out and drew the curtains by my bunk to see where we were, just as a girl in a stationary train alongside did exactly the same. We were near enough to have touched had we been able to. But we waved to each other instead, and as the cries of 'All aboard' from the guard sent her train on its way, she blew me a kiss. I can see her now, a ship that passed in the night, but for a few seconds we felt very close. I lay awake for a long time thinking about her, wondering if she was doing the same.

It had all seemed incredibly romantic – like something out of a film – and in the end it was probably of more value to me than if I had stayed at school and gone on to university, as I'm sure my parents would have wished. Life is what you make it.

While I had been away the second front had taken place, Paris had been liberated, and after five years of black-out the lights had come on in Piccadilly. It had been officially revealed that German flying bombs had started to fall on this country; they were christened 'doodlebugs'. Glenn Miller had just been reported missing over the English Channel, and there were rumours that a bomb of unparalleled power was being created.

There was a lot of news to catch up on and with luck I would be home in time for Christmas.

CHAPTER 7

A Private on Parade

The army ages men sooner than the law and
philosophy; it exposes them more freely to germs,
which undermine and destroy, and it shelters them
more completely from thought, which stimulates and
preserves.

H. G. Wells (1866–1946)

After a few days at home I was posted to the Isle of Sheppey, in the
Thames estuary, and spent Christmas Day in the middle of a snow-
covered field guarding a crashed German plane.

The natives were not friendly. To call Sheppey an island makes it
sound grander than it actually is. A more accurate description would be
an inhospitable tract of low-lying land surrounded by water, which at
some time or other someone misguidedly joined to the mainland by
means of a bridge. Or that's how it seemed in the winter of 1945, when
it was very, very cold.

Somewhere, deep inside the book of Service Regulations, there is a
ruling which states that in the event of the weather being so severe that
all the pipes freeze up and remain that way for a specified number of
days the main body of personnel can be sent home, provided always that
a small nucleus of staff is left behind to look after things.

At least, that's what our 'barrack-room lawyer' told us.

Nucleus-wise, I once again drew one of the short straws, and along
with a couple of dozen others I waved goodbye to the lucky ones.

Other than the fact that it looked rather small, I don't know what
sort of plane it was I was supposed to be guarding, or how it got there,
nor did I very much care at the time. It was covered in snow anyway. I

was more concerned with the immediate problem of pitching a tent in order to keep my body temperature hovering somewhere above freezing point.

Seeing smoke rising from what looked like a farm building a couple of fields away, I trudged through the drifts and knocked on the door.

The woman who opened it looked somewhat taken aback when I asked if she had anything to drink. Perhaps she thought I was a German spy or a smuggler with a poor sense of direction – the Isle of Sheppey has always enjoyed a reputation for strange goings-on – at any rate, she closed the door on me and turned a key in the lock. She returned a few minutes later carrying a jug.

Given the island's reputation and the fact that it was Christmas, I had been hoping for a tot or two of contraband rum, but all it contained was water.

I managed to start a small fire and made myself a cup of lukewarm milkless tea. I don't remember what I had to eat.

We had been posted to Sheppey while we made up our minds as to what we wanted to do next. The choice was a simple one: on the other side of the Channel the battle of the Ardennes was under way and General Montgomery was calling for reinforcements; back home there was a chronic fuel shortage – people were reduced to making 'brickettes' out of coal dust and cement – and there was an urgent need for more miners.

In short, we could either transfer our allegiance to the army or take an early discharge and go down the mines.

While one of our group, Oscar da Costa, played mournful tunes on a saxophone, we huddled round a coke stove in our Nissen hut as we weighed up the pros and cons. At times we managed to make it glow red-hot, so much so that one day I stood too near it and set fire to my greatcoat, but I wasn't greatly worried. I wouldn't be needing it much longer – or so I thought.

In the end the weather helped us make up our minds. The roads on the Isle of Sheppey were covered in black ice and the local coal merchants had gone on strike, refusing to make any more deliveries until things improved. As a consequence, the few of us remaining on the RAF base were called in to help.

A day spent slithering around Sheerness with sacks of coal on our backs, trying to bring help to people who in the main couldn't even be bothered to say thank you – and in the case of one woman, actually grumbled because she'd 'just polished the linoleum' – put most of us off coal for ever more. It probably had a similar effect on the woman who had complained, for she found herself left with a pile of wet nutty slack unceremoniously dumped in her hall.

That evening I decided the army had won on points and two weeks later, as we went our separate ways, I reported to an RAF maintenance unit situated – although I didn't realize it until long afterwards – in the grounds of Longleat House in Wiltshire, there to await my transfer.

Almost the first person I bumped into as I made my way through the main gate was the station warrant officer. He was about to go into the guardroom, but when he caught sight of me, his expression froze and he headed in my direction instead.

I suddenly remembered my greatcoat. It still had a large hole in the left flap. Until then it had escaped notice because I had managed to conceal the worst of it behind a carrier bag, but with a large kitbag containing all my worldly possessions slung over my shoulder, that was no longer possible. I tried turning sideways on, adopting a crab-like motion so that my best side was facing to the front, but it was too late.

I told him I had been in a fire, implying that it was lucky I was still alive, but he seemed to take the contrary view. He couldn't believe that I had actually been out and about dressed as I was, on view to the general public. Incineration was clearly too good a fate for me.

I was told to report to the orderly room as soon as I had been allocated a billet, but I never did. I discovered over a period of time that more often than not such threats were made on the spur of the moment and if you didn't turn up the problem went away, saving a lot of trouble all round.

Taking stock of the surroundings as I searched for my hut, I began to realize that everywhere I looked there were young and patently nubile WAAFS hurrying to and fro, many of whom seemed to be eyeing me with interest, as though I were some kind of being from outer space. It was a bit reminiscent of a Giles cartoon.

The few men I saw were all old – at least in their thirties, and that was *old*. To a man they looked as though, having achieved their lifetime's

ambition of being medically downgraded to C3, they were content to
stay exactly where they were for the duration.

There were very few places I was posted to during the war where there
wasn't a lecture by the MO on the lines of 'Steer clear of the local girls,
they're poxed up to the eyebrows.' I imagine in some places they were
by then, what with all the foreign soldiery around, although it wasn't
their eyebrows most of us were interested in.

No such lecture took place in Warminster; it simply wasn't necessary.
As far as the RAF was concerned, they weren't 'local girls', they were
WAAFS, and to us they were simply girls; normal, decent, law-abiding
girls; sex-starved and away from home.

Within a couple of days, without lifting a finger, I had an arrangement
with the driver of a NAAFI wagon, who promised that wherever I
happened to be she would make it her first port of call in the mornings,
along with a supply of Eccles cakes.

She was as good as her word, and later took me up on an invitation
to visit the camp cinema, causing much raucous amusement among her
friends when she turned up with a blanket under her arm – in case we
wanted to go for a walk by the lake after the national anthem.

Another girl, whom I took to a cinema in Warminster, first of all
slapped my hand for allowing it to stray during the trailers, then came
rushing up to me the next day bursting with the news that she had
written to her boyfriend in India breaking off their engagement.

Yet another, with whom, for reasons which Ben Travers or Feydeau
would have appreciated but the orderly officer didn't, I found myself
spending a totally blameless night on a deserted railway station in the
middle of nowhere, made great play of the fact that she wanted to get
her discharge and there was one cast-iron way of achieving it. Which
seemed to me a very good reason for spending a blameless night.

A few evenings later I was escorting a bombshell of a different kind,
blonde this time, back to camp from a local inn after closing time.
Suddenly, she burst into tears and between sobs let fall the information
that she had married a GI only the week before and that he had now
gone back to the States. She then tried to entice me into a field on the
grounds that she was missing him. I gave her a lecture on fidelity and
she didn't speak to me again. I felt very hard done by, especially as by
the time I was 'in my pit' I began to have second thoughts.

As at Heaton Park in Manchester, we sat on our beds in the mornings relating our previous night's adventures, only this time I was able to take a more active part in the conversation. I didn't tell them about the blonde for fear the others might not speak to me again either.

By the end of six weeks most of us weren't too sorry when our postings came through and we were able to make good our escape. We had begun to treat the permanent staff with new respect; they probably weren't as old as they looked after all – just worn out!

Before I left the RAF they recouped some of their loss by deducting the price of twelve shirt collars from my pay. It was the result of a ridiculous argument during my last kit check.

As always, items on the list were called out and we had to hold them up in order to prove they were still in our possession.

Part of the standard RAF issue was three collarless shirts and six detachable collars. When I went to Canada I discovered the RCAF wore collar-attached shirts, so I promptly did a trade-in: three collarless shirts and six detachable collars for three collar-attached shirts.

On the command 'Shirts, three, airmen for the use of,' I held up two shirts and pointed to the one I was wearing. But when it came to 'Detachable collars, six,' I naturally had nothing to show.

Trying to explain the reason for the deficiency, remonstrating that there was no point whatsoever in my having six detachable collars if I had nothing I could attach them to, was like banging my head against a brick wall.

In the end, I had to pay for twelve collars. The cost of the six that had been 'lost' and the cost of a further six needed to replace them. I looked round for the barrack-room lawyer, but he was nowhere to be seen.

In the nature of things, most RAF camps, being out in the wild, were of a temporary nature, built in haste to accommodate the needs of the service.

The army barracks we were posted to in Edinburgh was purpose-built and looked as though it had been there since the beginning of time. On 1 March 1945, I exchanged my blue uniform for one of khaki, gaining another digit in the process. To my nearest and dearest, I was now 14938882 Private Bond, and a less than happy one at that.

Gone were my collar and tie; boots replaced shoes. Gone were the steel-framed beds we had grown used to in the RAF. Instead, we were issued with trestles, three wooden planks, and what appeared to be a large sack, at which point we were directed towards some stables where the straw was kept; straw which, if the smell was anything to go by, no self-respecting horse would have considered eating, let alone sleeping on, except in a dire emergency. The blankets had seen better days, but fortunately I had thought to take with me a cotton sleeping bag, a relic of my youth hostelling days with Tim.

At dawn the next day we were wakened by the unfamiliar sound of someone playing a bugle. It took a little while before the truth sank in. Outside the window a flag began to unfurl at the top of a pole. It wasn't good news.

That morning I missed by the skin of my teeth being put on a charge for doing a crossword puzzle on parade. I normally like to start the day with a crossword – it gets the mind going. I was only saved by the fact that it was a very large parade and, as ever, I was as near the back as possible. By the time the sergeant-major reached our line the newspaper was well and truly concealed beneath my battledress and he couldn't remember which of us had been holding it.

It was history repeating itself really. My father was fond of telling a similar story, only in his case he hadn't been doing a crossword, simply daydreaming of home. He came to with a bump when his right eardrum was suddenly shattered by a sergeant bawling into it from a few inches away.

'You, I'm talking to. You! The pudding-faced idiot in the rear!'

The recollection of the story always made him laugh, although I doubt whether he had done so at the time.

Those of us who had been in the RAF received an unexpected bonus. Having already done our basic training, we were sent home on leave while the rest of the intake were taught how to march. On my return, I found I had been posted to Chester, where I was to join the Middlesex Regiment.

The first evening in camp I decided to explore the town and accordingly spent some time titivating myself before setting off.

As I was making my way from the billet to the main gate a dog came bounding up to me, wagging its tail. It reminded me of Binkie, so I bent down and gave it a pat.

Almost immediately a stentorian voice rang out. 'Come 'ere, you. At the double.'

On the far side of the parade ground I spotted the ramrod shape of what was clearly the regimental sergeant-major, a pace stick clutched firmly beneath his arm.

I did as I was bidden, covering the distance between us at record speed. As I drew near, I noticed his face had gone an alarming shade of puce. RSMs have a lot in common with Paddington. There are moments when they look as though they can hardly believe their eyes.

''Ow dare you cross the parade ground like that!' he bellowed. 'That's 'allowed ground, that is. Go back where you was and come round the outside. At the double! Go on ... move!'

Wondering what I could possibly have done to provoke such wrath, I set off and had barely covered a yard or two when I was stopped short.

'Not *that* way, you dozy man. Round the outside.'

It was some five minutes or so before I arrived back, the suave figure who had earlier been setting out to sample the fleshpots of Chester now reduced to a dusty, sweaty wreck.

The RSM looked me up and down. 'You 'orrible man. I saw you! I saw you! That dog you patted 'appens to be the CO's dog. You're not fit to touch an 'air on 'is 'ead. If I ever catch you doing that again you'll be on a charge. Right?'

It was an inauspicious start. Even the dog looked upset on my behalf, but I avoided his gaze in case he made a bee-line for me again.

I was beginning to wonder if I had made the right decision that day on the Isle of Sheppey. At least in a coal mine there were probably dark places in the face where one could hide.

In fact, as things turned out, I enjoyed my time in the army.

The Middlesex were known as the 'Diehards' and were equipped with Vickers medium water-cooled machine-guns mounted on Bren carriers. Along with their sister regiment, the Northumberland Fusiliers, who deployed mortars mounted on Lloyd carriers, they formed the two remaining infantry support regiments left in the British Army.

Having been classified as a driver/wireless operator, I was taken in hand by two driving instructors. They were as different as chalk and cheese. The first was a former London cabbie, a lovely man of the old school who had infinite patience and made learning to drive a pleasure.

The second was a dyspeptic ex-long-distance lorry driver who, when I first encountered him, was fondling a large piece of timber. It didn't take long to discover the reason. The gear boxes on Bren carriers were not only fitted back to front, so that the gate was reversed, but they lacked any form of synchro-mesh, which meant that if you didn't get the revs exactly right it was all too easy to miss a change.

Punishment for missing a gear change was swift. Hardly had the noise of grinding metal died away than it was punctuated by the heavier sound made by timber making contact with a tin hat. As a form of ulcer-transference therapy for the instructor it probably had a lot to recommend it, but for the hapless driver sitting alongside him it made for unhappy outings at the wheel. Our hearts always sank whenever he beckoned us, and on those rare occasions when I'm tired and miss a gear I still instinctively cringe as I await the blow.

Driving along the highways and byways of north Wales in our tracked vehicles, we perfected the technique of changing drivers whilst travelling at speed – something which would have wiped the smile off the faces of approaching car drivers had they realized what was happening, for it wasn't easy in hobnailed boots.

Another useful skill I learnt was how to take an open-sided tracked vehicle over the side of a sheer cliff without killing all the occupants. It's quite easy really. All you do is drive up to the edge, close your eyes, grip the steering wheel until your knuckles show white, then put your foot gently on the accelerator. Gravity does the rest.

When it came to being taught the rudiments of radio communication and the army discovered I not only had a good grounding in the subject but that I knew the morse code, I narrowly escaped being made an instructor for the duration, which would have been bad news.

I even enjoyed learning how to take a Vickers machine gun apart, reassembling it in record time with my eyes closed. Viewed as a piece of mechanical engineering rather than as an instrument of death, there is a certain elegance about the mechanics of weaponry.

I also discovered an aptitude for rifle shooting and won myself a marksman's badge. It struck me as a mixed blessing and when I sewed the badge on to my uniform I used easily detachable stitches in case I was ever captured by the enemy. Uncle Jack had many tales to relate about snipers receiving short shrift.

There were times when training felt as though it could be even more dangerous than active service. At least when the enemy lob a grenade into your trench it isn't entirely unexpected. When one of your own side removes the pin and then drops one at your feet out of sheer fright, as happened on two occasions, there is cause for legitimate complaint. The first time I owed my life to an alert range sergeant; the second time I saw it coming. The 4–5-second delay is longer than it sounds, but you cannot afford to fumble the pick-up and it's only afterwards that you start to sweat.

Doing fatigues in the guardroom one rainy day, I spent the morning polishing some fire buckets until I could see my face in them, only to have them thrown out of the door into the nearest pool of mud by an ill-tempered sergeant on the grounds that they were filthy; which they certainly were by the time he had finished with them. One acquired a certain stoicism in the face of such indignities.

Stoicism was a much-needed quality when it came to doing route marches carrying the bits and pieces for a Vickers machine-gun. Normally mounted on a Bren carrier, it required three people to manhandle it. The barrel with its supply of water for the cooling jacket weighed forty pounds, the tripod another fifty pounds, then there was the ammunition. After twenty or so miles it was impossible to say which was the worst item to be lumbered with.

At the end of the day we used to fall into our bunks exhausted and sleep like proverbial logs.

After about six weeks there was a minor diversion when I was sent to Eaton Hall, the Duke of Westminster's home in Cheshire, on a WOSB (War Office Selection Board) for potential officers.

I was a bit embarrassed to tell the rest of the platoon for fear they might rag me about it, which of course some of them did, calling me 'Sir' long after lights-out.

The first evening after I arrived we all sat down to dinner at an immaculately laid table in what must have been the duke's dining-room, where we were served dinner by a bevy of poker-faced ATS girls while an officer prowled around peering over our shoulders and entering notes on a clipboard.

It was an uneasy occasion; a far cry from my first meal in Regent's Park Zoo when I asked for one portion of mashed potatoes instead of two, and it was certainly a welcome change from eating out of mess tins.

Apart from morning coffee with Auntie Ethel at the Tudor Restaurant in Newbury, where we all had to be on our best behaviour, the only time I ever remember being taken out to eat when I was small was at a fish restaurant in Margate. While the grown-ups were busy talking I decided to put some pepper on my cod, but when I shook the pot the top came off and the entire contents fell on top of my fish. I was too embarrassed to tell anyone, so I ate it all up as best I could, along with copious draughts of water. Afterwards I was asked if I was feeling all right because I looked as though I had caught the sun.

On the other hand, I had been rigorously schooled in table manners, not only by my parents and Auntie Ethel, but also by Auntie Annie. She was a stickler for always having a correctly laid table, with things being properly served on plates which had their patterns set at exactly the same angle, so I wasn't intimidated by the large array of cutlery laid out before me. I simply started at the outside and worked my way in. Fortunately someone else had to start passing the port at the end of the meal and we all carried on sending it round in the same direction, pretending we did it every day of our lives.

In the event that first dinner was to be the high spot of the few days we spent at Eaton Hall, so it was as well we made the most of it.

The rest of the time was taken up with other tests: wading through mud and water up to our armpits while idiot fresh-faced officers just out of school took great delight in aiming thunder-flashes at our heads. Never have I been more thankful for a tin helmet. Having made my way along a narrow plank some twenty feet off the ground only to come face to face with the prospect of either taking a leap into space or going back the way I'd come, I took a quick look round to make sure no one was looking and opted for the latter. Just as my fingers clasped a convenient rope I caught sight of an officer looking up at me. He made an entry on the inevitable clipboard and I knew I had landed on the metaphorical snake in the draughtboard of life; the long one which takes you back almost to GO.

Later that day I forfeited a few more moves when we all took part in a series of banal psychological war games.

Question: You are a prisoner of war somewhere in Germany. Whilst in the camp commandant's office there is an air raid during which a bomb drops nearby killing all the other occupants of the room. You are about to make good your escape when you notice the drawers to the filing cabinets have been blown open. Do you carry on or do you lose valuable seconds gathering up as many papers as possible?

Since I didn't speak a word of German, and since it seemed to me highly unlikely there would be anything of importance there anyway, and I didn't see myself charging around the German countryside weighed down with bundles of office files, I opted for making good my escape. Another note was added to my report form.

Question: As a group you have been sent to an unnamed town in Germany where all the services, electricity, water, gas, transport, have been rendered inoperable through bombing. What would you do about it?

Drawing lots for the various positions of authority, I found myself in charge of transport. Dipping my toes in first, I put up what I thought was a spirited argument in favour of getting the trams working so that people could get to their factories on time, but I was shouted down by the others with cries of 'Let the buggers walk. Serves them right! Do them good!' and 'What factories?'

I must say that in my heart I rather agreed with these sentiments and hoped I might earn a few bonus points for being reasonable about it, but I'm not sure that I did.

The last nail in my coffin came at the final interview when I was asked: 'If you are successful, would you be prepared to sign on for seven and five!' (Seven years active service, followed by five on the reserve).

Clearly, from the air of finality with which my file was snapped shut, 'No' was not the right answer.

I arrived back at camp and climbed into my bunk feeling somewhat relieved, glad to be back among people I had grown to respect and identify with. To have moved over to the other side, as it were, would have seemed like a betrayal.

I had been born into a west of England family who through unconsidered loyalties always voted Conservative. 'They' knew what was best for us. My few days at Eaton Hall had, for the first time in my life, brought me face to face with the British class system. The services – particularly the army and the navy – perpetuated the established order of things and my brief encounter on equal terms with the so-called officer class and the superior attitudes that went with it had suddenly made me aware of the unwritten barriers which exist.

On the other hand, I had to admit there were moments when I had enjoyed the experience.

Doing guard duty with a Durham miner shortly afterwards, he questioned my views about life and the rights and wrongs of a system which allowed for so many inequalities. Finding myself unable to answer any of his questions with conviction, I was left feeling even more confused, particularly when I remembered my father's occasional bitterness at the incompetence of those who by virtue of their birth had been in command during the First World War and had sent so many millions to a certain death.

But in some respects it all became academic anyway. While we were still at Chester the war in Europe came to an end, and a few months later, at 8.20 a.m. on 7 August 1945, the Allies dropped the first atomic bomb on Hiroshima. The largest bomb ever dropped until that day had been the British 'Grand Slam', which weighed 11 tons. The one at Hiroshima was the equivalent of 20,000 tons of TNT, and killed over 80,000 people outright. Two days later a second bomb obliterated Nagasaki and the Japanese surrendered. It was hard enough to take in the fact that after six long years the war was over, let alone absorb the enormity of the means by which it had been brought about.

In November 1945 I returned to camp after fourteen days' embarkation leave and joined an assembly in the main drill hall to hear our fate. We were, announced a red-tabbed brigadier, who had travelled down from the War Office for the sole purpose of addressing us, 'bound for a British possession in the Indian Ocean'. He painted a rosy picture of what life would be like once we got there, and of how we were to consider ourselves, each and every one of us, ambassadors of our country. Above all, he stressed how lucky we were to be going to such a wonderful place.

As we came to attention and the crash of several hundred army boots signalled our approval, he saluted and returned to Whitehall.

Our enthusiasm was immediately dampened.

The sound of the brigadier's departing car had barely died away when a staff sergeant brought us to attention again. 'Don't take any notice of all that bollocks,' he bawled with relish. 'There's been a little mix hup at GHQ. You lot is 'eading for Heegypt, where it's not only bleedin' 'ot, but the natives is distinctly unfriendly on account of wanting to get rid of the Raj.'

And so it was that one cold but sunny November day in 1945, I stepped off the gang-plank of a cross-channel ferry on to French soil, en route for the Middle East. Suddenly, after what had been a comparatively short journey, I found myself in a totally different world. The people looked and behaved in a different way; most of the men were clad in blue dungarees and some of the women wore the shortest skirts I had ever seen. The architecture was different, the language was different, and the food – the little there was – was certainly different.

It was a case of love at first sight, and unlike some other love affairs, it has stood the test of time. Over fifty years later it shows no sign of waning.

The train journey across France was taken at a snail's pace and lasted several days. There wasn't much left of the French rail system – four-fifths of the engines and rolling stock had been destroyed, not to mention hundreds of miles of track – and we were constantly being diverted or brought to a halt for one reason or another.

I had plenty of time to absorb my new surroundings; from the flat, shell-shocked plains of the north, down through the Rhône Valley, past vineyards and distant snow-covered mountains, onward to the red-tiled roofs and relative warmth of the south. I lay awake at night, not wanting to miss any of it.

I knew that one day I would return, for despite the intense cold of travelling huddled up in a windowless carriage, sheltering from a draught which was so biting some people were sick, I felt strangely at home and at peace with the world.

We spent a week in a transit camp in Hyères, and I managed to make several excursions into Toulon, where I wandered the streets, forgoing the prospect of a hot meal back at camp in exchange for a slice of ersatz bread and a glass of the local wine in whatever candle-lit street café took my fancy. I was blissfully happy.

The usual MO's warning had fallen on largely deaf ears. We boarded a P & O liner bound for Port Said and soon after we left a good proportion of those who had earlier regaled us with stories of visits made to a local nightspot in Hyères known as Nob Hill, began queueing up outside the ship's hospital in order to pay the price.

But once again, as I leaned over the ship's rail, I hardly noticed. Before I left England everyone had told me what a nice sea the Mediterranean was. 'Nothing to worry about there,' they said. 'Lucky old you!' Little did they know. I was beginning to tire of people who said 'Don't think about it'. They were worse than the ones who recommended swallowing a piece of fatty pork on the end of a string. At least the latter were trying to be funny.

On arrival at Port Said we boarded a train for Cairo and the more enterprising were soon hard at work flogging blankets to the native population swarming the platforms. At the very last second, as the train began to move, a great battle would break out, with the troops grabbing the money while at the same time hauling the blankets, already firmly secured by rope, back into the carriage.

At the first station we came to the train slowed down to a walking pace and we were stoned by the local populace, who had turned out in force to waylay us. I could see their point, and I also began to see why the Egyptians might not be sorry to see the back of us.

Stones figured large on the horizon soon after we reached Heliopolis.

I never ceased to be amazed at the ingenuity and imagination displayed by regular NCOs in the army. A group of us were marched out to the boundary of the transit camp where we were brought to a halt.

Not far away, outnumbering us by several hundred to one, a group of German prisoners of war, mahogany brown from long exposure to the African sun, eyed our white knees with ill-concealed contempt as those of us who had gone through our fifty-a-week cigarette ration searched desperately in the sand for any discarded butts. They were probably wondering how on earth they had ended up on the losing side. Fortunately a barbed wire fence separated us or they might have exacted their revenge.

'That there', said the sergeant, pointing to a seemingly endless expanse of sand and rocks, 'looks bleedin' untidy. I want them stones cleared before the end of the afternoon. Right? Get cracking.'

It was a variation on the old army motto: 'If it moves, salute it. If it doesn't, paint it.' It would have been more to the point if we had mounted a concerted attack on the bedbugs which inhabited the ancient barracks in which we were housed. Flat as a pancake by day, they were plump with blood fresh from the UK by morning. Some inveterate gamblers used to organize races with those that could still move.

We were to spend some time in and around Cairo. The occasional military forays we made into the city when trouble broke out were more than enough for some, who were content to spend their evenings in the NAAFI downing the local chemically made beer, or eating fried-egg sandwiches while listening to the Andrews Sisters singing 'Drinking Rum and Coca-Cola'.

I much preferred the bright lights of Cairo. It had its downside: the never-ending noise of car horns, the hordes of pickpockets, horses condemned to spend their entire life between the shafts of a gharry, the occasional dog covered in mange, professional beggars and their families of small children trained to press their faces against restaurant windows watching your every mouthful as you ate, or pressing the stump of an amputated leg against yours while you waited at a bus stop; all of which was at times hard to ignore. But it also had a lot to offer.

The forces at that time were bursting with talent waiting to escape and there were theatre groups and music societies and opportunities galore only a tram-ride away from camp for those willing to make the effort. Open-air cinemas proliferated and it was in Cairo that I saw my first French films; usually Tino Rossi playing twin brothers after the same girl; you could tell which was the bad one because he always sported a pencil moustache and had his hair slicked back. Scorpions occasionally scuttled across the screen and the biggest laughs were reserved for the ones which happened to run up Betty Grable's legs. The air would be filled with cheers and the ribald comments of licentious soldiery.

There was also Groppi's, where I used to call in for an ice-cream sundae called 'Three Little Pigs', and on the way back to camp late at night there was the Brazilian Coffee Shop in Solomon Pasha where they made what I still think of as the best coffee I have ever tasted.

But there was a feeling of change in the air. There were periods when Cairo was out of bounds for days on end, and even when it did open up again one was conscious of the resentment of the population at large. Troops were allowed out only if they were wearing civilian clothes. Not that it deceived the locals. Short cuts down dark alleyways – not to be recommended at any time – were best avoided.

In February 1946 came the first of the large-scale orchestrated riots outside Kasr el Nil Barracks, and the Victory Club where I had spent many happy hours was destroyed.

One day when I was confined to camp I borrowed the office typewriter and wrote a short story. I called it 'Captain Hazel's Piece of String'. It told of a recruiting officer's machinations as he tried to persuade a soldier to sign on for a further seven years, baiting his trap with a story set in a sleazy Cairo bar. It was inspired more by the dusky maidens one saw beckoning from behind many a bead curtain than the touts outside who seemed to have cornered the market in the supply of 'Young virgin English schoolteachers – fresh out from the UK'. For some reason this was always regarded as the very height of temptation, although with memories of Miss Campion still fresh in my mind, the idea of finding her lying in wait for me had the opposite effect.

I wrote the story very quickly and sent it off to a magazine called *London Opinion* as it seemed their kind of material.

The weeks went by and I had almost forgotten the whole thing when I received an envelope bearing a London postmark. On opening it, out fell a letter saying my story had been accepted for publication.

Cashing the accompanying cheque was another problem. I had never seen one before and wasn't quite sure what to do with it. The clerk in the post office felt the same way, eyeing with suspicion the words '*London Opinion* will pay Michael Bond seven guineas', and the local Arab traders, who had never heard of the word 'guineas', didn't want to know.

I wish now I'd had it framed.

What was more important, however, was the fact that at last I had found my true vocation. The way ahead was suddenly clear. A glittering future lay before me; a future paved with golden guineas. I had read somewhere that Ernest Hemingway was being paid 7s.6d a word for his dispatches. One day . . .

In the meantime, after months of sporadic and often very violent rioting, the British were preparing to move out of Cairo. On 4 July 1946 the Citadel, which we had occupied for sixty-four years, was handed over and I found myself ensconced like a prisoner behind barbed wire in the Canal Zone. Almost immediately, having survived a thousand ice-creams in the parlours of Cairo, I went down with amoebic dysentery.

As I made countless journeys shuffling through the sand between my tent and the nearest open latrine, carrying a long ribbon of sulphur tablets in one hand and a roll of precious toilet paper in the other, I must have looked a sorry figure. But sympathy was thin on the ground.

All my immediate friends had been demobbed and I didn't even have Bismarck for comfort.

Bismarck, my constant companion, had disappeared in the wash. In my debilitated state I accidentally left him in the top pocket of a battle-dress shirt. When it came back he had gone. I rushed to the *dhobi wallah* and searched through the remaining pile of laundry in case he had fallen out. But it was in vain. The man doing the ironing didn't know what I was talking about and anyway he had his mouth full of water as he made ready to spray the next item. It was my last link with N.K., who the previous year had written to say she had got married.

I felt very miserable and seized on the chance of a month's leave in the UK.

It seemed like a good idea at the time, but it got off to a bad start. By then I had been made a corporal and had grown a moustache in the hope that it might impart an air of authority. There were quite a few latitudes in dress in the Middle East at that time. Brown shoes had become very popular – some even got away with suedes – and along with some hand-made brogues I persuaded a local tailor to widen my trouser-leg bottoms in the current fashion. Taking advantage of my rank, I had also let my hair grow longer, tucking it up under my beret when I was on parade. In short, it wasn't quite the image the army was wont to use on its recruiting posters.

When I reached Port Said, I heard my name being called over the tannoy telling me to report to the orderly room where a telegram awaited me. Thinking it must be urgent, I made haste there, removing my hat as I entered.

The sergeant-major was sitting at a desk facing the door and as I entered he looked up.

'Well I never,' he exclaimed, calling the attention of everybody in the room to the new arrival. 'Look 'oo's 'ere. Yeoody Menuin isself, come to give us a concert. We *are* honoured. Where's yer violin? Come on, Mister Menuin. Don't just stand there. Give us a tune.'

There was a lot more in like vein and I waited patiently until all the musical possibilities had been exhausted, at which point I mentioned that I had a boat to catch.

'Oh, no, you 'aven't,' he bellowed. 'Not until you've 'ad your 'air cut. You will report 'ere at seventeen-thirty 'aving 'ad it off. Right?'

I collected my telegram and fled. It was from Pamela, wishing me *bon voyage*! It could have been the end of a beautiful childhood friendship, but it wasn't. The boat was due to leave at sixteen hundred hours and I made sure I was on it.

It was probably rough justice, but as I scrambled up the gang-plank I was waylaid by an officer with a clipboard and found myself detailed to escort some British army prisoners as far as Malta. They were already in the brig and I was warned to exercise great care. They had set fire to the last boat they were on, and one of them had already broken the arm of a guard, wrapping it round a bar of the cell when he'd taken them some water.

I got together enough 'volunteers' to form a twenty-four-hour guard and consulted a plan of the ship. The brig, when I found it, was roughly triangular in shape, and it was triangular for the very simple reason that it was right up in the bow, just below the water-line. My heart sank when I saw it. Even in harbour the room seemed to be moving up and down in an alarming way.

Mindful of the fact that we were all going on leave and needed to keep our limbs intact, we took great care of our prisoners, treating them as though they were lions in the zoo at feeding time, pushing their plates under the bars with the aid of a broom handle.

When the time came to say goodbye we wished them well, and, seeing the military police with their shaven heads and sun-bleached webbing who were waiting on the quayside to collect them, we meant it.

The Mediterranean Fleet was at anchor in Valletta harbour, a sight probably never to be repeated. The next time I saw Malta, years later, it was almost devoid of shipping; a sad shadow of how I remembered it.

In Gibraltar, where we stopped for a few hours, there was a small open ship moored a little way apart from all the others. It was packed to suffocation with Jewish refugees, men, women and children making their way to Palestine, and for the first time as I gazed down at them I felt ashamed to be British, for clearly they were crying out for help, and equally clearly they were unlikely to get it.

The story of the plight of the Jewish people in many such ships, of which the *Exodus* was perhaps the most heartbreaking, has been told many times, but after the horrors of Belsen and other such places it still seemed wrong that they should be treated that way, even if it was with the best of intentions. Man's inhumanity to man knows no bounds.

Back home, England was slowly recovering from one of the worst winters ever recorded. For a time continual blizzards had stopped all shipping in the Channel. Over three hundred roads had been blocked by deep snowdrifts; fifteen towns cut off. Power supplies had failed, and for a while the country almost ground to a halt in sub-zero temperatures – at times down to minus sixteen degrees Fahrenheit.

Many people, my mother included, blamed it on the atom bombs disturbing the atmosphere, just as people had laid the blame on continuous gunfire in the First World War. They could be right, of course.

After the thaw came the floods. Coal and gas fires were banned. The meat ration was down to one shilling's worth a week. The bread ration had been cut. Beer production was down fifty per cent. Eggs were scarce and the Ministry of Food issued an edict saying that if you bought one and it turned out to be bad – which it often was – you could take it back and it was the supplier's duty to change it.

All around posters exhorted the nation to work harder, but strikes were rampant.

My parents didn't grumble, but listening to them talk I realized that by and large things had been much easier for me. I had been away from home for nearly four years and during that time my mother had gone completely grey and I had grown up; grown up and grown away from them. England was no longer the green and pleasant land they had brought me up in. It had become very grey and I felt a stranger in my own country. Although the war was over, things were worse than they had ever been and the population seemed thoroughly demoralized. The divorce rate soared as men returning from abroad full of hope became disillusioned by what they saw.

It seemed a long way to have come for so little.

Back in the Canal Zone the talk was all about discharge and demob numbers. Mine was 57 and I still had some time to go, although having seen what it was like in Britain I felt tempted to sign on.

In August 1947 my first story appeared in print. Shortly afterwards I received a copy through the post. It was accompanied by a muted letter of congratulation from my mother, who ended by saying she hoped all was well, clearly believing it wasn't.

Her letters were in the style of Gertrude Stein, like streams of consciousness written from the heart, with little or no punctuation, and although she didn't say it in so many words, my fictional tale of life in the raw in a backstreet Cairo bar had obviously been taken seriously.

If it demonstrated the perils of writing in the first person, at least it also showed I had the potential to make a work of total fiction ring true.

CHAPTER 8

A Taste of France

There are three difficulties in authorship: to write
anything worth the publishing, to find honest men to
publish it, and to get sensible men to read it.

Charles Caleb Colton (1780–1832)

In October I made the final journey back to the UK, trading in my
uniform for a grey pinstripe utility suit, which in the event nobody liked,
and which turned out to be too small anyway, although the tailor had
assured me it was a perfect fit. After an army beret, the trilby hat felt
very odd and I never wore that either. Later on, when money ran out,
I sold both for a few shillings to a second-hand clothes dealer. From the
look of his storage rails I wasn't the only one.

The England I returned to in 1947 was, if anything, in an even worse
state than when I had last seen it. There were shortages of practically
everything. The bacon ration had been cut to one ounce a week and
potatoes to three pounds. The weekly milk ration was down to two and
a half pints. Ration books were needed if you stayed longer than two
nights in an hotel. Pleasure motoring was forbidden, and there was a
flourishing black market. With the war over, people had fewer qualms
about making use of it. There had been a change of government and
nationalization was taking place left, right and centre. Most ominous of
all, there was a chronic shortage of dollars with which to pay for imports.

'Export or Die' and 'Work or Want' were the slogans of the day.

Ironically, the big hit song of the moment was 'They Say It's Wonderful', from *Annie Get Your Gun*.

No private building had taken place during the war and by the end
of it in London alone over one and a half million houses had been

destroyed or badly damaged. Troops returning home in their thousands found rented accommodation almost non-existent, so for the time being I went back home to live until I had sorted myself out.

Foreign travel was about to be banned, so my dreams of going to France had to be temporarily shelved. With my demob money I bought myself an old upright Remington typewriter, a packet of quarto typing paper and a supply of carbon paper, and set to work with a pin cleaning out the pockets of dirt in the typeface ready for the off. Even if I wasn't able to do the real thing, it needn't stop me writing about it.

After Egypt, England seemed very tame. I missed the constant bustle of Cairo with its cafés full of old men sitting hunched over their hookah pipes or sipping cups of coffee over endless games of backgammon. I even found myself missing the wailing voice of the mullah calling the faithful.

There was nothing like that in Reading. The muffin man had disappeared at the outbreak of war and I never came across our local vicar.

A few of us who had served together arranged a reunion in London, but it was an uneasy occasion. Out of uniform, I suppose we had all reverted to type. One ex-drinking partner of many a riotous evening turned out to be a customs officer and looked as though our past friendship would cut very little ice if he ever caught me trying to smuggle anything past him. Another, whose tales of amorous exploits on a beach in Cyprus had once kept us enthralled, now worked for the Bank of England and dressed accordingly. He regarded my French beret with a certain amount of envy. A third member of the party, who had miraculously survived having a bullet enter the back of his neck and exit through his mouth without losing a single tooth, and with whom I'd shared many a laugh, had little to say for himself.

All were either married or about to be married and had trains to catch because they had promised to be back by seven o'clock. We went our separate ways, saying we must do it again, but knowing in our hearts we never would, and that was that.

Tim was already home, having been invalided out of the military police. He had accidentally stamped on his own left foot whilst doing drill; a not uncommon occurrence. He was in the process of taking over the family mineral water business, and for a while I helped out in the bottling plant, loading crates on to conveyor belts and generally making myself useful to the sound of *Music While You Work*. It was, I told myself, all good material for a budding author, although for the time being an effervescent story-line set in a lemonade factory eluded me, and still does for that matter.

I wasn't unduly distressed: writing is one of the few occupations where lack of commercial success carries with it no great social stigma – rather the reverse – and being a Capricorn I was determined to get there in the end. In the meantime I grew proficient at recognizing the dull thud of returning manuscripts from a distance of fifty paces or more.

In order to keep body and soul together, and to pay the return postage on my manuscripts, I went back to the BBC.

The transmitter in Reading having closed down at the end of the war, I was sent to join the Monitoring Service, which had moved from Wood Norton Hall in the Vale of Evesham to Caversham Park, just outside Reading. It turned out to be a refreshingly cosmopolitan oasis in an otherwise grey world.

The hub of the whole enterprise – the listening room – consisted of long rows of communication receivers staffed by foreign nationals whose job it was to record news bulletins from stations around the world, afterwards translating them into English. By the end of the war, when Gilbert Harding was one of the editors producing a daily digest of foreign broadcasts for the War Cabinet, they were monitoring more than a million words every day in thirty languages, and it was at Caversham in May 1945 that the first news of Germany's capitulation was received. In an increasingly unsettled post-war world it still had its ear tuned in on behalf of the government to what other countries were thinking and saying, and performed a useful and at times highly valuable service.

Winston Churchill's warnings had come to pass and the Soviet Iron Curtain now divided Europe in two, so there was a large Russian section, but there were also Poles and Germans, Chinese, Greeks, Arabs, Hungarians . . . practically every race under the sun was represented. Some were more British than the British; their sports jackets had a broader weave, their pipes were more firmly clenched between their teeth, their clipped accents often too good to be true. Others remained steadfastly loyal to the land of their birth and could be spotted a mile away. Many had fled their own country at the start of the war, and nearly all of them had a story to tell.

The engineers who looked after the technical side, of whom I was one, were British to a man, much given to wearing corduroy trousers, sweaters – if you could find a girlfriend to knit you one – and Harris tweed jackets with obligatory leather patches on the elbows. Mine was topped by a government surplus duffle coat which arrived in a vast cardboard tube and doubled up as an additional bedcover at night.

It was yet another bitterly cold winter, made worse by the fuel shortage, and at night, lying in my officially prescribed four-inch maximum depth of water, I used to balance an electric fire on the side of the bath in order to keep the top half of me warm while I took stock of the situation and tried to decide what the future held.

It makes me shudder now to think of it. I didn't even have the excuse of being unaware of the risk I was taking. It was a form of Russian roulette without the advantage of knowing that in a well-oiled gun the odds are in favour of the one full chamber always ending up at the lowest point, away from the firing pin.

There was yet another hazard connected with taking a bath. The gas-fired geysers which had been installed when the houses were built had mostly come to the end of their useful life. Years without any kind of maintenance had taken its toll and explosions were commonplace, particularly on a Friday evening.

The only splash of colour, for Londoners at least, came towards the end of 1947 when the wedding of Princess Elizabeth and Prince Philip took place. Princess Elizabeth was granted extra clothing coupons for her wedding dress, but went on her honeymoon minus a trousseau owing to the cloth shortage.

Cold wasn't the only hazard during the immediate post-war winters. Fog – thick, damp and all-embracing – was often the norm.

Driving a car at night it was possible to enter a roundabout and before you were a quarter of the way round find yourself completely lost. Pedestrians took to covering the lower half of their faces with a knotted handkerchief. Between 26 November and 1 December 1948, London suffered one hundred and fourteen continuous hours of it. (There was worse to come: four Decembers later clouds of a singularly evil colour began to form over London, heralding the arrival of smog, that lethal mixture of smoke and fog. It stayed for four days and during that period the death rate was seven times greater than normal.)

*   *   *

It was 1949 before things started to look up again. That year the Tate Gallery reopened and in March clothes rationing ended. There were sales everywhere in celebration. Olivier's *Hamlet* deservedly won no less than five Hollywood Oscars, including the first-ever British award for 'Best Picture'.

The following month chocolate and sweets came off ration (although they were to go back on again in July).

Carol Reed had a hit with *Odd Man Out* starring James Mason, and an even greater one later in the year with *The Third Man* – which would still be on my list of the ten best films ever made.

It was possible to take the train up to London of an evening for four shillings return, so after work I began catching up on all the theatre I had missed out on and became an avid galleryite, arriving back long after the last bus had left. But it was worth the mile and a half walk home.

I saw Olivier's wonderful *Richard III* at the Old Vic and Gertrude Lawrence in *September Tide* at the Aldwych. I discovered Ibsen and Chekhov, Priestley and Shaw, Maugham and Rattigan.

Robertson Hare, a surviving member of the great pre-war Aldwych farces team, was appearing with Alfred Drayton in *One Wild Oat* at the Garrick. Years later, when I was living in Haslemere, he used to come down at Christmas to stay with his daughter and son-in-law who lived next door. His favourite drink was a lethal cocktail called a 'Trinity' – one part each of red and white vermouth, one part gin. After he had partaken of a modest few he would sometimes consent to say 'Oh, calamity!' in the way that only he could deliver it. In a sense it was his catch phrase and he must have uttered it a million times. But he always maintained it was something you had to feel – it had to come from within.

By far the most exciting theatrical event that year took place on 9 May, when Christopher Fry's verse play *The Lady's Not for Burning* burst on the scene. John Gielgud and Pamela Brown headed a star-studded cast, which included a young Richard Burton, Claire Bloom, Norah Nicholson, Eliot Makeham, Harcourt Williams and Esmé Percy. I remember laughing so much I had pains in my side.

For a while everyone wanted to write like Christopher Fry, but of course they couldn't, any more than a run-of-the-mill violin maker can turn out a Stradivarius. There came a period when even Christopher Fry lost his touch for a while, and the style had gone out of fashion anyway, but at the time he couldn't put a foot wrong.

I saw *The Lady's Not for Burning* several times and I even bought tickets for my parents as a treat. I could only afford seats in the upper circle and as my mother didn't like heights she kept her eyes closed all through the performance. Since she also didn't really hold with being out after dark, the evening wasn't a great success and it must have been her last visit to the London theatre.

Meanwhile, back in Reading, the Caversham Electric cinema was enjoying a new lease of life with programmes aimed at the captive foreign audience populating the BBC monitoring station.

Picking up where I had left off in Cairo, I dabbled in the many delights of the French cinema of that period; films by Jean Renoir and René Clair, and Marcel Pagnols's wonderful trilogy, *Marius*, *César* and *Fanny*, with Pierre Fresnay, Fernand Charpin and the late, great actor Raimu, who was to become a role model for a character in books to come.

At the beginning of May the overseas travel allowance was increased from £35 to £50 (during the winter of '47 it had been cancelled altogether) and I was able to take a holiday in France for the first time. My 'companion' and I (to use a phrase which was far from current at the time) travelled to Brittany via Air France. The plane was propeller-driven and on the journey out the pilot flew low over Mont St Michel before circling over the Rance estuary, banking steeply to show us with pride the various sites we could visit after we had landed, which couldn't be soon enough as far as I was concerned. It brought it all back to me, along with my breakfast. The startled air hostess clearly didn't share the pilot's earnest hope that I would be among those flying Air France again very soon when I handed her my sick bag.

Apart from the fact that Pamela had promised her grandmother 'no misconduct would take place' – a promise which no amount of grumbling or cajolery on my part could persuade her to break – we had a lovely, carefree time.

We stepped off the plane into a France which, outwardly at least, was very little different to that of the thirties. All through the war the intellectual elite had been taking advantage of their enforced idleness to plan for the future, but their ideas had yet to be put into practice;

the country was still recovering from years of occupation and the moral shame of all that had happened. Governments came and went and de Gaulle, who had also spent much of the time planning for the future, had yet to pull it up by its boot-strings and give it back its pride.

The plumbing was idiosyncratic to say the least, the telephone system was notoriously bad, nothing ran to time, the great autoroutes and the rail system with its high-speed trains were still a dream away. It was all as I had pictured it to be and I loved it; from the wonderfully ornate seaside architecture along the Brittany coast to the scents and smells and the cobblestone streets I remembered from my first visit.

One day we decided to take a trip up the River Rance to Dinan. It was long before the great hydroelectric barrage, and when we left Dinard in the morning we wondered why the boat was following such a tortuous course, crossing and recrossing the wide waters in seemingly haphazard fashion, as though the captain had gone to sleep or, worse still, was drunk at the wheel.

The reason eventually became clear when we began the journey back. The tide had gone out and we realized that we had, in fact, been following the course of a deep but very winding, narrow channel. All of which meant that we didn't arrive back in Dinard until after three o'clock in the afternoon, when all the restaurants were closed.

Wandering through the back streets we came across a small café with a few tables and chairs on the pavement outside, so we sat down and ordered a drink. I happened to mention to Madame in my halting French that we hadn't eaten lunch and wondered if perhaps she had a sandwich.

'*Ooh, la, la! Pas de déjeuner!*' Raising her hands in horror at the thought, she bustled off into a back room.

A basket of bread arrived, followed by a bottle of red wine and we waited again, wondering if that was to be it. Two sets of knives and forks wrapped in a red napkin appeared and gave us cause for hope.

When Madame eventually returned she was carrying two large silver platters. Full of apologies because it was all she had, she placed them reverently before us. On each there was a thick slice of perfectly grilled bacon, two fried eggs and a large pile of *pommes frites*, crisp and golden on the outside, soft as butter within.

It was a memorable meal, not simply because it was delicious but for many reasons: the difference in the attitude of mind and the sense of priorities compared with what we were accustomed to, the pride of doing things as they should be done, and the genuine concern that it was to our liking. There was no question of take it or leave it.

I'm sure it was all she had to offer and that it had left her larder unexpectedly depleted, but simple though it was, it was a meal which wouldn't have disgraced a presidential table.

Basking in the sunshine, we used what was left of the bread to wipe our plates clean, drank the last of the wine, sipped our coffee, and felt very privileged.

We were charged a modest sum, I forget now how much, but to me it said more about France and the French than any brochure or guide could possibly convey and confirmed all my feelings that this was how life should be.

On our way back to the hotel, wandering near the beach, we came across several tiny rabbits playing in the grass. We bent down and picked them up and they gazed at us with total trust in their eyes, for they were too small to be anything other than interested at this strange new development. We stroked them for a while and exchanged a few words of franglais, then put them back by their burrow.

I often wondered afterwards what the mother thought when she returned home and found her family smelling of bacon and eggs, and hoped they weren't in too much trouble.

In September the pound was devalued by thirty per cent and banks and stock exchanges closed for a day while they got over the shock. Life was like a game of snakes and ladders and this time the country had landed on a very long snake which took it to the bottom of the board again. In the way that popular music reflects the mood of the moment, Frank Loesser scored a hit with 'Baby, It's Cold Outside', but at least I ended the year with three more short stories in *London Opinion*.

The following June, I returned once more to France, this time as a married man.

My first wife, Brenda, worked in the BBC Reference Library at Caversham, and a great deal of our early courtship had taken place standing up. My mouthing sweet-nothings into her ear while pretending to be looking through an upside-down copy of the *Financial Times* eventually caught the attention of the engineer-in-charge. I realized my number was up one morning when out of the corner of my eye I saw him give a double-take as he passed the library window and caught me at it for the third time. His sense of humour had more to do with jokes about mixing up the colour coding of resistors and condensers than hi-jinks among the book shelves, especially in the BBC's time, so I was called into his office and given a stern warning.

Clearly if we wished to avoid spending the rest of our lives talking out of the sides of our mouths – and we both agreed that was so – something had to be done. Besides, the BBC had places for people like me: remote transmitting stations situated on the Yorkshire Moors or worse.

The wedding reception was held at the home of Brenda's delightful parents. She had made no promises whatsoever to her grandmother or to any other members of the family, which was probably just as well because on the day I nearly blotted my copybook when I caught her Auntie Cis unawares in the toilet. Fortunately I had the presence of mind to say 'Sorry, Pop!' before beating a hasty retreat, but she gave me some very funny glances for a long time afterwards.

Brenda and I spent a carefree honeymoon at the Hôtel du Centre in St Briac-sur-Mer, a few kilometres along the coast from Dinard. In those days it was a pretty, unspoiled village with two small beaches and a square where in the mornings everybody met to talk while they went about their shopping. There were several modest hotels dotted about the place, but ours was the nicest. It had a star in the *Michelin Guide*, mostly for its lobster dishes, but we couldn't afford those because the travel allowance at the time was still only £50.

On that kind of money it wasn't possible to push the boat out and we had to make our wine last. After each meal waitresses automatically marked the level on bottles belonging to English guests, making a pencilled line on the label to show how much was left. Financially, it was touch and go, and before going to bed there was the nightly ritual of counting out the francs, making sure we had enough left for one grand meal at the end of our stay and the autobus back to the airport.

It was in the Hôtel du Centre that we encountered our first artichoke. As with bananas, artichokes had disappeared off greengrocers' shelves during the war, and if you have never seen one before it isn't immediately obvious what to do with it. Had it been *mange-tout* we might well have sent them back because they were undeveloped, but as it was we ploughed on. Fortunately there was only one to a plate, but they were large and firm, about the size of a regulation tennis ball. I lost count of the number of leaves we chewed our way through, but after ten minutes or so it seemed hardly any smaller.

I daresay the person who discovered the first artichoke had a similar problem, but he might have left some instructions.

Being, as ever, first down to dinner, we acted as trendsetters. Soon others followed our example and the room grew unusually silent. Waitresses came and went, exchanging glances and talking to each other in whispers.

After about twenty minutes the chef appeared in a doorway, clearly wondering what was holding things up. He stared at the scene for several long moments before disappearing back into his kitchen in a state of gloom.

Some years later, Brenda and I acquired a waste disposal and almost the first thing we did was cause it to jam when we tried to dispose of some artichoke leaves. I wasn't at all surprised; we were certainly jammed pretty solid that evening in St Briac, and for several days afterwards.

It must have looked as though a lot of penguins were waddling round the village looking for the ark as two by two the guests set out on their post-prandials. Shadowy figures, who until that moment had scarcely acknowledged each other's presence, made sympathetic groaning noises as they passed each other like ships in the night. All the same, as an ice-breaker it was hardly to be recommended.

Artichokes were never served again while we were there, and I doubt if any of us looked one in the eye for a long time afterwards. The francophiles amongst us had been tested to the limit, although I like to think I wasn't found wanting. If you truly love something, or someone, or some*where* in this case, you either find excuses for their occasional deficiencies or else ignore them altogether.

Back in England we moved into our first flat. It was on the upstairs floor of a semi-detached house near my old school. There was no question of our having a waste disposal other than a bucket, nor was there a fridge or a washing machine. The kitchen was in the spare bedroom, so there was no water – it had to be fetched from the bathroom, where washing-up was also carried out in the hand basin.

The landlady, who lived downstairs, had a habit of banging on the ceiling with a broom handle if we had the radio on too late at night and used to drop dark hints about how the whole place needed repainting if only she could find somebody to do it. Nevertheless, we were very grateful, for accommodation was hard to come by, and we were luckier than many newly married couples. Because she knew me she knocked 2s.6d. off the weekly rent of £3.os.od.

Earlier in the year I had received a contract from the BBC confirming my appointment to the permanent staff. It covered most things, including the possibility that I might invent something – which I suppose a lot of people in engineering did over the years – in which case they would pay me £10. (If they formed a favourable opinion of the validity and utility thereof, there was even the possibility of a further *ex gratia* sum as the Corporation might deem fair and reasonable.) There was also a lot of talk about what would happen if I gave away any secrets or committed gross misconduct.

Such were the disciplines at the BBC in those days. When a colleague committed what in the Corporation's eyes was just such an act, he was sent straight home and forbidden to communicate with other members of staff by any means whatsoever until his case had been duly considered. The charade went on for several weeks; every time he tried ringing up to find out his fate all he got was a click as the receiver at the other end was replaced. It's hard to picture it happening nowadays, although he did eventually end up as a personnel officer, dealing with similar problems himself.

My pay – or remuneration as it was referred to in the contract – was £6.10s.6d. a week. The term 'week' was defined as meaning any period of seven consecutive days, something I should have picked up when I read through the document, because when we returned from our honeymoon I found myself doing shiftwork at a satellite aerial station in the middle of Crowsley Park, some five or six miles from Caversham, so Brenda and I barely saw each other from one day to the next except in passing.

To make matters worse, I was bottom of the holiday list, so for a while summer holidays were out. But one winter we went to Paris instead, staying in an old hotel *sans* restaurant in the Boul' Mich, eating our morning croissants at the counter of a small *boulangerie* opposite and drinking steaming coffee out of the kind of vast cups the French had a liking for at the time.

Afterwards we discovered the joy of wandering and sitting in a city which is made for such things, and I took lots of pictures of bare trees in the Luxembourg Gardens and of shop windows full of cheese and of bridges across the Seine and of the frosty sun shining on the golden dome of Napoleon's Tomb, and of many other things which to my great joy are still there today, unchanged.

I transported myself to and from work on a government surplus paratroopers' scooter, aptly called a Corgi, for it was very low on the ground and had a distressing tendency to fold up while it was going along, as though dying to relieve itself against the nearest tree. My duffle coat reached nearly to the ground and actually did one day when the saddle stem slowly collapsed under my weight as I was going up a steep hill.

The talk amongst the foreign staff at Caversham Park was largely about food, and through Brenda's contacts in the library our gastronomic horizons were considerably extended. In the house of some lovely Hungarian friends we were introduced to the culinary delights of the old Austro-Hungarian Empire: chicken paprika made with paprika and cream, and proper beef goulash, again with paprika, along with potatoes and onions – accompanied by tiny dumplings or grains of dried pasta, boiled and then browned with chopped onions. Afterwards, over *apfel-strudel*, made with pastry so thin you could see through it, we listened to talk of life in pre-war Budapest and shared their sadness at the loss of its carefree café society.

There were Russian parties which started off full of gaiety, with vodka flowing like water, but which gradually grew gloomier and gloomier as our hosts began reminiscing of the land they knew they would never see again. Russians seem to be born to suffer.

Austro-German friends regaled us with *Palatschinken* – delicious pancakes stuffed with creamy curd cheese and nuts and jam, and home-made cakes made with love and echoes of old Vienna.

With Greek friends we drank ouzo and afterwards devoured stuffed vine leaves by the dozen and ate lemon soup and taramasalata, followed by moussaka, which shouldn't be mentioned in the same breath as shepherd's pie, and baclava, followed by coffee with *rahat lokum* – Turkish delight of a quality which made all I had ever eaten before seem like a mockery of the name.

With Italians I ate home-made pasta for the first time. Until then the only pasta I knew of was macaroni, which was always long and hard and came wrapped in blue paper. As a small child I was often allowed to break it up when my mother was making a milk pudding. I also used it from time to time as drinking straws, but the end usually went soggy before I got to the bottom of the glass.

With all of them we drank the wine of the country, smuggled in after holidays spent abroad or in diplomatic bags. Having friends who 'knew someone at the Embassy' was a great bonus.

Afterwards we scoured through recipe books and the shelves of wine merchants trying to decide what we could give them in return, and I began collecting cuttings about wine and food and even writing the occasional article on the subject.

But all this was over a period of time, for in the beginning if you didn't have friends at ambassadorial or even diplomatic messenger level, food rationing called for a great deal of ingenuity. Most of my foreign travel was done vicariously in restaurants recommended by those who knew a thing or two.

The London restaurant scene had hardly changed since before the war. One that I used to patronize from time to time, because of the large helpings, was Madame Maurer's in Soho. Madame Maurer owned a rather dreadful, unhygienic-looking mongrel she had acquired from the Battersea Dog's Home. It had developed a vested interest in what was going on in the dining room and was the canine equivalent of '*Le patron mange ici*' (the literal translation of which could well have been: 'The owner's mangy dog likes the food'). I happened to give it a passing pat the very first time I went there, in much the same way as I had greeted the commanding officer's dog at Chester, only on this occasion it was out of fear that he might turn nasty if I didn't, rather than as a display of affection. I don't think anyone had ever done such a thing before and from that moment on I could do no wrong in either Madame Maurer's eyes or the dog's, and it was always more than ready to help me out with my beef olives.

One day I was ploughing my way steadily through lunch in an otherwise deserted restaurant when a couple of tourists came in and committed the cardinal sin of shooing the dog away as it went over and sniffed them. Madame Maurer came out from behind her counter and began shouting at them in her guttural English, 'Go avay! Go avay! Ve are full up! Can't you see!' She then literally chased them out into the street with a carving knife.

They didn't know how lucky they were, for she had perfected a rapier-like skill with the knife and when she returned I saw her kill a blowfly with a single thrust. The fact that she didn't wipe the blade afterwards, but simply carried on cutting up some meat, put me off her cuisine and I never went back.

For Turkish food there was the Blue Windmill in Great Windmill Street. The 3s.6d meal was recommended by John Arlott in an early *Good Food Guide*, but for five shillings one could really go to town, with a huge plate of moussaka, followed by shish kebab, a Turkish sweetmeat and coffee. Afterwards I wandered the streets of Soho, gazing at the amazing government surplus radio bargains in Lisle Street; things that must have cost millions of pounds to design and produce going for a song. Radio magazines were full of articles on how to make television receivers with tiny green screens out of old radar equipment.

For Greek food it was always the little Akropolis in Charlotte Street, and there was a wonderful old French restaurant in Soho where the menu outside was handwritten in purple ink.

The first espresso coffee bar in England opened in Frith Street and I wrote an article about it which I sold to *Men Only*. That was followed by another one on making coffee which was taken by what was then the *Manchester Guardian*. We used to get our coffee from H. R. Higgins in South Molton Street. Mr Higgins senior had made an agreement years before with the Chagga tribe in Africa and was very knowledgeable on the subject. To me, good fresh coffee is one of the joys of life; fresh orange juice too. I can't understand anyone who can afford it going through life making do with things out of packets, but I suppose the truth is that deep down a lot of people don't really care.

I took a trip on the *Jason*, the first canal boat to ply the Regent's Park Canal between Little Venice and Camden Lock. On the way the owner pointed out a house in Blomfield Road where Christopher Fry lived, and I thought how nice it must be to live by a canal, never dreaming that one day I would be living there myself. That, too, was turned into an article.

Around that time I wrote a short story called 'Sausages for Breakfast', which I sold to the BBC for their mid-morning spot. It told of the adventures of a mythical uncle staying in a small hotel in Paris. I was

going to call him Uncle Paddington, but I called him Uncle Parkington
instead.

One day, having decided it was time I got myself an agent, I stuck a
pin in the *Writers' and Artists' Year Book* and fate guided my hand towards
a name which meant nothing to me at the time.

Harvey Unna was born in Hamburg of middle-class Jewish parents
and by the early thirties was well set on a promising legal career, but in
1933 he was dismissed from the Civil Service on racial grounds and fled
to England.

He arrived in this country with five pounds in his pocket, and for
fourteen years worked in the scrap metal trade. Then in 1947 the War
Office appointed him Head of Translations for the War Crimes Unit
and he served at the trial of von Manstein.

During that period the seeds of another career were sown when Lance
Sieveking, Drama Editor at BBC Radio, commissioned him to translate
a number of German plays for possible use in England. At the same time
he began directing for the amateur theatre. All of which led him in 1951
to set up business as an agent, specializing at first in radio but gradually
adding theatre and television.

As an agent he had a wonderful gift of making every client feel as
though they were the only one he represented, and although I was one
of his earliest, I began to realize from the number of first nights he went
to that his portfolio of famous names was growing.

Scrupulously honest, firm but fair in his dealings, a strict upholder of
protocol, I couldn't have wished for a better or a wiser person to look
after my interests.

He had a system of rewarding his clients at Christmas with gifts of
wine, allocating them according to their previous year's performance,
much as Michelin award crossed knives and forks and rosettes in their
guide. Starting with a bottle of Beaujolais – the equivalent of crossed
knives and forks – it was possible to rise to the dizzy heights of three
bottles of champagne – three rosettes – but for a long while I remained
strictly on mineral water: not worth a detour.

For several years we were Mr Bond and Mr Unna, then it became
Michael Bond and Harvey Unna. The day it became Michael, and then
'my dear boy', I felt I had arrived. A gift pack of Beaujolais that Christmas
confirmed it.

Harvey was then in partnership with Nina Froud, who was part Georgian Russian, and extraordinarily fluent in many languages. The author of numerous cookery books, she had been partly responsible for translating *Larousse Gastronomique* into English, and from her I learned about Chinese food. Her beautiful daughter Tamara, now working for the United Nations, impressed me greatly one evening when we were dining in a Thai restaurant and a waiter brought her a note from a man at another table asking if he could take her out. I would never have dared to do such a thing for fear of what the waiters would think if I were turned down.

Together, Harvey Unna and Nina Froud were a formidable combination.

Bored with the routine of maintaining the same pieces of equipment week in, week out, and feeling the need to do something more creative, I applied for a job with British Forces Broadcasting as a scriptwriter-cum-continuity announcer.

The words 'Died Waiting', carved on the wall of a singularly down-at-heel waiting room where I had to report for an interview, should have served as a warning.

The board was seated round a long, polished table – one of the longest I had ever seen – and it was presided over by a senior officer with red tabs and a hearing aid. It clearly wasn't a very good hearing aid, or it needed a new battery, for he kept tapping it and everything had to be repeated several times over, but at least it gave me time to answer the questions, which grew more and more technical as time went by.

Eventually I plucked up courage and enquired what over-modulation of the primary stage of a transmitter had to do with writing scripts.

There was a long silence, broken only by plaintive bellows from the opposite end of the table: 'What's the feller sayin'? What's the feller sayin'?'

On the basis of my answers, I think I could have been in the running for a job as engineer-in-charge of a radio station in Cyprus – I felt I knew more about the subject than most of those on the board – but that wasn't what I had applied for, or indeed what I wanted to do.

I left them trying to explain to the president that there had been a 'bit of a mix-up, don't you know. Wrong feller – wrong job.'

Transferring from one department to another in the BBC wasn't easy. Understandably, having trained you for one job, they have always been reluctant to waste their investment, so I began looking outside.

The Locust Control Commission in Rhodesia didn't bother answering my letter, and when I recalled a very small cloud of locusts I had once encountered in Egypt, I wasn't too sorry. It had been difficult to avoid stepping on them and they made a nasty crunching noise underfoot.

I tried putting a 'Go anywhere – do anything' advertisement in the *New Statesman* and received a lot of strange replies, most of which suggested a preliminary meeting under the clock on Victoria Station.

In desperation I even toyed with the idea of taking a job with the US War Graves Commission. Rumour had it that they were paying £80 an hour to have bodies of ex-servicemen exhumed for return to the USA, but it was literally a dead-end job, so I never checked up on it.

Sadly, I returned to the typewriter, and widening my net tried my hand at radio plays.

Writing is a long process of distillation, of cutting and pruning and rewriting until you get it right. Less inspiration than perspiration. The wonderful thoughts you wake up with during the night or dream up on top of a bus disappear the moment you commit the first words to paper, which is where the perspiration comes in. Radio was a wonderful means of learning the trade and of getting a feel, not only for writing dialogue but for the 'geography' of the characters' surroundings and the motivation behind their actions. It's a great pity it has become the poor relation of television, especially as in my experience people remember something they have heard on the radio far longer than anything seen on television.

In 1955, according to records I kept at the time, I wrote four articles for the *Manchester Guardian* and one for *Men Only*; three radio plays – one for New Zealand and two for Radio Ceylon – and a half-hour children's play for BBC Television which, including a repeat fee for the latter, brought in a grand total of £171.19s.6d. (less ten per cent agent's fees).

Not much money for a lot of work, and as far as Harvey Unna was concerned it probably didn't even pay the postage. He must have regarded me as something of a loss leader, although he never said so, and I shall always be grateful that he never lost faith in me.

Partly for his sake as well as my own, I determined to try to double my earnings by the end of the following year, which in fact I did. But before that happened I received an entirely unexpected stroke of good fortune.

The Monitoring Service is financed independently of the viewers' licence money. Instead, it receives a Grant in Aid from the government, which is subject to review at the end of each financial year. In 1956 there was a savage cut, and economies had to be made. Volunteers for transfer to other departments were sought.

I jumped at the chance and before the week was out found myself walking through the entrance to the BBC's Lime Grove studios and into the make-believe world of television.

A few months earlier, our Astronomer Royal announced that in his opinion the idea of space travel was 'piffle', but by 1969 the Americans were cock-a-hoop when they proved him wrong by successfully landing the first man on the moon. I felt as though I had beaten them to it by more than a decade.

CHAPTER 9

Entering Another World

Television is more interesting than people. If it were
not, we should have people standing in the corners of
our rooms.

Alan Coren (1938–   )

As a non-party-going person myself, I know just what Alan Coren means.
A television set also has the advantage of possessing an on–off switch;
you can't always get rid of people that easily.

He might also have said that working in television is often much more
interesting than watching it.

I was fortunate to join when I did. BBC Television was just beginning
to emerge from years of being kept on a tight financial rein by the old
guard in Broadcasting House, many of whom regarded it as an upstart;
something which by rights ought to be put down.

The televising of the coronation of Queen Elizabeth II on 2 June 1953
changed all that, and the imminent arrival on the scene of Independent
Television provided the final catalyst. There was a big exodus of key
staff who were being offered all manner of inducements by the new
companies: immediate promotion, better pay, cars, interest-free mort-
gages, to name but a few, so I found myself thrown in at the deep end
of a rapidly emptying pool.

For new entrants who stayed the course, promotion was rapid. The
normal progression via general dogsbody, camera-tracker grades three,
two and one; then, if you were lucky, being allowed to try your hand at

The Home Guard.
Father (with pipe!)
is second from
right, front row.

All that was left of
the People's Pantry
in Reading after it
was bombed on 10
February 1943.

Cairo, 1945.

Mother with one of
her 'little artfuls'.

Rivers, Manitoba
1944. I am second
from right, front row.

Cutting the cake
with Brenda,
29 June 1950.

Harvey Unna.

Below: On set with
Tito Gobbi, BBC
Television Centre.

Ivor Wood in the Herb Garden, with Sage the Owl.

Right: Shirley and Eddie Clarkson and friends.

Below: Roger and Emma on board the *Queen Elizabeth*, New York harbour.

Dick Miller.

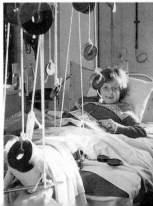

Karen grinning and bearing it in 1962.

Eve.

Anthony at one week, February 1977.

operating a camera, went by the board. Progress up the next rungs of the ladder, via various grades of cameraman until finally, as a senior cameraman, you had your own crew, which in the past had been largely a matter of waiting for others to grow old and retire, was considerably accelerated as new crews were formed in order to cope with demands brought about by longer programme hours and the increase in the number of studios available. When I joined, seven crews were responsible for almost the entire studio output in the UK. Ten years later, as a senior cameraman, I helped form the seventeenth crew in London alone.

For a number of years BBC Television had got by with two small studios at Alexandra Palace. In 1950, having bequeathed them to the News Department, the main body of BBC Television had begun the move to the old Gaumont British/J. Arthur Rank film studios in Lime Grove. Four out of the five existing studios – D, E, G and H – were converted for television use and put into service. Studio F, with its boarded-over water tank, where before the war in the A. E. W. Mason epic *Fire Over England*, Elizabeth I's navy overcame the Spanish Armada, was now a scene dock.

The old Empire Theatre, round the corner at Shepherd's Bush Green, was also taken over and became known as the Television Theatre.

Later, pending completion of a new Television Centre at White City, there would be two more studios at Hammersmith: Riverside 1 and 2.

I never lost the feeling of excitement that came over me whenever I entered a studio in those early days. The contrast between what was appearing on the screen and the reality of the surroundings was the realization of my childhood dreams; all those months spent building my marionette theatre and hours sitting in cinemas. If only the kapok-covered walls of Lime Grove could talk, what tales they could tell: stories about *The Wicked Lady*, *Fanny by Gaslight*, and all the other films which had been made there in its heyday, including many of Hitchcock's early thrillers, like *The Thirty-Nine Steps*.

Crossing the invisible line drawn between the red plush seating of the Television Theatre to mingle in the wings among the acts waiting to go on never failed to give me a kick. That I was actually being paid to do something I enjoyed so much seemed almost too good to be true.

Studio H, the smallest studio of all, was where most cameramen cut

their teeth. It was where you could do the least harm whilst gaining the
most experience in the shortest possible time.

It was home to a multitude of presenters, from Barry Bucknell, the
BBC's tame 'Do-it-Yourself' man, to Percy Thrower, the resident gardening expert, who regularly nailed his onions to batons of wood concealed
beneath a layer of peat in case they fell over on the night.

And from studio H came *All Your Own*, a programme devoted to
children who showed a particular talent in some way or another. One
week a young John Williams brought his guitar along.

Although in later years he chose to forget the fact, it was how Huw
Wheldon first made his name as a presenter. He had a brisk, no-nonsense
manner which went down well with the viewers. Once in an unguarded
moment over coffee in the canteen he let slip the information that if
any of the participants showed signs of being difficult before they came
on they were threatened with a quick Chinese burn. The recollection
prompted one of his inimitable guffaws of laughter.

The tip came in handy some years later when I found myself making
a promotional film for Penguin Books along with a seven-year-old who
was determined to get out of a taxi by the wrong door. It worked wonders
and saved a re-take.

Whether or not Huw Wheldon's story was true or tongue in cheek,
there were occasions when even he didn't have the last word.

Having interviewed a small boy who had built a life-size working
harpsichord entirely out of matchsticks, Wheldon turned all avuncular
and posed the obvious question: 'And what are you going to make next?'

While waiting for an answer, he placed one hand on the instrument
– rather heavily it seemed to those of us watching through our view-
finders. Sure enough, there was an ominous crunching noise from somewhere deep inside.

'Another harpsichord,' came the sad reply.

Then there was the time when an interviewee brought along his two
prize pets – a mouse and an eagle. Huw Wheldon launched into a long
dissertation about how interesting it was that in the wild the one was
the mortal enemy of the other, yet there they both were, getting on like
a house on fire. At which point the eagle promptly ate the mouse!

It was in studio H one evening, after moving in high over a trestle table
in order to show a close-up of a piece of equipment being demonstrated by

Baron, the society photographer, that the producer called for a lower shot. The camera-mounting on the dolly was on the end of an arm which the tracker could raise or lower by means of a wheel. My tracker, who was doing the job for the first time, panicked and, before I could stop him, began winding the arm down as fast as it would go. There was a loud splintering noise as we landed on one end of the table.

Making a grab for the opposite end in a vain attempt to hold it down, Baron, who had cultivated an upper-class accent for television, reverted to his humble beginnings rather quicker than it normally took him to recommend 1/50th at f11.

His cry of 'Gorblimey!' made headlines in next morning's papers.

Towards the end of 1956 the government ended the so-called 'Toddler's Truce' – a blissful period between six and seven every evening when screens went blank so that parents could put their children to bed – and studio H became even busier.

In between all the other programmes this hour was to become an important arena in the battle of the ratings when in February 1957 the formidable Grace Wyndham Goldie, then Assistant Head of Talks, scored a bull's-eye with a programme called *Tonight*.

The early evening news was still only ten minutes long and *Tonight* was the equivalent of a daily newspaper's middle pages. The items were short and there was something for everyone.

Hosted by Cliff Michelmore, who had graduated from producing *All Your Own*, it went on the air at five past six every weekday evening and quickly established itself with a regular audience of eight million. Part of its strength came from the fact that it was one of the first programmes to question those in authority on behalf of the viewer.

In the beginning Cy Grant led off with a topical calypso – often contributed by Bernard Levin. Derek Hart and Geoffrey Johnson Smith conducted most of the studio interviews. In time they were joined by Kenneth Allsop, Christopher Brasher, Julian Pettifer, Brian Redhead and Polly Elwes (who got into television in the first place because her birthday fell on 29 February and she happened to write in suggesting an idea for a special programme for others like her).

The bearded Fyfe Robertson regularly took to the road, reporting on strange goings-on from Land's End to John o' Groats; Alan Whicker made his television debut on *Tonight* and never looked back; and film cameraman Slim Hewitt contributed deadpan cockney pieces written by Tony Jay.

For a time it was directed by the supremely unflappable Ned Sherrin. He needed to remain calm, for more often than not the programme was literally put together on the air, while filmed reports were being biked across London or the sound was dubbed elsewhere in the building.

The running order was constantly revised in order to include last-minute items – like the appearance of Christine Keeler and Mandy Rice-Davies on the day the Profumo scandal broke, or the sudden arrival in England of a young ballet dancer named Rudolf Nureyev, who had defected from Russia via Paris.

MacDonald Hastings, Trevor Philpott and John Morgan added their contributions on film, while film editor Tony Essex beavered away behind the scenes. It was a formidable array of talent and in retrospect the credits read like a miniature *Who's Who?* of television.

Chaos wasn't always confined to the gallery. The cameras had seen better days and breakdowns were frequent. When that happened there would be a mad rush to change the whole unit or to cannibalize even older equipment while the programme was still going on. They were also relatively insensitive by present-day standards, requiring a great deal of light, and it wasn't unknown for the sprinkler system to be set off. Another hazard for the cameraman was that if you didn't keep the picture moving it 'stuck' to the tube and had to be 'burnt off' by pointing the lens at the nearest bright light. On the other hand, if you accidentally caught a light in your shot, or even a bright reflection, the whole picture would 'peel' away, so any reflecting surfaces had to be sprayed down beforehand.

Cables were at least twice as thick as present-day ones and weighed a ton. No one had thought of having guards round the base of the dollies, so if you did accidentally run over your own umbilical cord it was a case of waiting for a suitable moment between shots to get back over it again.

A pair of cans (headphones), a stick of thick yellow crayon for marking floor positions, some string and a reel of adhesive tape – no cameraman worth his salt was ever without any of these things.

Despite all the problems, old diaries I kept at the time, which are mostly filled with working schedules, show the enormous variety of programmes being put out in the fifties.

Studio G was reserved for bigger epics, the largest of which was undoubtedly *The Passing Show*, a series of five 90-minute extravaganzas covering popular entertainment over the first fifty years of this century. Those who worked on them still recount the experience with awe.

They were the dreamchild of Michael Mills, the doyen of Light Entertainment producers, who had a penchant for pushing things to their absolute limit.

The most successful and still the most talked about episode was *The Story of Marie Lloyd*. By then I was number one tracker on the crew and it was my first real taste of being under pressure in what at times seemed like total chaos.

Pat Kirkwood, who played the lead, had so many costume changes they completely filled three six-foot rails. There was no room for a quick-change tent, so she spent half the time dashing wildly about the studio, stripping off as she went in order to be ready for her entrance in the next scene.

There were over a hundred different sets, the vast majority of which had to be stored in the adjoining scene dock. The huge soundproof doors leading to it were permanently manned, opening and closing like Harrods on a sale day as sets came and went while the programme was on the air. At one stage the action got so frantic a cameraman found himself shut out of the studio along with his camera and dolly, and could only get back in when the next set was struck. On another occasion a group of scene hands were taking a much needed breather when they suddenly found themselves part of the action, but since it took place in a working-class living-room and there was a party going on, no one noticed a few extra guests with their sleeves rolled up.

At the end of it all, Pat Kirkwood received that very rare accolade, a totally spontaneous ovation from everyone in the studio – cameramen, sound crew, scene hands, electricians, make-up girls, dressers and the rest of the cast.

Playing the part of Marie Lloyd's manager was the actor Peter Bull, who had enjoyed a great success on stage, first in *The Lady's Not for Burning*, and then in Samuel Beckett's *Waiting for Godot*, and was consequently in demand. For various reasons, mostly to do with the fact that he became a well-known collector of bears, our paths were to cross many times over the years, but one occasion which sticks in my mind was when, for some reason which totally escapes me now, he had to toss a very small baby up into the air and then catch it on the way down.

Peter was a lovely man, but I doubt if he had ever been near a baby in his life, let alone touched one, and he was terrified of dropping it; a fear which was clearly shared by the child.

The two or three inches of freefall he managed was not enough for the director. He kept calling for more, and the baby's real mother, who was standing just outside the shot, alarmed at the thought of losing the performance fee, kept hissing, 'Don't worry! Higher! Higher!'

Despite Peter's protestations, the combination of Mammon and Mama was a force not to be denied. I daresay the baby has grown up with a nervous tic.

In direct contrast to *Marie Lloyd*, I returned to studio G one evening after an early dinner break in order to work on an interview with a visiting American senator. The studio was bare apart from a table, a couple of chairs, and a background flat. Pushing open the soundproof door, I found my way barred by a large, lantern-jawed individual with a crewcut and a suspicious-looking bulge under his jacket.

'Where are you going, bud?'

Having pointed out to an area somewhere level with his breast pocket that I happened to work there, I was all set to dislike the subject of the interview on sight. But when he came into the studio, instead of going straight to his seat and ignoring everyone else in sight, as politicians usually did, he came across to the camera and shook me warmly by the hand, greeting me by my first name.

It didn't actually make me want to buy a second-hand car from him, but it was an interesting lesson on how a committed professional like Richard Nixon did his homework in order to get the best out of people at all times. In my experience the only politician to behave in an equally courteous manner, but for different reasons, was Harold Wilson; he was just naturally polite, although he was as aware of the tricks of the trade as anyone.

Before a television interview it was a case of 'Cue Mr Wilson.' Pause. 'Fade up camera one,' so that he could be seen in avuncular mood lighting his pipe as the programme went on the air.

The long-running *Juke Box Jury* began life in studio G, and on Sunday, 2 February 1958, another Grace Wyndham Goldie programme was launched. It was called *Monitor* and once again Huw Wheldon was to impose his own stamp on the presentation. A film school in its own right, it gave many directors their first chance. John Schlesinger's *Circus* was in the opening programme, and he followed it with some memorable films, including one on Georges Simenon. After him came Ken Russell, who produced a wealth of items before he went on to bigger things.

On one edition devoted to Kurt Weill, I remember tracking through the bead curtains of a nightclub set in order to isolate Lotte Lenya singing 'Surabaya Johnny'. As she began to move towards the camera, I gave the signal to start the track back, but to my horror nothing happened. I learned later that the dolly had lost its power, however at the time all I was aware of was Lotte Lenya's face registering alarm as it grew larger and larger in my viewfinder. That made two of us, but fortunately she carried on singing and afterwards I was congratulated on the unusually tight close-up.

Tight close-ups were the hallmark of *Face to Face*. They were considered daring at the time for they broke the accepted rules of composition, cutting foreheads and chins as the camera went in to show the subject warts and all. Directed by Hugh Burnett, with John Freeman doing the questioning, they set a new standard in the art of interviewing in depth which has never really been equalled.

On days off, inspired by a new Vespa, I took to writing about scooters for the *Manchester Guardian*. I also began scouring the collected works of W. W. Jacobs and Guy de Maupassant, looking for stories which hadn't yet been adapted for radio or television.

There weren't many left, but one afternoon I was able to slip into the Television Theatre and watch the dress rehearsal of an adaptation I had made of Maupassant's 'The Decoration' being performed by Tony Britton, André Morel and André van Gysegem.

That same year I had a field day when Harvey Unna sold six half-hour radio plays and two short stories to Hong Kong. They paid thirty-four guineas for the lot, so we didn't get very fat on the proceeds, but at least my list of credits was growing.

I was still commuting between Reading and London, and late one evening I arrived at Paddington Station and came across an empty compartment at the front of an otherwise crowded train. Admittedly there were no lights on in the entire carriage and for some reason the heating appeared to have been turned off, but I settled down, glad of the chance to unwind in relative peace.

The guard blew his whistle, and as we began to move I glanced out of the window. To my surprise, an imposing figure waiting near the end of the platform suddenly removed his top hat and stood reverently to attention. Clearly I was travelling in exalted company.

It wasn't until we were about halfway to Reading that I heard a door being unlocked. It was followed by the sound of footsteps coming along the darkened corridor towards me. As they drew near I cleared my throat.

When the ticket collector had recovered from the shock, he looked at me accusingly through the gloom and let fall the information that I wasn't supposed to be there. Why? Because there was a coffin containing a dead body in the next compartment!

Having made my peace, I elected to stay put for the rest of the journey. But when I was on my own again with the door at the end of the corridor locked, the carriage suddenly seemed even darker and colder than before; distinctly eerie in fact. It struck me that perhaps someone, somewhere, was trying to tell me something and it was time to make a move.

Mrs Chambers would have felt at home in the one-roomed garden flat I eventually found near the Portobello Road – it was a bit like living in a caravan. The kitchen had to be tucked away in a cupboard at night and during the day the bed was used to provide extra seating for visitors. But the market was just around the corner, and Holland Park, with its peacocks and its shady walks, was only a short distance away.

Outside the window there was a tiny patio with a pond and a fountain, and beyond that some communal gardens. On sunny days people came out on to the balconies of the flats on the far side of the gardens, and over the seasons I watched their comings and goings as I sat at my typewriter in search of inspiration. Life was uncomplicated and for two years Brenda and I were very happy there.

One spring morning, not long after we moved in, I sat down and wrote the first of what became a collection of eight short stories, enough to form a book, which I entitled *A Bear Called Paddington* and sent to Harvey Unna.

I hadn't ever intended writing for children, and it really came about through Harvey. I sent him a radio play about a small boy who found a capsule in the street and, having mistaken it for a sweet, became radioactive, causing havoc wherever he went. The play was rejected by the BBC on the grounds that it might not set a very good example, and it was then that Harvey suggested writing for children might be a fruitful area.

Following up his suggestion, I'd already had one children's play produced on television and shortly afterwards I wrote another. Both came from studio E, where most children's programmes originated.

The fifties were the start of a golden age. In the beginning *Children's Hour* had only gone out on a Sunday, but in 1950 it was increased to three days a week, and later to every day.

For the very young there was *Watch With Mother*. Johnny Morris told stories in his role of *Hot Chestnut Man* and Sooty appeared regularly on the *Saturday Show*. Before the end of the decade there would be *Crackerjack* and the first *Blue Peter*. For older children there were live plays and serials, including *Billy Bunter of Greyfriars School*. A young Michael Crawford played one of the Famous Five for a while, and fittingly Gerald Campion, who played Billy Bunter, eventually became a restaurateur in Brighton.

Programmes involving anything to do with marionettes were always the worst to work on. Whereas with humans there is always some indication of when they are going to make a move – a momentary tightening of the lips, or a slight movement of the eyes – puppets take off without the slightest warning, their arms and legs often going in wildly different directions. Cameramen used to sweat more on a half-hour puppet show than they ever did on a Sunday night play.

Because children's programmes went out early in the day, lack of rehearsal occasionally caused problems.

It was during an episode of a serial called *Potts in Perovia* – a modern adventure story set in a fictitious Ruritanian country – that Humphrey Lestocq produced a memorable ad lib. In every episode there was at least one unrehearsed disaster, often more. One week the script called for a final shot in which a large chandelier would come crashing down on the hero's head. All necessary precautions were taken to make sure that the chandelier, which was attached to a rope and pulley, would stop a few inches short; far enough away to ensure the star's safety, but close enough to leave the viewer in a state of suspense until the following week, wondering whether or not he had been killed. On transmission the rope became snarled up and the chandelier stopped some distance short of its target. In the split-second's silence before the end credits started to roll, Humphrey Lestocq looked up and cried: 'Good God! Another six feet and it would have been curtains!'

Studio E was also the venue for Fanny and Johnny Cradock's *Kitchen Magic*. Fanny Cradock was the most professional of performers. It's one thing putting together a half-hour cookery programme in an editing suite, picking and choosing shots from a multitude which have been taken on video tape over a period of time; it's another matter to cook an actual meal live and still come out on time, which is what she did week after week. The programmes were also recorded on 16mm film for archive purposes and on one occasion, after she finished exactly to the second, we were relaxing while waiting for the OK to wrap up when word came down that the sound supervisor had a problem and could it be done all over again.

Mrs Cradock didn't suffer such things lightly. Picking up a carving knife, she waved it at the microphone.

'Where is he?' she cried. 'Bring him to me. I'll have his goolies off and fry them in batter!'

Needless to say, the fault cleared itself in record time.

One of the most charismatic people I ever had the privilege of working with was General Sir Brian Horrocks, who took what to many people might have been a dull sounding subject, 'Men in Battle', and by peppering his talks with personal anecdotes and leaning towards the camera lens as though speaking directly to the viewer, brought them instantly to life in a totally riveting way.

He always saw the studio in military terms, giving everybody a rank, so that he had the hierarchy firmly established in his mind. Despite his age and the severe wounds he had suffered during the war, he was extremely active and, apart from the problem of maintaining focus as he leaned backwards and forwards, he also had a disconcerting habit of leaping to his feet at intervals and striding over to a wall map, exclaiming as he went: 'So, I said to Montgomery . . .' *pause* 'Then, he said to me . . .' before shooting back to his desk and carrying on from where he had left off.

He refused to use an autocue, but insisted on learning the script off by heart while walking in Hyde Park, arriving in the studio word perfect.

He was a lovely man and a truly inspirational person. One could readily picture those under his command being prepared to follow him to the ends of the earth if need be.

The phrase 'It can't be done' didn't have a place in his vocabulary, or indeed of anyone else who worked in television in those pioneering days; everyone was prepared to have a go.

On one occasion a sound engineer had the bright idea of placing a microphone in one of the toilets at the Television Theatre in order to use it as a makeshift echo chamber. All went well until in the middle of a musical number someone from the audience went in and pulled the chain!

In the days before portable tiered seating was available in the studios, the Television Theatre was home to practically all the audience shows of the time; everyone from Joyce Grenfell – who always brought along a huge bag of 'sweeties' for the crew – to Count Basie, who was so pleased with the result he offered the sound supervisor a job on the spot.

One coffee break during a rehearsal of *This is Your Life*, I went up to the tiny canteen at the top of the building and found it was already occupied by the entire set of the then knights of the theatre gossiping round a table and I listened enthralled to Sir John Gielgud in full anec-dotal spate.

It was in the Television Theatre that Eamonn Andrews uttered his immortal phrase 'This is your life' to Danny Blanchflower, who replied 'Oh, no it isn't!' and that night we all went home early.

Gilbert Harding used to complain loudly about the heat from the lights. It often put him in a bad mood for *What's My Line?* and he was apt to take it out on some poor unfortunate who was being tardy with his mime. He once told a contestant he was tired of looking at him.

One day, when he was in a particularly bad mood, an enterprising lighting supervisor rigged an extra and entirely unnecessary lamp pointing straight at him and after a lot of complaining agreed to turn it off. From that moment on all was sweetness, if not light, and 'Gilbert's lamp' became part of the standard rig.

In those days viewers still wrote in to complain whenever male ballet dancers appeared on their screens wearing tights, although what the BBC were meant to do about it was hard to say, but the *Black and White Minstrel Show* survived the odd complaint from 'Disgusted of

Cheltenham', asking why the BBC couldn't make use of decent English boys to dance with the gals on the programme, and ran for eighteen years.

Paradoxically, music hall, which had been killed off by television, found a new home there for a while, largely through the efforts of Richard Afton. Richard Afton was a theatrical impresario-cum-agent turned television producer and a natural showman of the old school, who always directed rehearsals from behind a cloud of cigar smoke in the stalls. He liked nothing better than to dress the Television Toppers as nuns and have them sing 'Ave Maria' as they walked down the catwalk carrying all before them. He had also cornered the market in unlikely turns, the sort of acts Woody Allen portrayed with love and affection in *Broadway Danny Rose*.

They were the backbone of variety – the kind of acts I was brought up on as a child at the Palace Theatre in Reading – but sadly, most of them were living on borrowed time. One brief appearance on television and that was that.

When I was small, the fireplace was the focal point of any living-room and if you were lucky the window looked out on to a garden. Now the fireplace has been replaced by a television set and people have become very blasé.

When Perry Como brought his show to London he was so laid-back that for the morning camera rehearsal he had a stand-in who sang well enough to have had a show in his own right. But his role in life was to say things like: 'At this point Perry moves stage right and sits here.'

Sammy Davis Jnr was a walking, talking, singing, dancing essay in how to hold an audience in the palm of your hand and he could do no wrong.

Frank Muir and Dennis Norden used to think up ingenious and often hilarious ways and means of enabling Jimmy Edwards to partake of some liquid refreshment during *Whack-O!*, the series which exploited the Englishman's obsession with his schooldays. There were occasions after the final run-through when the star needed to be taken for a brisk walk round Shepherd's Bush Green before the start of the show.

It was in the Television Theatre that Charlie Drake, having survived countless hair-raising episodes of his show, dived head-first into a bookcase and didn't come out the other side. I remember panning down with him as he fell to the floor, expecting him to get up and try again. But for once he didn't, and that, for a long time, was the last of the *Charlie Drake Show* and almost the end of Charlie Drake.

Benny Hill was born to remain one of nature's bachelors, but he certainly surrounded himself with numerous possibilities were he to change his mind. Each week the crew used to lay bets on who would be the lucky lady. After the show he always invited me round to his dressing room so that he could provide the wherewithal to buy the crew a round of drinks, 'Just in case I'm busy'. It was a speedy, if sometimes embarrassing way of finding out the answer to the bet, and in the end I gave up going.

By contrast, an after-the-show drink with Tommy Cooper would be a very downbeat affair, full of introspection and self-doubt. 'Did you think it was funny? Did so-and-so work? No, but seriously, did you think it was funny? Are you sure?'

Ted Ray brought a rehearsal to life one dull Sunday afternoon by the simple act of removing his violin from its case and blowing on it. At which point a cloud of dust rose into the air. He must have done it many times before, but it immediately endeared him to all the crew.

Television drama came – appropriately enough – from studio D, and of all the different types of programme making it was probably the most demanding, for in effect it was the art of making in an hour or an hour and a half of real time what took a film company many weeks or even months to do. Film inserts were a luxury; only resorted to if there was no alternative, and then only if the budget allowed.

Once the action had been cued there was no going back. There were occasions when for one reason or another rehearsals had gone badly or had become so bogged down a complete run-through had never been achieved – fast moves from one end of the studio to the other had been impossible to make in the allotted time, or lens changes in a quick-cutting sequence hadn't been achieved – so there was no knowing whether it would work at all, but somehow it always did. The adrenalin flowed. Colds which had flourished during rehearsals totally dried up on the night.

To most outsiders the complexity of it all, the fact that anything ever came out of such apparent chaos, was a source of wonder, too hard to grasp in one visit. Often, if you took someone on a guided tour all they could think of to say at the end was: 'Where does the man who reads the news sit?' It was a bit of a let-down to say 'Alexandra Palace'.

Attacks of temperament were surprisingly rare; there simply wasn't time and they received scant sympathy.

Rudolph Cartier was a director of the old school and a genius at tackling productions on a grand scale, producing effects far in excess of the resources he had at his disposal. Born in Vienna, he served his apprenticeship in the pre-war Berlin UFA Studios, and he had a short way with anyone who complained. Once, during a break in rehearsal while some technical problem was being sorted out, a forlorn-looking extra rose up out of a foot-thick layer of cloud from the dry ice machine and gasped a request via the studio manager to stand for a while.

The response was short and to the point. 'Certainly not! Tell her zis is her chosen profession!' It always comes to mind when I hear anyone complain about their job.

Most of these rejoinders lost something in translation. 'Tell her zis is her chosen profession' became simply: 'No, I'm afraid not.'

Producer Douglas Moodie's, 'Tell that girl she's not getting value for money at her acting school', became, 'Would you mind doing that again?' 'F****** Hell!' got watered down to: 'Hold it there, everyone!'

It was part of a studio manager's job to keep everybody happy.

Pre-planning played a vitally important part in live productions. Lights had to be placed so that they performed more than one function. The shooting script often required the use of all the cameras. The normal routine would be to release one of them shortly before the end of a scene so that it could be in position ready to start the next, then the others would follow on behind as quickly as possible. With four cameras and often as many microphone booms in the studio, all the moves had to be worked out in advance, often with pieces of string on a floor plan of the sets, in order to make sure cables didn't knit together.

Actors and actresses, who until then had rehearsed in church halls, needed to accustom themselves quickly to the simplest of things – the opening and closing of a door as though it were something they did every day of their lives, or sitting down on strange chairs wearing voluminous garments for the first time in a costume drama.

For the technical crew it was a continual memory test; repeating at speed shots and camera positions that had been carefully worked out during rehearsal and remembering the names of the characters and much of the dialogue. It was also a test of manual dexterity, of being able to bring all your faculties into play at the same time – panning with one hand while focusing with the other, watching out for shadows or shooting off the set or microphones dipping into shot; listening with one ear to instructions from the director and the all-important shot numbers being called out by his secretary, while the other ear absorbed dialogue and comments from the technical staff.

On the front of a camera crane it was also necessary to signal instructions to the trackers while keeping a wary eye open for hazards en route, such as passing under lights and throwing a shadow, or, worse still, knocking down an artist waiting to make an entrance. On smaller powered dollies with only one tracker, the cameraman also had to control the movement of the arm with his feet – one pedal for going up and down, the other for lateral movement.

With more than enough problems to occupy their minds, actors often displayed a touching faith in the ability of a large camera dolly to stop on a sixpence, sometimes only a matter of inches away from their faces.

After a particularly fast move across the studio from one set to another – a move which Paul, the tracker, had never made in rehearsal – we ended up hitting the end of a bed in which Felix Aylmer was about to die. To say he didn't bat an eyelid would be untrue, but as the vision mixer cut to us he did give an extremely realistic final tremor. However, he was a kindly man and he was very nice about it afterwards, although it must have put him off working in television for a while.

I don't recall a drama production ever totally grinding to a halt, although there were times when it came perilously close. There were also those occasions when one saw impending disasters and there was absolutely nothing to be done about it.

Once, when I was holding an empty shot of a window as seen from the inside of a room, an elderly actor, having done his bit, appeared on the other side of it as he made his way back to his dressing room. To everyone's horror, just as the director cut he paused and made a meal out of looking into the set to see what was happening.

Since the action of the play was supposed to be taking place on the thirtieth floor of a New York skyscraper, the air in the gallery was blue for a while.

It was even bluer during the closing stages of what had been a long courtroom drama, when the foreman of the jury returned to deliver the verdict. Focusing up on a tight shot of his face, I saw his eyes go dead; always a bad sign. Normally actors invented signals to warn the prompter when they had dried – stroking the chin or a quick tug at the right ear lobe – but with only one line to deliver it probably hadn't seemed worth it. There was a pause as he mentally tossed a coin. Heads for guilty, tails for not guilty. Mathematically it should have been a fifty-fifty chance, but the dice were loaded against the unfortunate actor and he got it wrong.

It was not a happy scene in the gallery as news filtered through from the duty officer that viewers were ringing in to complain.

In the early days it was always possible to tell when the person on the book pushed the button to cut studio sound in order to give a prompt because everything suddenly went noticeably dead, but later on studio 'atmosphere' was pre-recorded and automatically cut in so that it was impossible to tell a prompt from a dramatic pause.

Sometimes though, even that didn't work.

The longest dramatic pause I can remember happened during an episode of *Dixon of Dock Green*.

The scene opened with a shot of Andy Crawford reading a newspaper in George Dixon's living-room. On cue the door was supposed to open and a girl would enter.

As Peter Byrne turned first one page, then another, it became apparent that it wasn't going to happen. It was one of those occasions when there was nothing anyone could do to help. Every second seemed like an eternity. I could see his knuckles grow white as he returned to the front page and started again. Short of reading the headlines out loud there was little else he could do.

Shouts from Dougie Moodie in the gallery grew louder and more profane until our headphones were in danger of glowing red.

It turned out later that the actress had suffered a bad attack of stage fright and had shut herself in her dressing room. The studio manager made a wild dash down the corridor, gave her a quick slap, then literally dragged her back to the set and shoved her through the door. It was no wonder that when she finally appeared she was looking somewhat distraught. We all were by then!

Knowing my mother was an avid fan of the programme, I rang her that evening to see what she had made of it all. She said she thought it must have been an unusually interesting paper Andy was reading and did I know which one it was because it might be worth changing to!

Television crews – numbering around twenty or so specialist technicians – led a strange, slightly nomadic existence, moving from studio to studio, from production to production. For a day at a time, or perhaps two or three in the case of a play or a big light entertainment show, one worked in close proximity to other people, sharing their problems with an intimacy which was out of all proportion to the length of time one had known them.

For a few hours or days it was like being a member of a close-knit family, but it seldom went further than that. At the end of the show the lights would go out and there would be a rush to dismantle the sets and camera equipment in order to clear the way for the next production. Once away from the studio we all went our separate ways, knowing little more about each other than when we first met.

On 13 August 1958 an important event took place at Hammersmith Hospital in the shape of a girl called Karen Mary who weighed in at 6 lbs 12 ozs.

To find room for the new addition we had moved to a maisonette in Hayes and I lay awake at night wondering if I would ever pay off the £1,800 mortgage in my lifetime. My father was worried on our behalf because the lease on the property was only ninety-nine years. I pointed out I would be a hundred and thirty-one years old by the time it expired, but he wasn't entirely convinced.

Hayes also saw the start of a wine cellar. A few months earlier I had won twelve bottles of Liebfraumilch in a photo caption competition run by a magazine called *Lilliput*, but Brenda wasn't allowed alcohol, so there it lay until 13 October, exactly two months after Karen was born, when we had another piece of good news – the publication of my first book. In its dust jacket, *A Bear Called Paddington* weighed exactly 10 ozs.

Until then I had always half-heartedly tried to convince myself that since my own birthday fell on the thirteenth of the month I really ought to count it as my lucky number; now I knew it was true.

When Karen was born there was no question about whether or not she would be on display, but in the case of Paddington I went along to the Army & Navy Stores. When I couldn't see one anywhere I asked in a loud voice if they were getting any in. The assistant opened a cupboard behind the counter and there they all were, great piles of them. I was too embarrassed to say I simply wanted to look, so I had to buy one.

It must be an occupational hazard of the book trade having authors do the rounds, putting their book to the front. Speaking personally, I try not to look too hard any more. If the books are there it means they haven't been sold, which is depressing. If they are not, the chances are they weren't there in the first place, which is even worse.

In April the following year *My Fair Lady* hit London and was all the advance publicity promised it was going to be. Soon after it opened, Brenda and I spent a magical evening at Drury Lane, but the rain that was falling mainly on the plain in Spain, had started to descend on Hayes.

That month Karen went into hospital at Ascot to have an operation on a dislocated hip, and shortly afterwards the BBC sent me to Evesham on a training course. I had only just arrived there when Brenda broke her leg, so the year that had begun so well ended up being what it is now fashionable to call an *annus horribilis*.

What we none of us knew was that as far as Karen was concerned it was to last another four years.

CHAPTER 10

A Bear Called Paddington

Mr and Mrs Brown first met Paddington on a railway platform. In fact, that was how he came to have such an unusual name for a bear, for Paddington was the name of the station.

When I wrote those few words, I had no idea quite what a change they would eventually make to my life.

It was really a case of putting something down on paper in order to get my brain working that morning. If you don't press the typewriter keys no one else is going to do it for you.

My inspiration was sitting on the mantelpiece above the gas fire in our London flat. I had bought him as a stocking filler for Brenda the previous year. Taking shelter from the weather that Christmas Eve, I happened to wander into Selfridges and eventually found myself in the toy department. There I came across a small toy bear left on a shelf looking, or so it seemed to me, rather sorry for himself.

We called him Paddington because for some years Paddington Station had been my first port of call whenever I travelled to London, and it was also just down the road from where we were living at the time. Besides, it had a nice, West Country ring to it; safe and solid.

I hadn't intended writing any more than the first few words, but they caught my fancy and I carried on, trying to picture what might happen next.

Suppose Mr and Mrs Brown had been my own parents, what would they have done?

I suspect they would have behaved in much the same way as did the Browns.

To me, one of the saddest sights of any conflict is that of refugees, trudging along some dusty road, leaving everything they have known and loved behind them as they head into the unknown.

It was the memory of seeing newsreels showing trainloads of evacuees leaving London during the war, each child with a label round its neck and all its important possessions in a tiny suitcase, that prompted me to do the same for Paddington. *Please look after this bear* was a message the Browns could hardly resist, and the addition of *Thank you* said even more.

Having read the words on the label, and having then been told by the bear that it had come all the way from Darkest Africa as a stowaway in a ship's lifeboat, my mother would unhesitatingly have taken the line of 'first things first'.

The problem of deciding on a name having been disposed of ('Seeing we found you on Paddington Station – that's what we'll call you – Paddington'), clearly some kind of sustenance was required.

Before he knew what had happened, my father, one step behind as usual and worried about the legality of it all, but always in the market for a cup of tea, would have found himself sitting in the station buffet 'looking as though he had tea with a bear on Paddington Station every day of his life'.

On the very next page when Judy, home for the school holidays, arrived on the scene and was introduced to Paddington – by that time covered in jam and cream – it was a foregone conclusion that he would be going home with the Browns to number thirty-two Windsor Gardens (in my mind's eye Lansdowne Crescent – a quiet street of rather grand houses off Ladbroke Grove and close to Arundel Gardens where we lived).

From then on the story followed a simple but logical process of development, and before lunch I had written what was to become the first chapter of a totally unpremeditated children's book.

It seemed sensible to give the Browns two children, one of each, and both away at boarding school so that if necessary they needn't get in the way when they weren't contributing to the plot.

For the same reason, Mr Brown would be 'something in the City'; out all day unless required, at which point the market would unaccountably go slack.

It also seemed to me that any family who would take a strange bear home with them to live must be a pretty soft touch, so there was need for a stronger voice in the background. Someone of whom Paddington would remain slightly in awe.

Mrs Bird, the Browns' housekeeper, was an amalgam of Mary Gorden, who played Mrs Hudson in the Basil Rathbone Sherlock Holmes films, and a character from my school-days: Tim's Aunt Hetty.

Aunt Hetty was a familiar figure in England between the wars. There were a lot of them about. Not professional housekeepers in the strict sense of the word; they were among the many millions who had lost a husband or boyfriend in the carnage of the First World War and found themselves reduced to living with a relative in return for doing all the housework and cooking.

Like me, Paddington would have approved of Aunt Hetty's herring roes on toast, eaten in front of a roaring log fire in winter, usually while Tim and I were doing our homework. She made them taste as no one else ever has, either before or since. Some people have a knack for making even the simplest dish a cut above the rest. It was another culinary secret denied me.

The arrangement worked well enough for the first few chapters, as Paddington adjusted to his new surroundings and did various day-to-day things for the first time, like taking a bath, travelling on the underground, shopping for clothes in Barkridges, or decorating his new room.

With Mrs Bird keeping a watchful eye on them, the Brown family cheerfully bore the brunt of his early adventures.

The Mr Brown who kept putting off doing the decorating was very like my father, who used to spend so much time lighting his pipe when he was preparing wallpaper that the paste – made with flour and water in those days – had usually dried up by the time he started work. Once, having papered my bedroom at Gloucester Road, he announced that he had learned a few wrinkles. When I said I could see them he laughed as loudly as anyone and often repeated the joke.

Like Mr Brown he was probably secretly pleased by the knowledge that he wouldn't ever be asked to do it again.

In short, everyone was a bit too easy-going: there was need for some kind of conflict.

Mr Curry, the Browns' bad-tempered next-door neighbour, was no one person in particular but an amalgam of all the mean, intolerant and bigoted crosspatches I had come across over the years. As such, he is a constant thorn in Paddington's side, and of course, with Paddington's penchant for misunderstandings and getting into trouble, the reverse is true. Deserving all he gets, yet always coming back for more, Mr Curry was to become an invaluable source of plotting material.

Mr Gruber came about simply because it seemed to me that, kind and sympathetic though the Browns were, they would have no real idea of what it must be like to find oneself an immigrant in a strange country, with no money and nowhere to go.

Harvey Unna's simply told tale of his early flight to England always stuck in my mind.

Mr Gruber was born in Hungary and his antique shop in the Portobello Road is an oasis of peace and quiet in Paddington's life: a retreat where every day he can share his elevenses, discuss the world in general over cocoa and buns, and seek sound advice from his friend whenever the need arises.

I came across a number of Mr Grubers during my time with the BBC Monitoring Service, but of all the many different nationalities I encountered, Hungarians seemed to me to be the most civilized and philosophical about life's problems.

Paddington and Mr Gruber enjoy a formal yet very special relationship, one of mutual respect, always addressing each other by their surnames; it wouldn't occur to either of them that it could be any other way.

Paddington's old hat (handed down to him by his uncle) and his duffle coat were simply replicas of what I happened to be wearing at the time. The battered old leather suitcase with its secret compartment, the inside of which we never see, is reminiscent of the duffle bag belonging to the mother in *The Swiss Family Robinson*, indelibly imprinted on my mind from reading the book over and over again as a small child. The basket on wheels, which has become Paddington's trademark whenever he goes out shopping in the market, was an indispensable part of our own household equipment.

Fortunately, although I have read and enjoyed the Winnie the Pooh stories many times since, I had not read them at the time, otherwise I might have been tempted to make Paddington a toy bear. As it was, it didn't occur to me that he should be anything other than a real, live character.

His love of marmalade came about simply because I happen to prefer it to honey.

Always in the back of my mind were the things I had learned from reading the *Magnet*. Frank Richards respected his audience. He never wrote down and he never preached. His ideals and sense of values were implicit in the text and in the way the characters reacted to each other. He was also a deflater of pomposity.

Eight working days later, at the rate of a chapter a day, I realized I had a book on my hands. It doesn't sound very long, but then it had taken me twelve years to learn how to do it. After a few minor modifications and retyping I sent it off to Harvey Unna.

He promptly wrote back:

> I have now read your novel, *A Bear Called Paddington*, and I think it is quite a publishable tale and I like it well. My spies tell me, however, that you have slipped up in that there are no bears in Africa, darkest or otherwise. The race of bears in the Atlas Mountains has been extinct for centuries. Children either know this or should know this and I suggest you make suitable amends, for which purpose I am returning herewith the script. There are plenty of bears in Asia, Europe and America, and quite a few on the Stock Exchange.

A visit to Westminster Public Library, followed by a trip to the Regent's Park Zoo, eliminated most other bears on my list of possibles and I eventually settled on Peru. The few bears still existing there are about the right size and nothing much is known about them, which seemed a good thing. Making it Darkest Peru, with a capital D, added a touch of mystery.

Over the next few months the book went the rounds of publishers until finally it landed on the desk of Barbara Ker Wilson, the then children's editor at Collins, with a note from her secretary saying it had made her laugh on her way into work that morning. Fortunately it made

Barbara Ker Wilson laugh too, and went on to receive the blessing of
Sir William Collins himself. 'Billy' Collins was one of the old school
who followed his own judgement and took a keen interest in every title
he published. If he liked something, he expected everyone else to feel
the same way and to put their all behind it. At sales conferences he used
to tell the reps how many copies he expected them to sell and woe
betide them if they didn't. .

On 10 February 1958 Harvey Unna wrote to say *A Bear Called Paddington* had been accepted by Collins, who were offering an advance of
£75 against a ten per cent royalty.

There followed an invitation to lunch at which Barbara Ker Wilson
suggested Peggy Fortnum as a possible illustrator.

It isn't easy to capture a young bear's likeness in a few lines, but Peggy
does it to perfection with her pen-and-ink drawings. Her fluid style belies
all the effort that goes into her work; it is the artist's equivalent of a
writer's screwed up sheets of paper in the waste basket. She carries on
until she is satisfied, at which point that's it, take it or leave it. She
understands Paddington perfectly and with a few seemingly deft strokes
– perhaps portraying a back view of him walking down a street, lost in
thought – manages to convey a living, breathing creature. The eyes, the
shagginess, the slightly hunched figure, the purposeful air say it all.

We have never corresponded a great deal; there has been no need.
Apart from our first meeting she has never consulted me about her
drawings, and I have been perfectly happy for it to remain that way
because I respect her work. But sometimes at Christmas I receive a
specially drawn card – usually with a note of apology because she has
got a bit behind with her shopping that year or mislaid my address –
and they always give me a warm glow. Best of all, they make me laugh.

The following winter, soon after the book came out, I attended my
first signing session. It was at Fortnum & Mason and the previous night
there had been a heavy fall of snow over London. Piccadilly was as
deserted as I have ever seen it.

A few hardy souls taking refuge from the cold had made it to the
fourth floor and were gathered round the table where my book was on
display. Having swiftly disposed of them and dealt politely with a man
who wanted to know where the Biggles books were kept, I was reduced
to slowly signing copies for stock when the lift doors opened and a

slightly seedy, theatrical figure of what appeared to be the actor-manager *manqué* emerged. Brushing the snow from his cloak, he bounded towards me.

'Keep up the good work,' he boomed, enthusiastically grasping a right hand as yet unsullied by writer's cramp. 'We have two great books this year: Montgomery's memoirs and *A Bear Called Paddington*.'

I appreciated the gesture and the fact that anyone at all had bothered to make their way from Collins' offices in St James's in such foul weather, but I didn't believe a word of it. I wondered if all their authors received a similarly extravagant massaging of their egos.

After he had departed, I learned from Elizabeth Henniker Heaton, who ran the book department, that Fortnum & Mason's list of bestsellers put Paddington at number two, just behind Montgomery's memoirs. No wonder Billy Collins had been pleased.

The book was still doing well a few weeks later when I had my next signing two doors away at Hatchard's. The manager, Tommy Joy – doyen of London booksellers – gave me the visitors' book to sign.

General Montgomery had beaten me to it again. 'Montgomery of Alamein', occupied almost the whole of the left-hand page. Resisting the temptation to write 'Michael Bond of Hayes' underneath it, I inscribed my name on the opposite page. Even with my largest joined-up writing it still looked very insignificant alongside the other, perhaps reflecting our contrasting careers in the army.

Tommy Joy suggested I might like a gin and tonic before I began work and then hastily withdrew the offer in case, as he put it, I 'breathed fumes over any of the children waiting to get their books signed'.

I could have said: 'What children?', but I didn't.

By Christmas the entire first print-run of *A Bear Called Paddington* had been sold and in the following January *Books & Bookmen* listed it as the 'Best Children's Book of 1958'.

Barbara Ker Wilson wondered if I would consider writing a sequel.

As Paddington would say, 'I needed no second bidding', and soon afterwards I started work on *More About Paddington*.

Whether I liked it or not, my career as a writer had been mapped out for me and it was to keep me increasingly occupied for the best part of the next twenty or so years. But for the time being it was still very much a part-time occupation and I still had to earn my living.

By the early sixties the BBC Television Centre at the White City was gradually being opened up. For a while it was probably the biggest and best purpose-built studio complex in the world. The lighting was more sophisticated than hitherto and could be controlled at the touch of a button. Zoom lenses were all the rage. Video recording came into its own, and, more importantly, the means of editing the tapes quickly and relatively cheaply. And with it all came the opportunity to mount bigger and better productions to satisfy the needs of twelve million licence holders.

Eric Maschwitz took over Light Entertainment and immediately made his presence felt. A prolific writer of film and stage musicals, including *Goodnight Vienna*, *Belinda Fair*, and *Love From Judy*, he was also the lyricist of numerous hits like 'Room 504', 'A Nightingale Sang in Berkeley Square' and under the unlikely name of Holt Marvell, that perennial favourite, 'These Foolish Things'. He first joined the BBC in 1926 as assistant head of outside broadcasts, then edited the *Radio Times* for a while before becoming director of variety. One-time Hollywood scriptwriter, wartime member of Intelligence, sometime husband of Hermione Gingold, he brought more than a touch of spice to his job and they were boom years for the department.

Capitalizing on the fact that unlike ITV they were able to produce genuine half-hour programmes, that is to say without any advertising breaks, BBC television entered a prolific period of creating half-hour comedy shows and over the years they have remained ahead of the game. Such classics as *It's a Square World*, *Steptoe and Son*, *Hancock's Half-Hour*, *Monty Python's Flying Circus*, *Fawlty Towers*, set the pattern, and the list could carry on almost indefinitely.

But perhaps the area which benefited most from the new facilities at the TV Centre was music. Opera singers, who until then had fought shy of the medium, began to be attracted by the possibility of performing to much larger audiences and under Patricia Foy's direction the BBC mounted a series of large-scale productions, many of which I was lucky enough to work on.

Often a law unto themselves, opera singers are almost always lovely to work with; the most generous of people when it comes to passing on their immense knowledge to others.

Tito Gobbi, who has played most parts in his life, was not above stopping a rehearsal in order to show some humble extra how carry a hurricane lamp.

'No, no, no! Not like-a that. Like-a this!' And we would all wait while he demonstrated exactly how it should to be done.

One suddenly realized that here was someone who had performed in front of some of the most demanding audiences in the world; a perfectionist, who knew every move and every gesture. One realized, too, what a strain it must be – an actor can fluff a line and no one will notice; an opera singer has only to miss a note and even the least musical member of the audience can spot it at once.

Before the start of a programme there was always an air of excitement and anticipation; the orchestra tuning up – usually in an adjoining studio – the sound of singers relaxing their voices would filter through from the dressing rooms and from make-up. The last-minute production notes would be run through.

It was impossible not to feel moved as one carried out a long, slow camera movement in time to some of the most beautiful music ever written, counting the bars, trying to end the track at exactly the right moment; impossible not to feel enormously privileged at being part of it all.

But in the nature of things such moments were becoming fewer and farther between.

One night, towards the end of 1965, obeying a call of nature before I began the long drive home, I happened to say to the man standing next to me, 'I wonder what the weather's going to be like tomorrow?'

Five minutes later, as I struggled to free myself from a mass of warm fronts and occlusions, I began to wish I had bothered to look before I asked. If I had, I might have recognized one of the weather men.

It also struck me on the way home that maybe I was getting a bit jaded. Television had its moments, but a lot of the excitement had gone out of the job. In some respects it had lost its magic, the knowledge that what you were watching was actually happening there and then. With the coming of recording, that feeling had been lost for ever. Knowing that it was no longer a total disaster if you didn't get things right first time meant the adrenalin did not flow in quite the same way. In short, the Television Centre had become a programme-making factory. And as it grew, so more and more paperwork crept in. Having a crew to manage meant there were annual reports to make out, and quarterly reports and monthly reports on the newer entrants, plus leave charts to administer. You could be tracking in on someone giving their all and a voice would whisper in your ear, 'Can I have next Thursday off?'

We had moved house again, this time to Haslemere in Surrey. There was decorating to be done, and a quarter of an acre or so of wasteland to be knocked into shape; not helped by the oldest inhabitant, who took great joy in learning over the fence to watch me digging, saying things like: 'Ah, I see you've reached the bit where the old garages were. They knew how to mix concrete in them days. Made to last it were!'

In the words of Charles Dickens, the previous two years had been the best of times and the worst of times, and it wasn't over by a long way.

Karen, having suffered a botched operation on her dislocated hip when she was eight months old, was still in hospital, this time at the Wingfield in Oxford, beginning what was to take another two years of surgery to put it all right. It was in the days when a half-hour visit in the afternoon was the maximum allowed – anything more was considered bad for the child and a nuisance for the staff – so they were precious, not to be missed moments. Miraculously, or perhaps partly because she is one of nature's Leos, she managed not only to survive it all but seemed to gain added strength, and to this day continues to embrace with open arms all that life has to offer in a way that is a pleasure to see.

My annual car mileage was around 40,000, which was so much wasted time and there weren't enough hours in the day to fit everything in. Something had to go, and since I had privately set myself the target of being a full-time writer before I reached the age of forty it was time I took the plunge.

During the years spent in television I had been lucky enough to meet, work with, photograph, or simply view at close quarters, practically everybody who was anybody, from prime ministers to pop stars, actors and actresses, musicians and dancers, the rich and the famous, or the simply infamous.

Out of it all I had learned one valuable lesson: the world doesn't owe anyone a living and the better you become at something the harder you have to apply yourself. Whenever a studio broke for coffee and there was a mad rush for the canteen, those at the top of their profession always carried on working.

By the time I reached home that night I had made up my mind. Brenda was totally supportive; my mother secretly relieved. I used to pass on to her copies of *Ariel*, the staff magazine, and her favourite reading was the obituary page. She was convinced that most people who worked for the BBC were not long for this world.

'I see four more have died this month,' she would inform me with a certain amount of satisfaction in her voice.

I was never able to explain to her that the only way to get a mention in the column was to kick the bucket, and that there were many thousands around who would make their retirement day. She didn't begin to understand, and when it came to hiring a car or taking out a mortgage it was clear that a good many actuaries agreed with her.

I was sad to leave the BBC, for it had been an enormously enriching experience. In the beginning they had been adventurous days: adventurous on both sides of the camera, with everyone – presenters and technicians alike – still finding their feet. The impossible was often asked for because everything seemed possible. Frequently it was a case of every man for himself, but also there was great pleasure in working as part of a team, knowing that when things went wrong help was close at hand.

Carrying out a long, smooth track from wide shot to a big, pin-sharp close-up is very satisfying, just as making a smooth landing in a plane must be. In both cases, no matter how many times you repeat the manoeuvre, there are always those occasions when you know you could have done it that little bit better – you lose focus momentarily, or touch down a second too soon, and afterwards the trackers or the cabin crew avoid your eye.

A cameraman on a big camera crane is only as good as those at the back, and when I first reached the dizzy heights I was blessed with two of the best, Colin and John, who also helped make the crew a happy one. We had a lot of fun and I remember them all with great affection.

But nothing is for ever and people move on.

On 1 April 1966 I returned to the real world.

The hit song of that particular year was 'Strangers in the Night', which, sad to relate, was beginning to have echoes at home.

CHAPTER 11

The Herbs and Others

You must write for children in the same way as you write for adults, only better.

Maxim Gorky (1868–1936)

One morning, soon after I left the BBC, the telephone rang and an unfamiliar voice asked me how I was getting on.

It was Doreen Stephens, the then head of Children's Television. They were thinking of revamping *Watch With Mother* and did I have any ideas?

It so happened that a few days earlier I had been sitting at my desk gazing out of the window when I happened to glance at the herb bed, and in much the same way that one can often see pictures in the glowing embers of a fire, it struck me that the leaves of parsley blowing in the breeze looked not unlike a lion's mane.

I was by then into writing my sixth Paddington book and had the first book in a new series about a mouse called Thursday scheduled for publication. But given the lesson I had learned in television, it didn't cross my mind to turn away the possibility of more work, so I naturally said, 'Yes, it just so happens that . . .' and found myself outlining an idea in which all the characters were named after herbs.

It was reminiscent of past occasions when I had attended BBC job boards and, having been asked a question, heard my voice gradually become detached from my body, trailing away into some far corner of the room as it played for time on my behalf. At which point one's real self usually took over and came out with something desperately banal like: 'Would you mind repeating the question?'

On this occasion, none of these things happened. It all seemed perfectly feasible and the more I talked the more enthusiastic I became about the idea.

'Good!' came the brisk answer. 'Can you let us have a pilot script as soon as possible? Shall we say in two weeks' time?'

Wondering what I had let myself in for, I hot-footed it down to the nearest bookshop where I bought some books on herbs.

Culpeper's seventeenth-century *Complete Herbal* lists around four hundred different varieties, so finding enough characters to populate a television series was no problem at all; rather the reverse.

The setting would be an old-fashioned walled garden owned by Lady Rosemary – tall, willowy, aristocratic and blessed 'with a tough bark' – together with her husband, the equally aristocratic, but rather bumbling, huntin', shootin' and fishin', Sir Basil, 'with a smell so excellent that it is fit for a king's house'.

Since Parsley had inspired the whole thing and was 'completely beneficial to man and to other animals who sense what is good for them', he was a natural for the central character.

He would need a friend, of course; someone who could also act as a foil. Dill, 'a magician's herb' and a 'favourite on the Continent' sounded a suitably cosmopolitan partner. 'Dill the dog' rolled easily off the tongue and the appearance of the herb itself was wild and devil-may-care.

The garden would need someone solid and reliable to look after things and keep the place tidy. 'Neither witch nor devil, thunder nor lightning, will hurt a man where a Bay Tree is', suggested a gardener called Bayleaf.

Knapweed, 'good at restraining distillations of thin and sharp humours from the head', was sworn in as Constable Knapweed – a kind of Dixon of Herb Green.

Sage, with its 'aromatic colour and bitter taste', became a dyspeptic, somewhat bloody-minded owl; one of nature's squatters and well placed to give a bird's-eye view of things going on in the garden.

Other characters would follow, but I had enough material to write a pilot episode.

Two weeks later I found myself sneaking back into the Television Centre for a meeting with Doreen Stephens and two other members of her department – Joy Whitby and Ursula Eason – both of whom I knew, having worked with them in the past. Joy Whitby was the inspiration behind the highly successful *Jackanory* series. Ursula Eason, who had once been a Radio Auntie – Phoebe rather than Ursula, which was judged too sibilant for early microphones – was the guiding light behind *Vision On*, the highly successful programme for deaf children. I couldn't have wished for a better audience.

All three said they liked the script but wondered how I saw it being done.

Originally I had pictured opening each episode in a kitchen, with an actor playing the part of a chef who would tell the story over a mixing bowl, adding a dash of dill here, a bayleaf there, in order to help the plot along and at the same time provide a relatively painless educational element. Somewhere along the line this idea was dropped on the grounds that the budget for *Watch With Mother* was strictly limited.

For the same reason, cartoon animation was out.

What did I think of string puppets?

Despite an early love for marionettes, my experience as a cameraman had put me off working with them. They were lumbering, and their movements too jerky. They would restrict the story lines.

Glove puppets?

It seemed too much like Sooty. Besides, there would be a lot of characters to handle in a small space.

Ursula Eason had been responsible for suggesting Eric Thompson for *The Magic Roundabout*, which was enjoying a cult following at the time, and the possibility of using a similar method of stop-start animation came up. The thought prompted Joy Whitby to suggest I go and see someone called Graham Clutterbuck who had just arrived in London and was in the process of setting up a company. He, in turn, had working for him a Frenchman named Ivor Wood, who had been involved in animating the original Serge Danot series, *Le Manège Enchanté*. They might be interested . . .

It seemed an unlikely combination. Clutterbuck sounded like a pre-war northern comic, and the name Wood hardly reeked of Gauloises and garlic. But the type of animation interested me because it fitted in with the style of script I had in mind in which a simple tale would unfold, with the narrator doing all the voices, much as parents do when reading to their children at bedtime.

The problem with animated children's programmes then, and it remains true today, is that the cost of making the films far outweighs the limited budget allocated by most television stations. Generally speaking, this means they are often made at a loss by outside production companies who have to take a chance and hope that profits will come later out of overseas sales and merchandise spin-offs, which doesn't always happen.

As I came away from the meeting I sensed that, although in many ways it had gone well, the BBC were distancing themselves from the possibility of actually paying me any money and that my calculations of future earnings based on minimum payments listed in the *Writers' and Artists' Year Book* might prove to be a trifle optimistic.

It was in a spirit of not knowing quite what to expect that I presented myself at the offices of FilmFair in Poland Street. They looked and, as things turned out, were indeed only temporary.

There was an outer office which housed an umbrella in a stand and an extremely elegant, long-legged, mini-skirted, blonde PA named Jillo, who, from the look of her desk, didn't seem exactly overburdened with work – which she probably wasn't as she hadn't been there much longer than me.

Opening a door leading into a second room, she ushered me into the presence of a slightly more lived-in, classical elegance. Old, well-worn tweeds; shirts from Turnbull & Asser, with just a hint of wear at the cuffs; shoes from Lobb. There was a fleeting glimpse of immaculately suspended silk socks as the wearer leapt up from behind an even emptier desk and came round to greet me. It wasn't at all what I had expected and my M & S cotton and nylon mix felt distinctly loose around the ankles.

Although I didn't realize it at the time, it was the one and only occasion when I was to see Graham Clutterbuck behind a desk. He didn't like being pigeonholed and desks came under the same heading as briefcases; they didn't suit his image. Business was normally conducted from a sofa in an office furnished like a living-room.

Accepting a seat, I sat back and listened, first to profuse apologies for the lack of anything to drink – the refrigerator hadn't arrived – then, via a series of compliments on the brilliance of my idea and how much his company was looking forward to producing it, to an outline of the kind of deal they – meaning Clutterbuck, since he *was* the company –

had in mind. As we entered the realms of percentages, my dreams of the golden pot at the end of a comparatively short rainbow plummeted still further. Even to a mind unschooled in the workings of the film world, they sounded distinctly on the low side as far as I was concerned.

Something about the look on my face must have triggered off warning bells, for he suddenly paused in mid-flight, looked me straight in the eye, and said: 'Of course, if I were wearing *your* hat I couldn't possibly accept a deal like that!'

Over the years I was to grow accustomed to the fact that Graham had a large selection of hats, which were trotted out as the occasion demanded. The hats and the equally disarming expression, 'You're absolutely right!', served him well throughout his life.

We parted on a warm handshake, and although from time to time there would be situations when others felt it necessary to involve lawyers, with their forty- and fifty-page contracts covering every possible eventuality including references to future developments yet to be invented, that was all we ever needed.

It was only later, as we grew to know each other better, that Graham admitted that in the beginning his knowledge of the facts of life concerning the market for children's animated films had been even hazier than mine. Fortunately for both of us he was a quicker learner.

In Paris, he had for a while enjoyed the title of Directeur-Général, Les Cinéastes Associés, before setting up the European arm of FilmFair, a Los Angeles company involved in making television commercials. When that folded, more as a result of the workings of French television than for any other reason, he left his offices for the last time feeling so shattered he didn't know whether to turn to the left or to the right. In the end he did neither: he boarded a plane to California and persuaded the parent company to let him set up an office in London, with no salary, but on a percentage-of-profits basis. My visit was a lucky break for both of us, lending weight to the theory that there are some events in life which in retrospect seem almost preordained.

When Graham and I next met it was at the BBC and this time Ivor Wood put in an appearance, having flown over from Paris with the first of the puppets – Sir Basil and Lady Rosemary. Once again, I felt an immediate rapport.

Ivor not only looked French but thought French too. Although born in Leeds of Anglo-French parents, he was brought up in a small village near Lyon, before going to art school in Paris. Stop-start, three-dimensional puppet animation had long been popular in Eastern Europe, but he was one of the first animators to apply it to children's television in France and the UK.

Constructed on a wire frame, fully articulated, with ball-and-socket joints, his puppets are very distinctive. The human characters, with their high, domed foreheads are instantly recognizable and, as befits their parentage – Ivor's wife, Josiane, being very chicly French – are always dressed with enormous style.

The animation is painstakingly done a frame at a time, each frame recording a tiny movement of the puppet, so that when the completed film is run at normal speed, persistency of vision makes it seem as though the movements are continuous.

Unlike a book illustration, where if need be you can ask the artist to make minor changes, it was necessarily a case of take it or leave it. With thirteen 15-minute films already commissioned and on the point of being written into the schedules, it was no time to suggest making fundamental changes. Fortunately, I found myself dealing with a perfectionist, who would never show anything until he was totally happy with it himself, so at no time did the question arise.

The animation was being carried out on the kitchen table of Ivor's and Josiane's Paris flat, so he rushed straight back on the next plane to start work on building the set and designing the rest of the puppets.

Back home, I followed the example of a friend and neighbour, Ronald Rideout, and got myself a second desk in order to begin writing the scripts, leaving my usual desk free for Paddington, Thursday and anything else that came along.

Ronald Rideout enjoys an entry in the *Guinness Book of Records* for being the world's most prolific writer of school textbooks. He used to commute between his two work stations by means of a chair on a set of rails. I never got around to doing that, although there were moments when I was sorely tempted, but having two desks did mean I could switch both mind and body between *The Herbs* and other projects quite easily and painlessly.

With animated films the dialogue is normally recorded first so that the result can be timed overall and if necessary edited before the animation begins. At that stage the music and sound effects are also added.

Each puppet was to have its own distinctive four-line introductory song, which could be varied to suit the situations. Tony Russell, who composed the score for *The Matchmaker*, was commissioned to write the music and, under her maiden name of Johnson, Brenda wrote the accompanying lyrics with great facility.

There was an immediate and frantic search for a suitable voice.

Just as the big marionette companies of old knew that fat people tend to think 'fat' and thin people tend to think 'thin', casting their puppeteers accordingly, so fat people tend to have 'fat' voices and vice versa. Gordon Rollins, a lovely north countryman of saturnine appearance, fitted Ivor Wood's creations admirably. He belonged to that small group of anonymous people who earn their living doing 'voice overs'. One sometimes wonders what they would have done had television not been invented, or what television would do without them. Highly professional, they remain totally unfazed whatever is thrown at them.

Gordon Rollins is the only man I have ever met who actually turned up at a studio one morning, dead on time as always, but wearing an icepack on his head following what he gloomily called 'a bit of a do' the previous night. Until then I had only seen such a sight in pre-war American 'B' movies.

Unfortunately, the script that day was a complicated one which revolved around a surprise birthday party being given for Parsley. At the very end all the inhabitants of the Herb Garden had to sing 'Happy Birthday', each line being rendered in a voice of a different character. As I remember it, Gordon sailed through the script with a minimum of retakes, although at one point the sound engineer did complain about strange rattling noises every time he moved his head.

Graham, Ivor and I continued meeting from time to time, Ivor flying in with his latest creations, which he produced out of his case like a magician taking rabbits from a hat: Aunt Mint, who was for ever knitting and offering good advice; sergeant-majorish Mr Onion and his lovely, if perennially tearful, lady wife, along with their long-suffering family of ten chives; Belladonna, the witch – ultimately written out at the request of a nervous BBC; Sweet Cicely, everybody's singing niece; Signor Solidago, her music master; Tarragon, the dragon – who used to blow real smoke rings out of his nostrils; Good King Henry; and last but not least, for he was a very useful character to have around when the writing reached a sticky patch, Pashana Bedhi, an Indian magician.

Although India is home to many spices, the inhabitants are not deeply into herbs, so I called into Veeraswamy's restaurant off Regent Street to ask their advice. It was early morning, and the consensus of opinion among the off-duty waiters was that such a herb did exist and one of them even wrote the name down for me, but I have to admit I've never come across it in any cookery books.

Somewhere along the way Ivor began sending me photographs of the latest puppets – the journey to and fro between London and Paris had become too time-consuming – politely pointing out at the same time that his Paris apartment was only small and, understandably, Josiane was becoming a trifle restive.

In short, could I please not think up any more characters for the time being and, 'to tell you the truth', could I also go easy on the chives, who had a tendency to march across the screen at intervals to no great purpose.

It was the classic situation of the writer putting in camera instructions which take only a few seconds to type, but which land the animator with a day's work or more.

The Herbs began weekly transmissions in February 1968.

In the very first episode I allowed Sir Basil's gun to go off by accident and in so doing blow Parsey's tail away. The underlying intention was to put children off playing with firearms, which I hope it did. Unfortunately it also put a sizeable number off watching with mother. Tears flowed and many a set was switched off in desperation without waiting to see the happy ending when Parsley's pride and joy was returned to him courtesy of Sage, the owl, and he was once again able to sing, 'I'm a very friendly lion called Parsley, with a tail for doing jobs of every kind.'

Fortunately the viewing figures recovered the following week. But it taught me not to put messages in stories. As Sam Goldwyn once wisely said: 'Messages are for Western Union.'

The Adventures of Parsley, a series of thirty-two 5-minute films starring Parsley and Dill, contained no messages at all, and was commissioned by the BBC to help fill the prime spot between *Children's Hour* and the early evening news.

From the writing point of view it was a valuable exercise in the disciplines required for that kind of slot. In practice, because they were scheduled to go out before the evening news, the BBC requirement was for four minutes and forty-five seconds, which would allow time for a trailer. Take away, say thirty seconds for beginning and end titles and credits, and it didn't leave much time for the story. There was no question of the news starting late, so if you went outside these limits you knew the programme would be faded.

All the same, despite the restrictions they were fun to write. Knowing that most children go through a period of liking corny jokes, I was able to indulge myself and the series evolved into a kind of Morecambe and Wise cross-talk act.

They were a good example of stories which almost write themselves. With the characters firmly established in the original series, it was possible to wake up in the morning without the ghost of an idea, sit down after breakfast and pluck a line out of the air – 'Today isn't a Monday, a Tuesday, Wednesday or Thursday . . . it's a Friday.' Almost immediately Friday would become *Fly*day and by coffee-time I would have hammered out a workable plot about flying. A quick rewrite after coffee and the finished script would be ready by lunch-time.

After he had finished filming *The Adventures of Parsley*, Ivor went on to make *The Wombles* and I returned to my other desk.

One of the nicest things about writing for children is their total acceptance of the fantastic. However, the parameters of a series are established with the very first story and there is no going outside them.

The action of *The Herbs* takes place within the four walls of the garden. While we are within those four walls anything can happen, for it is a magical place and herbs are known to have special powers. But we are privileged visitors and at the end of our quarter of an hour stay we are ushered out again; the door closing on Parsley waving goodbye.

Paddington, too, quickly established his credentials as a solid citizen of West London. Apart from occasional excursions with his friend, Mr Gruber, or an outing with the Brown family, that is where he belongs. He would certainly be the last person on earth to think of going to the moon. His first thought would be to wonder whether or not he would be able to get his favourite marmalade.

It was largely because I felt the need to free myself of these constrictions that I began writing a series of books about a mouse called Thursday. Arriving out of the clear blue sky hanging on the end of a balloon, Thursday established himself straight away as a go-anywhere, do-anything character. To him all things are possible. However, for some reason he never emerged from the pages as a born leader. In most of his adventures it is Harris, a water vole he meets early on, who tends to make the running. Sometimes characters take over and stubbornly refuse to behave in the way you want them to and there is nothing you can do about it.

Another problem with the genre is that, as with James Bond, there is a natural tendency to try to cap each story with something even more fantastic and there comes a point where a line has to be drawn.

The last of the four books, *Thursday Goes to Paris*, was set in underground Paris: the catacombs, the sewers and the post office *pneumatique* – a system by means of which messages placed inside metal containers used to be propelled by compressed air to other offices in Paris via a complex network of interconnecting pipes.

At the time of writing it, neither the catacombs nor the sewers were open to the general public, and not many people living outside Paris knew about the *pneumatique*. However, those in charge were very kind and helpful and only too willing to show me what went on behind the scenes, although I don't know what they would have thought had they known the plot involved the blowing-up of their city by a gang of fiendish oriental mice who planned to send high explosive along the pipes. Fortunately the books didn't get translated into French and perhaps it's just as well the system is now defunct, having been rendered redundant by the fax machine. It might give real-life terrorists ideas.

When I first began writing I often had radio plays and short stories returned with a note scrawled across the rejection slip saying: 'Sorry, we don't accept fantasy.'

With Paddington I learned the simple truth that it isn't sufficient for the author to believe in the story – the other characters must believe in it, too. If just one character expresses disbelief it can be fatal. Looking back, a lot of my early work seemed to be about young men finding themselves staying in a small French village where the statue of a beautiful young girl miraculously, and usually for one night only, comes to life. There was always a full moon, of course. But to a man, the heroes made the fatal mistake of expressing surprise.

And yet it would be hard to find anything more fantastic than a bear living in Notting Hill Gate, able to speak perfect English, doing his daily shopping in the Portobello Market and living a perfectly normal life. However, because he is totally accepted by all those who meet him and no one is ever surprised when they find themselves dealing with a bear, he becomes, in turn, totally acceptable to the reader.

The same is true of Thursday. I took it as a compliment when I came across the books one day in the wildlife department at Foyles, although of course they could have been put there for other reasons.

Another basic truth is that stories should arise out of the central character and not the other way round.

For that to happen one needs a role model, however slight.

Paddington was based on a toy bear which has very little physical resemblance to the character who finally emerged from the pages, but without him I could never have written the books. Thursday and his friend, Harris, metamorphosed in a similar way, and the Herbs really came to life, first from drawings and descriptions of real herbs, and then through Ivor Wood's interpretation of them.

In the case of a guinea-pig called Olga da Polga, which was my next project, the term 'role model' would be an understatement. It was more a case of following her around, notebook in hand. What finally emerged was the pig, the whole pig and nothing but the pig. A 'touch of Bunter and Falstaff' to quote the *Times Literary Supplement*. Bunter would certainly be a good name for most guinea-pigs, for they are basically eating machines. There is no question of their saving the best until last.

She was bought for Karen in 1965 at a cost of four shillings and sixpence in old money and came from a pet shop in Basingstoke. We called her Olga for the simple reason that the children who lived next door had one they called Boris. Playing about with the name, tossing it around like a tennis ball in my head, it came out as Olga da Polga.

After we'd had her for about a year, following a chance meeting with the editor of a local freebee magazine called *Mere Views*, I began writing a series of very short stories. They were a labour of love, and in the beginning not much more than a record of a typical day in the life of a guinea-pig, describing how she lived, what she ate, how to build a hutch and an outdoor run, along with a list of dos and don'ts connected with keeping a small pet. But gradually the series took on a different shape and plots began to form.

In terms of parameters, it threw up the challenge of how to weave stories around an animal whose life was contained for the most part within an area of a few square feet. In the end I fell back on the simple expedient of developing Olga into the kind of character who lives in her own fantasy world, bossing not only the other animals around her – Noel the cat, Graham the tortoise and Fangio the hedgehog – but the humans as well, bending them to her will, which was exactly what she did.

Many of the stories were based on normal everyday happenings in a typical English household – like the day we returned from holiday and having decided to cook some *pommes frites*, I set fire to the kitchen. Olga watched wide-eyed as I dashed past her house carrying a flaming chip pan, but of course in her dream world she saved the day.

Then there was the time when I was taking her back to her hutch and a sudden clap of thunder directly overhead caused her to leap out of my hands in fright and land on the concrete, where she lay spread-eagled in a puddle of water, to all intents and purposes not long for this world. Fortunately there was a happy ending, and Olga lived to inspire many another tale.

One of the nice things about being a writer is that you can get some sort of mileage out of even the worst events.

The stories ran for a year and then later on at the suggestion of Kaye Webb, the editor of Puffin Books, I rewrote them to form a book.

Kaye at that time was the leading force in quality children's books. Founder of Puffin Post, she was Queen Puffin to a whole generation of children. She loved them and those who were lucky enough to come into direct contact with her – and there were many, for she went out of her way to meet them – adored her. Emotionally involved in all aspects of her work, she was also immensely shrewd and demanding and, in the beginning, managed to acquire paperback rights from many of the major publishers, including Collins.

In a way her success proved her own undoing, for in time they came to realize the potential of the market and gradually reacquired the rights. Olga came to Kaye's notice shortly after the Paddington titles reverted to Collins, so it helped fill a gap in her list.

The Tales of Olga de Polga, the first of what was ultimately to become a series of four books, was published in 1971. Once again I was lucky with the illustrator. Kaye suggested Hans Helweg, who not only brought them delightfully to life but became a life-long friend.

Paddington apart, of all the children's stories I've written, the four Olga books are the ones that have given me the most satisfaction and sense of achievement.

It is impossible to know what guinea-pigs talk about amongst themselves; food mostly, I suspect. It's also hard to know what they are thinking. That they *are* thinking is obvious to anyone who spends any time at all observing their behaviour. Over the years I have owned, or been owned by, a number of them and they have all been different, with highly developed individual personalities. At the end of the day, as with most things, you get out of your relationship with any animal what you are prepared to put in. But it would be wrong to ascribe to them thought processes similar to that of humans.

Olga nearly became an early victim of this kind of muddled 'politically correct' thinking when the second book in the series was taken by an American publisher.

In the opening chapter of *Olga Meets her Match*, she goes to stay with Boris, transferred for purposes of plot from his hutch in the house next door to a more impressive abode near the sea, where he lived in some splendour. Although she certainly wouldn't admit it, despite Boris's boastful nature and her natural inclination to pooh-pooh much of what he says, Olga is very smitten. So smitten is she, in fact, that in the final chapter of the book, much to her own and everyone else's surprise, she gives birth to a family of three.

I thought I had handled the whole thing very tastefully, glossing over all the sordid details about goings-on in the hay. However, the American publishers thought otherwise and wrote saying that if they were to take the book they would like me to insert a few paragraphs allowing Olga the opportunity to discuss with Boris the possibility of having a family before the two of them retired for the night.

I put my foot down on behalf of my characters. For better or worse, I don't think any animals are deeply into family planning, and guinea-pigs rather less than most. I saw Boris as a male chauvinist pig not much given to discussing such matters at the best of times. He is one of life's doers in a world where it is every pig for himself and you live for the moment, taking your pleasures whenever and wherever you can. I certainly didn't feel my hackles rise on Olga's behalf. From personal experience I knew she was well able to look after herself, and if she had wanted to say no, she would have done so. A sharp nip in the right place works wonders.

An impasse was reached, with both sides digging their heels in and refusing to budge. Fortunately it was only a temporary hiccup and another publisher was quickly found. *The Tales of Olga da Polga* went on to win the American Library Association's 'Notable Book' citation and I began work on a third collection of stories.

A worse fate was to befall Big Ears when the BBC tried to sell the television series of *Noddy* in America. The buyers objected to the name on the grounds that physical abnormality is no joking matter.

Having many a time been dubbed 'big nose' when I was at school, I can certainly vouch for the fact, but I always drew comfort from people like Jimmy 'Schnozzle' Durante who made a virtue out of it, taking the line: 'So what – dere's a million good-looking guys in the world, but I'm a novelty.'

A few years ago I set about making an Olga series for television. Video cameras had yet to reach the present state of the art, so I planned to shoot it on 16mm film. Since film is expensive and I intended using live animals, it involved a lot of pre-planning.

First it was a case of making a variety of modified hutches with removable doors and windows for Olga. Then a semi-portable raised area of paving and grass was constructed, which would solve many of the problems involving low-angle shots.

Next, the cast had to be assembled.

The first Olga having died of old age many years previously, Olga II was acquired.

Graham, the tortoise, came from Whipsnade Zoo. I suspect they may have been glad to see the back of him, for he turned out to be pretty bloody-minded, although to be fair he was the easiest of all to film. The shortest distance between two points being a straight line, he let nothing stand in his way and soon became known as 'One-take Graham', although he did develop an annoying habit of disappearing when wanted.

Fangio, the hedgehog, arrived quite literally out of the blue one morning when he fell down some steps into the basement area of the house in Pimlico where Karen and her husband were living. He not only stayed around for the filming but happily for the rest of his life.

Noel, the cat, was played by Marble Jankel, who became part of the family when Tony and Karen were married, so he was available on request.

Filming small animals has its problems, but it wasn't until I started work that I began to realize just how many there would be.

A basic fact of life is that they all have minds of their own and do what *they* want to do. Olga, in particular, had flashes of temperament and took to disappearing into her bedroom whenever she saw a camera approaching. The only way round that kind of situation is to prepare a basic script knowing it won't work, then modify your thoughts as you go along, rewriting it completely in the light of what actually happens. There are no such thing as 'rehearsals', but animals often unwittingly provide one with shots one wouldn't dream of attempting.

Over two summers of variable weather, a 'pilot' was completed, plus enough material for another six or seven 10-minute episodes.

In the end, the filming of Olga turned out to be more like a miniature *Ben Hur*. There was a whole catalogue of disasters.

The narrator went to India for a holiday and picked up some rare disease which caused his voice to change, so the soundtrack had to be done all over again, this time using two voices: Joanna David playing Olga and Tim Hardy doing the narration and all the other characters.

But then we lost the star, who quite simply died of old age. (The place felt so empty without her, she was soon followed by Olga III, who is as different again. Born a Leo, she displays all the characteristics of her sign. Interested in everything going on around her, she would know the correct exposure for every shot and there would be no point in arguing, for it simply wouldn't occur to her that she could be wrong or that others might think differently!)

Fangio, who must have been older than we first thought, became white-haired under the chin and also died of old age.

Marble had to have a leg amputated, and now copes remarkably well, but there is a limit to the number of rewrites you can do.

Worst of all, during the comparatively short time it took to shoot the film, the whole nature of children's television underwent a change and the market for that type of programme dried up.

But it's all there, lying in a vault somewhere in north London, so who knows? One of these days, when I am at that elusive loose end which somehow never seems to happen . . .

Back-tracking in time a few years, by 1974 I had completed the tenth Paddington book, and although I was by no means tired of him, he had done most things and I had no wish to be accused of scraping the barrel.

I had come to be considered something of an expert on bears – which I certainly am not – and as arctophilists in various parts of the world began baring their souls, fan mail started to include a fair sprinkling of letters beginning: 'Dear Sir, I have never told anyone this before, but . . .' They come in all shapes and sizes and ages.

Signing books in Liberty's one lunchtime I was confronted by a man who, like Mr Brown, was clearly 'something in the City': dark suit, bowler hat, and with an unmistakable air. He produced an out-of-date passport in which he had replaced his own photograph with one of Paddington. Much travelled, wherever he went he had always had it stamped by the authorities, who had clearly entered into the spirit of things. Bears, as I was beginning to discover for myself, are an open sesame.

Signing sessions had become signing tours and they were not without their hazards. Marmalade sandwiches figure large in any kind of Paddington promotion and there were times when I wished I had given him a liking for something a little more exotic, like truffles or even out-of-season asparagus, but it was too late. It wasn't so bad in winter, but in summer it could become a problem. I still recall a school fête somewhere in the Cotswolds where an emergency squad of sixth-formers was last seen disappearing over the brow of a hill carrying a large trunkful of sandwiches, hotly pursued by a swarm of angry wasps.

Signings are unpredictable events anyway, very much at the mercy of the world outside; an unforeseen local needle match, the weather being either too hot or too cold, or too wet; a rival 'event' in the next town; a native uprising on the other side of the globe; something better on television.

What could have been the high spot of one particular tour took place in Glasgow and was timed to attract children on their way home from school. Expecting a modest turn-out, Collins advertised free marmalade sandwiches, and the good ladies of the book department did their stuff during their lunch break. Unfortunately, not only did the event attract children on their way home from school but mothers out shopping and sundry passers-by with pushchairs descended on the store in droves. To make matters worse, the children's book department was on the top floor.

By the time I arrived the supply of sandwiches had long been exhausted and the police had been called to control the crowds outside. Forcing my way up a narrow, winding staircase packed with harassed mothers and their screaming infants, who probably didn't like marmalade anyway, my heart sank. The noise was deafening, and most of those present clearly held me entirely responsible for the debacle. The only bright spot as far as I was concerned was that there was no time for 'messages' – just a quick flourish of the pen as the queue shuffled past. Adding messages in Glasgow can be a nerve-racking experience to southern ears untuned to the broad accent.

At least there hadn't been any Waynes.

No children's book-signing is complete without a Wayne. They usually arrive late, just when you have got down to signing a few copies for stock.

The shop door opens and you hear a woman's voice, loud and clear, calling: 'Come along, Wayne. Come and get your book signed.'

Without even bothering to look up, there are a number of things you can safely say about Wayne. He will be dressed in a cowboy outfit, and not being one of the world's great readers, he will have no desire whatsoever to get his book signed. However, hours of target practice with his six-shooter have honed his eyesight to a point where he can spot your average rickety book-signing table at a glance, and having made a beeline for it he will proceed to rock it gently to and fro while you try to write. He will have a horrendous cold and it goes without saying that he won't have blown his nose for several days. Resisting the temptation to add a suitable dedication, like: 'When did you last see a handkerchief?' in case he wants to borrow yours, you carry on as best you can. Last, but not least, having watched you sign his wretched book, he comes out with: 'Don't spell it that way.'

His mother backs him up with a steely gaze. 'He's quite right. We spell it with an "i" instead of a "y", don't we, Waine?'

The only consolation as you remove the offending germ-ridden object between thumb and forefinger and with averted gaze reach for a replacement, is that for the rest of his life the problem will be his, and his alone, and he will have to live with it, again and again and again.

Then there was the time when a tour of the West Country culminated in my being asked to switch on the Christmas lights at a town in north Devon. As often happens, someone had dressed up as Paddington for the occasion and stood proudly alongside me on the mayor's balcony as I performed the ceremony.

During the photo call which followed I was asked by someone from the local press if I would mind having the bear sit on my lap while they took a picture.

Anxious to get things over and done with, I extended my arms and once Paddington had made himself comfortable I gave him a big hug while jogging him up and down for the camera. During the inevitable argument as to whether or not the flash was working, I whispered into its ear: 'And how old are you?'

To my alarm a girl's voice said, 'Seventeen.'

I could see the banner headlines: CHILDREN'S AUTHOR MOLESTS SEVENTEEN-YEAR-OLD GIRL!

Mud sticks. FIFTY-YEAR-OLD AUTHOR DENIES CHARGE would carry little weight among those who see evil everywhere they look.

I THOUGHT IT WAS A BEAR! sounded even less convincing. Animal rights protesters would be down on me like a ton of bricks.

It was time to lie low for a while.

Fortunately, help was at hand in the shape of Ivor Wood. Having completed work on the first Wombles series, he invited me out to lunch one day and after a lot of humming and hawing and 'to tell you the truths', let fall the fact that he had been playing around with a way of animating Paddington, and what did I think about the possibility of making some films?

To tell you the truth, I was beginning to think he would never ask, and although there would be moments in the years to come when I almost wished he hadn't, I jumped at the chance. Life is nothing without a challenge and in the end it's the lost opportunities one regrets.

CHAPTER 12

Paddington on Screen

You're absolutely right!

Graham Clutterbuck on numerous occasions between 1966 and 1986

Ivor wasn't the first person to suggest making a television series about Paddington, but he was the first and only one who gave me the feeling of being on exactly the same wavelength and in whom I had total trust.

For a long while I had been tied in with a producer of the old school, an early associate of the Children's Film Foundation, who had never adjusted to the fact that television was here to stay, as inevitable as the arrival of the wheel, whether people liked it or not.

Alec Snowden never accepted it and lost no opportunity in making everybody he came into contact with aware of the fact. It didn't exactly endear him to the programme buyers, but he was caught in a time warp and there was no changing him.

Because he lived in Brighton and I was still living in Haslemere, we often held our production meetings at his London club, which again didn't help; it was against the rules to discuss business so we had to leave our briefcases in the cloakroom and talk in whispers. At least I discovered where many of the old music-hall artists went before they died. There they all were, propping up the bar of the Savage; Wee Georgie Wood, Leslie Sarony, Fred Emney and other well-known figures from the past.

It was always Alec's ambition that as soon as the films took off, as he optimistically phrased it, he would put my name up for membership, but

Karen and Brenda.
Graduation Day,
Exeter University,
12 July 1979.

With Koala Bear,
Australia 1979.

With Graham
and Sue, Fattie's
restaurant,
Singapore,
August 1979.

With Graham and Sue, 8 July 1981.

Nicholas Durbridge.

Left to right: Deborah, Stephen Durbridge and his wife, Jane, newly acquired half-sister, Gilly, Nina Froud, Alfred Bradley and self.

The restaurant 'Pic', Valence, France. The birthplace of Monsieur Pamplemousse.

Anthony leaving for Kathmandu, January 1996.

Robyn, India and Harry.

School days 'best
friend' Tim.
Jersey, 1947.

Sir Michael Hordern,
for many years the voice
of Paddington.

With Kaye Webb.

Bears don't need a
postcode!

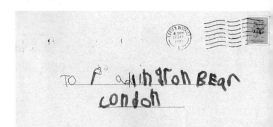

TO Paddington Bear
London

rather to my relief it was never to be put to the test. I'm not basically a clubbable person and another rule of the Savage is that no member shall ever be left sitting on his own, which would be my idea of hell – even worse than Oxford Street on the opening day of the winter sales.

The production of a half-hour live-action pilot film got off to a shaky start. British Rail wouldn't let us use Paddington Station, and in the end we had to make do with Marylebone on a Sunday morning. It wasn't exactly the hive of activity I had suggested in the script: '. . . crowded with people . . . trains whistling . . . porters rushing to and fro . . .', but at least it provided a good reason why Paddington looked so forlorn when the Browns found him.

Alec was convinced the character could be portrayed only by a midget dressed up in a bearskin, but the simple truth was that however good it looked off camera – and to my mind that was a very moot point – on film the tiniest fault was magnified. Seams, almost invisible to the naked eye, showed up as great scars, making it look as though he had been involved in a nasty accident on the way over from Peru and had subsequently been stitched up by a drunken ship's doctor in the Bay of Biscay. Anything less like the bear of my dreams would be hard to imagine.

The actor playing the part may have started off par for the course midget-wise, but by the time he was dressed up and the head was in place he looked like an oversize reject from a Disneyland audition. Attempts to compensate by casting the other characters as tall as possible failed miserably. Nothing could disguise the fact that he was too big. Nobody in their right mind would have taken him home to live with them.

There were other practical difficulties. Communication was impossible. The person inside the skin couldn't hear what was being said to him, let alone see where he was going. Once the call 'Cue action' went up, that was it. He could raise his hat, which must have been all of size 42, but he couldn't feel where his head was in order to put it back on.

Midgets also tend to be temperamental; they like to build up the part. Bereft of any possible facial expression by virtue of being inside a papier mâché head, they tend to resort to falling over backwards with their legs in the air whenever they need to register even mild surprise. Anything more startling and they start running round and round in circles. And who can blame them? Apart from the pantomime season, work isn't exactly thick on the ground – although they never seem to lack British Standard full-size girlfriends when they are resting.

Following the making of the original live-action film, when it was patently obvious that Paddington wasn't actually speaking his lines, it was decided to construct an artificial head which could be used for close-ups. Basic movements such as shaking it to and fro or nodding in order to signify disagreement or approval were carried out using a system of hand-operated gimbals. Electronically operated lip-synch for the dialogue worked up to a point but in the end only underlined the fact that on the whole bears are not great conversationalists, preferring tried and tested methods of communication handed down over the years: tight-lipped grunts or the occasional deep-throated growl.

For emotional scenes the eyes could be made to roll by means of remote control using a joystick, but when it came to giving the lids a random blink rate there were other problems. For reasons which now escape me, Alec enlisted the services of a man who had invented an automatic lawn mower.

In the case of the mower, you placed the machine in the centre of the lawn and pressed a button on a remote control, whereupon it set off towards the edge, turned left and, while it was trundling round the perimeter in an anti-clockwise direction, programmed itself to the required size and shape. Having done that it carried on in ever-decreasing circles until it ended up where it had started and switched itself off. All of which was fine if you were lucky enough to have a lawn like the proverbial billiard table; if you didn't then one bump and it was a case of chasing the machine through the flower beds before it did untold damage to the dahlias.

On the whole, dedicated inventors tend to be very single-minded – they probably need to be – but the one thing they all seem to have in common is a complete inability to accept the possibility of there being anything basically wrong with their brainchild.

When it came to the eyelids both certainly blinked in random fashion, but no one had thought to mention that in an ideal world they should both do it at the same time, with the result that the bear not only looked as though it had a particularly nasty tic in each of its glass eyes, but as if it were constantly winking at passers-by. Combined with the curling of the lips when it spoke, the overall effect was not what we'd had in mind. As the lids were also flat, made of aluminium, and emitted a whirring noise whenever they opened or closed, the overall effect made Boris Karloff's Frankenstein look like a cuddly toy.

The art of making television characters that are a sophisticated mixture of electronics and live animators had a long way to go before the arrival on the scene of Jim Henson and his Muppets set new standards.

On and off over the years, at Alec's behest, I wrote innumerable scripts: half-hour, twenty-minute, fifteen-minute and finally ten-minute versions which could be joined together to form any possible permutation according to the way the wind was blowing in the market place.

Woody Allen has said somewhere that he gives his characters short names because he doesn't like typing. When it comes to writing scripts, he has a point. The sheer mechanics of having to spell out every minor detail concerning the location and the weather and the time of day is tedious enough as it is. And that's before you start on the dialogue!

Alec was nothing if not persevering, and in his constant search for financial backing I found myself in all sorts of strange places, often sitting at vast tables in conference with the moguls of Wardour Street, forced to listen while they took my creation apart from behind a thick pall of cigar smoke.

On one memorable occasion, in the space of about a quarter of an hour, Mr Gruber's antique shop became an emporium selling old army uniforms (the designer just happened to have a relative who owned such an establishment in the Portobello Road and was sure he could book it on favourable terms), and Jonathan and Judy gained a few years in order to become teenagers with a drugs problem (I seem to remember that idea came from the director, who was clearly speaking from first-hand experience).

There were moments when it wouldn't have surprised me if someone had got up and demanded to know what a bear was doing in the story. I sometimes wondered myself!

Light relief came my way in the early seventies when I collaborated in writing a stage version of Paddington with Alfred Bradley, then a BBC Radio drama producer in Leeds. It was a fruitful experience, not least because Alfred was a lovely man who combined a very genuine enthusiasm and generosity of spirit with a great love for his craft and a never-ending fund of theatrical stories which one never tired of hearing.

Totally indefatigable in his search for new talent, over the years he had discovered, nurtured or simply helped on their way in passing a whole host of others he thought of as 'his writers'. People like Alan Ayckbourn, Keith Waterhouse, John Arden, Stan Barstow, Willis Hall (with whom I once shared a credit on a radio play), Alun Owen, Roy Clarke and Alan Plater to name but a few, and he always took enormous pleasure from their success.

The play was first staged in 1973 at the Nottingham Playhouse, and the following year it opened in London at the Duke of York's Theatre. Brenda wrote the lyrics for the songs, this time to music by Herbert Chappell.

Once again, the lead part had to be played by someone dressed up in a skin, but one advantage the stage has over film is the factor known as 'suspension of disbelief'. Provided everything else works and is seen to work, and provided the other actors enter into the spirit of the thing, it doesn't have to be perfect and audiences quickly accept what they see.

Even so, there were times when for one unforeseen reason or another the play didn't work and not only did disbelief have to be temporarily suspended, but everything else as well, including the production.

On one occasion the actor playing Paddington was wearing a half-mask and in order to lend verisimilitude to the part, came up with the idea of gluing a black ping-pong ball to the end of his own nose. It worked well enough until he caught a bad cold and the glue dissolved. The sound of a bear's nose bouncing all over the stage hotly pursued by its owner is unique and won a well-deserved round of applause.

Then there was the time in Scotland when the company borrowed a trolley from British Rail for the opening scene on Paddington Station. Unfortunately, it didn't arrive until just before the curtain rose. What they hadn't bargained on was its being of a kind normally seen only in railway museums; enormously heavy and with a mind of its own. The stage had an unusually steep rake to it, and no sooner had the unfortunate actor playing the part of a porter made his entrance than it moved off of its own accord, rapidly gathering speed as it headed towards the footlights. As it disappeared into the orchestra pit there was an enormous crash and everything went black.

The noise level in children's productions is normally quite high, but that night it must have broken all records.

The inevitable late start was all the more unfortunate because Brenda and I had taken my father up to see it and we had to leave early to catch the last plane back. My mother was to have come too, but the thought of flying had kept her awake all night with palpitations, so she stayed at home.

It was the first and only time my father went up in the air and we never really discovered what he thought of it. During the journey up to Scotland I kept pointing out items of interest, like unusual cloud forma-tions, but he was much more concerned with the contents of his food tray and all he kept saying was: 'Yes, very nice.'

On the way back he couldn't wait to tuck in again.

When we got him home, my mother was waiting at the front door, clearly 'all keyed-up inside' as she called it. She greeted us with, 'Thank God you're back safely!', and that was that. The front door was closed on air travel for the rest of their days.

Since I shared the writing honours with Alfred Bradley, it's only fair that I should share the blame for any faults in the play's construction, but the truth is that when it came to be written it underlined one very fundamental fact which I had managed to gloss over in the film scripts.

Paddington himself doesn't normally have a lot to say. The humour lies mostly in the reader being a privileged party to the workings of his mind. Once you start giving Paddington too much dialogue you run the risk of making him seem either foolish or rude, both of which are totally out of character.

With this in mind, and given my unhappy experiences with live-action filming, I was very much open to suggestions when it came to television.

Ivor's plan, which he unfolded over a plate of squid and a bottle of wine in a local Greek restaurant, was to combine stop-frame animation of a fully articulated three-dimensional model Paddington with animated two-dimensional cardboard cutouts for the other characters, in a three-dimensional setting.

It was a simple idea, but it hadn't been tried before – certainly not on a large scale.

'Would it work?' Knowing Ivor it was a silly question.

'To tell you the truth . . .' After lunch he went back to his studios at FilmFair and he showed me some experimental footage.

There it all was on the screen. A living, breathing, tactile Paddington, as near to the original Peggy Fortnum illustrations as possible. Being three-dimensional, and wearing his traditional blue duffle coat, he naturally stood out from the other characters, but above all he had dignity and warmth. It was possible to get pleasure simply from watching him in repose or walking across a room. The sets, intentionally muted in colour, gave the effect of a sixties Peter Brook stage production, when splashes of brighter colours directed the eyes of the audience to what they were meant to see.

The BBC agreed that it had been worth waiting for and immediately commissioned thirty 5-minute episodes. Of course, all of us – Graham Clutterbuck, Ivor Wood and myself – inwardly rubbed our hands and breathed a sigh of relief. Who wouldn't? That's what we had all been hoping for, and I rubbed mine as hard as anyone.

The BBC pencilled in a date on their schedules and moved on to other problems, as is the wont of television schedulers the world over, and we all went back to Graham's office to celebrate.

Graham had moved several times before finally installing a rapidly expanding FilmFair in a row of mews cottages near Marylebone High Street.

His first-floor office was much more in keeping with his chosen image. The thickly carpeted floor sported an antique Chinese rug in the middle. Table lamps were dotted around the room, and through the glass one could see windowboxes full of freshly watered flowers. Pictures adorned the walls, including some delicate drawings made by his son, Micky, of whose work he was rightly proud; mostly heads and hands executed in sepia crayon in the style of Michelangelo.

There was no sign of a desk. Instead, there was a sofa along one wall, where Graham spent most of his working time, taking telephone calls, dictating letters, wheeling and dealing, bargaining and cajoling, while metaphorically wearing one or other of his many hats.

Disliking arguments of any kind, 'You're absolutely right' became his stock phrase. It was the ultimate soft answer which turned away the wrath, cutting the ground from beneath anyone who showed the slightest sign of being difficult.

On the wall behind the sofa there was a vast blow-up of the historic, never to be repeated photograph taken at MGM's twenty-fifth anniversary luncheon, when all the stars were present. Like me, Graham had been brought up during a period when cinema-going was a way of life, and he liked nothing better than being able to identify Hollywood players of the thirties and forties. I think he also secretly enjoyed the thought of all those famous names watching him at work.

As with many extrovert characters, he was a shy person at heart and the various trappings with which he surrounded himself made a useful conversational gambit whenever someone new paid him a visit.

A well-stocked refrigerator completed the decor, and although I didn't realize it at the time, the room was to become a kind of home from home for me too as pressures mounted; a haven of lunch-time peace where we could share our sandwiches and our problems.

Graham's experience with the Wombles, together with the years I had spent working in television, should have warned me of what might be in store. Not that it would have made me change my mind, for it was already made up and after so many abortive attempts in the past, I was keen to accept the challenge of something I knew could be made to work.

The natural length for the Paddington stories is around twenty minutes' reading time. Many of the plots depend for their effect on a slow build-up, splitting the reader down the middle as disaster looms, one half wanting to call out and warn Paddington to stop right where he is, the other half secretly wanting him to carry on in order to see how he gets out of trouble – which, or course, he always does. It was beginning to sink in that five minutes, minus perhaps forty-five seconds for the credits, was no time at all in which to convey all this.

In some ways, fixed time slots are the curse of television, for they often over-ride artistic considerations, but one has to work with things as they are, not as one would like them to be.

Ivor was anxious to see something on paper so that he could begin work as soon as possible in order to meet the deadline. As it was, he knew that the opening episodes would most likely be going on the air while he was still filming. Graham's mind was already on cash flows and the hundred and one other things to do with producing a series.

Having stuck out for using narration, it was once again a case of looking for the right voice.

Anyone who has ever read a story out loud to a child has their own idea of how voices should sound, just as most people reading a story to themselves can 'hear' the characters in their mind. The nearest I came to hearing a definitive Paddington voice in real life was on an almost deserted beach in Crete when an extremely elderly German strolled past talking to his wife in what can only be described as a 'high-pitched, gruff voice'. The Beatles one-time Indian guru came a close second. But in the end, since it doesn't exist, it can go in any direction.

It was another good reason for using a narrator. Not only would it allow one to be a party to Paddington's thoughts and idiosyncratic powers of reasoning, but when he did speak it would be a kind of arm's-length transaction, leaving the viewer with the option of accepting it or substituting their own voice as the spirit moved them.

Of the many possibilities we auditioned over the next few weeks, Harry Worth stays in my mind. But as he said somewhat apologetically before he started: 'I'm afraid I shall turn it into the *Harry Worth Show*,' which he promptly did. Great fun, but not what was needed.

He put his finger on a problem which besets many British comedy films. We have a large pool of 'characters' who are called on to do their act, which they do to perfection, but it's not always what the author had in mind and it doesn't necessarily produce a smooth and integrated whole in the way that many American or Continental films do.

It was Monica Sims, by then head of children's programmes at the BBC, who suggested Sir Michael (then plain Michael) Hordern. His opening comment, delivered in sonorous tones as he settled himself down at the microphone and glanced through the script was, 'I don't do voices.'

But, of course, in his own quiet way, with little changes of inflection here and there, he did. Very soon, I found myself hearing his voice when I wrote and began tailoring the scripts accordingly. It was a rewarding way of working, for he was a wonderfully professional actor, totally devoid of airs and graces, and always giving of his best, no matter what. Having him read the scripts with his unique and immediately recognizable delivery was an enormous privilege, and one which I am sure Paddington himself would appreciate no end.

Once, when we were leaving the studios after recording half a dozen episodes, he confided to me that it was a funny old world. 'I'm just off to the Television Centre to play the part of God!'

I'm sure the Almighty was as delighted as he was.

An ever-present problem when transferring a subject from one medium to another is that of pacing and of trying to retain the natural rhythm of the original. What can take several pages to describe in a book can be shown in a matter of moments on the screen. Similarly, but in reverse, dialogue which takes only a few seconds to sight read can easily stretch into minutes.

Armed with a stop-watch and going through the motions of the camera directions as I wrote them down, allowing roughly a minute per page, I knew that if Paddington wasn't out of trouble by the end of page four, Ivor would be in an even worse state.

There were other things to watch out for. Objects passed between Paddington and another character meant cutting away to a reaction shot so that it could change from being three-dimensional to two-dimensional, or vice versa. Any kind of shot involving running water was out. The only saving grace was that none of the cast belonged to a union, none of them expected to be paid overtime, and there were no displays of temperament when their best lines were cut. The sole casualties were the girls who had to make the hundreds of cardboard cutouts needed to create the illusion of movement. Most of them went home at night with bandaged fingers.

There was also a problem with Paddington's fur. As the star of the show he was on screen practically all the time and with between six and seven thousand separate pictures per episode he had to be handled very carefully in case he wore out before the end of the series.

In a curious way, because Paddington was a puppet and very watchable even in repose, it was possible to create the effect of time passing in a rather more leisurely fashion than it did in reality.

An episode called 'Paddington Makes a Bid' was a good example of how much could be packed into a short space of time without its ever looking rushed. In just over three and three-quarter minutes, Paddington, paying his first visit to some auction rooms with his friend, Mr Gruber, raises his hat to all and sundry while taking his seat and finds to his astonishment that he has bought a carpentry set. After Mr Gruber explains to him that it is dangerous to make any kind of movement at an auction, he sits very still for a while until he realizes his friend is bidding for an old highwayman's pistol. In his excitement, Paddington starts bidding against him, forcing the price up far beyond what Mr Gruber originally intended paying. However, later on Paddington makes

up for his mistake when he acquires a silver preserves stand for ten pence
– causing consternation among hardened dealers in the process, many
of whom had their eyes on it too.

At the end of it all, Paddington still finds time to test his purchase
over elevenses back at Mr Gruber's shop – philosophizing on the fact
that eating marmalade out of an antique makes it taste even better than
usual.

The first series was transmitted in 1975. It was budgeted at a little
over £60,000, of which the BBC were to pay about one-fifth. For that
they acquired the right to unlimited transmissions over a period of seven
years.

It sounds a one-sided deal, but given Graham's need to bridge the
financial gap as quickly as possible by the sale of merchandise, their early
evening spot was hard to beat. It caught the tail end of the children's
programmes with a guaranteed audience of several million, plus a growing
number of adults arriving home in time to catch the news.

Letters addressed to 'Paddington, 32 Windsor Gardens, Lundun', or
simply 'Paddington Bear, England', started to arrive even quicker than
if they'd had a postcode.

In the beginning, if a child had laboriously written to me in capital
letters I did the same in reply, hoping he or she would be able to read
it, but very soon they all got joined-up writing, and then even that
became too time-consuming and they had to be typed.

Fan letters, in fact, became an increasing problem. All deserved a
reply, but many wanted at the very least a signed photograph of the
author together with a picture of Paddington, plus answers to long ques-
tionnaires. All very flattering, but very few enclosed the return postage,
let alone a stamped addressed envelope. I was determined not to resort
to a standard printed reply, but given the time involved in writing back,
plus the mounting cost of servicing all the requests, there were moments
when I found myself wondering how many books would need to be sold
that day in order to pay for it all.

I felt better about it when a letter arrived from a certain J. B. Scranton
in California thanking me for taking the trouble to write back, saying
he knew my letter was genuine because he could feel the bumps on the
back of the notepaper!

And on the same side of the coin, by way of thanks other faithful fans, like Jason Schiller, must have spent a great deal of their pocket money searching out bigger and better cards to brighten my Christmas – and still do.

The Herbs had been my first introduction to the world of merchandising, but that had been written for an audience which didn't have any great buying power, and at a time when manufacturers and others were not yet alive to how much free advertising they were being offered. Consequently, the films took a long time to recover their cost. Relying on the sale of merchandise to pay for the making of a series can be a risky business, and not really what it should be about.

The success of the Wombles changed all that and when Paddington went on the air it soon became clear that having kicked a ball into play, there was no stopping it. The most that could be hoped for was to try as far as possible to keep it heading in the right direction, avoiding any kind of excess.

Often manufacturers would jump the gun, turning up with samples direct from the production line almost before the ink on their contract was dry. In retrospect, many of the things I spent sleepless nights over at the time now have a curiosity value. All the same, I'm still glad to have turned down Paddington toilet rolls, not to mention a fur-covered wastepaper bin with a removable head, both of which were suggested in the early days.

Fortunately, the stuffed bear designed by Shirley Clarkson of Gabrielle Designs had been licensed long before the films went into production. Originally made one Christmas as a present for Shirley's and her husband Eddie's two children, Joanna and Jeremy, it remains a classic of its kind – one which still gives me pleasure whenever I see it – and it served as a kind of yardstick when judging other products. Some things, like Concorde and the Jaguar XK120 look right from the very beginning. Shirley's Paddington 'looked right' from the word go. It was created with love and it was born with that indefinable something known as 'star quality'. You either have it or you don't.

Soon after the Clarksons went into production, the brothers Richard and David Miller, co-owners of a company called Eden Toys Inc., flew in from New York, determined not to return home until they had secured the rights to manufacture Paddington Bear in America.

Perhaps it has something to do with the tactile nature of the end product, but whatever the reason, the makers of the soft toy Paddington have always enjoyed a special place in the scheme of things, an important part of 'the family' as Graham liked to put it, and in both cases they have become firm friends.

Eddie and Shirley Clarkson managed to surmount the ignominy of being the first 'pirates' on the scene and, until he was laid low by a debilitating bone disease, Eddie was indefatigable in his search for what he considered to be the right outlets for their product, touring the country, not simply *selling* Paddington, but deciding where it was right for him to be seen. Upsetting many potential stockists on the way, he remained firm in his resolve that nothing but the best would do. The bestowal of his favour was little short of a royal appointment.

Such exclusivity often breeds a desire for ownership and the Gabrielle Bear soon became something of a cult object, photographed in the arms of the rich and famous as they travelled the world. In 1980 the *Washington Post* listed Paddington among the 'In' people and things of the year, along with marriage, cotton undies, Meryl Streep and Bruce Springsteen. At the same time he began to appear in magazine advertisements, unnamed and unreferred to; his very presence in the background a symbol of integrity and reliability.

Richard Miller, who in time took over sole control of Eden Toys from his brother David, has always run an entirely different operation from the Clarksons.

If Gabrielle's strength lies in its having remained a cottage industry, then Eden Toys' lies in its ability to manufacture in quantity and with all the American expertise and bargaining power that goes with it.

The difference between the two can perhaps best be summed up by the fact that when the initial agreements were drawn up, both companies contracted to pay royalties on a sliding scale according to how many they sold. Gabrielle's go up, Eden Toys's go down.

The fact that over two decades later both versions continue to live happily alongside each other and can be found in most countries of the world, says a great deal for all parties concerned – especially perhaps Paddington.

If ever I had feelings of doubt over a product, I used to ask myself what Paddington himself would think of it. If I thought he would give it a hard stare, that answered the question. He was a great source of comfort, always keeping his feet firmly on the ground, and I still find myself seeking his advice from time to time.

Somewhere along the line it dawned on me that my life was no longer my own; in an indefinable way it had become public property. One brief appearance on a television chat show, and for a day or two afterwards people recognize you in the street. Taxi drivers tell you what's wrong with the world in general and with television in particular. People from far-flung parts of the world started burdening me with their problems; others would turn up out of the blue at unlikely times, taking it for granted that they would be invited in. In some cases, they became friends and have remained that way ever since, others simply went on their way, never to be seen again. In fairness, I have enough reciprocal invitations to last me the rest of my life, particularly from Americans, who are genuinely and sometimes overwhelmingly hospitable.

Hardly a post went by without there being some unforeseen, unpredictable, and in some cases totally unanswerable query of one kind or another. And there still are.

'I have recently come back from Australia where my friend has bought a business. The shop has vertical blinds with one section cut out . . .' The missing piece was in the shape of Paddington Bear! Where could the friend buy another blind?

Although fan mail can become a problem, letters from children tend to be short, sharp and to the point. No child is going to bother writing a letter unless it's to say they like something, so one shouldn't feel too flattered. All the same, it was hard not to feel a warm glow when I opened a letter one day which said: 'Your stories make me have pictures in my head.'

That, to me, made it all worthwhile, for it rekindled the joy and excitement I felt when my father first introduced me to the *Magnet*.

Another letter which gave me great pleasure at the time came from an adult. He said that what he liked about the Paddington books was my attitude to the colour question. Since I had never brought the subject up directly, I can only think he saw Paddington as a kind of universal outsider and took heart from the fact that he is accepted without question by an alien society. It would have been nice to have been able to show it to Neville Cohen's father.

Letters from charities and organizers of fêtes wanting items for auction soon denuded me of anything loose about my person.

The Japanese, who are nothing if not thorough, started bombarding me with questions no one had ever asked before, like: 'What is Paddington's name in Peruvian?' and 'What did his uncle do for a living?' – things I have to admit I had never even thought about.

When the first query came up it so happened I was staying in New York with my cousin Roger, who nowadays lectures on security at the John Jay Police College. Emma, his indefatigable Colombian wife, who likes nothing better than having a problem to solve and doesn't take 'No' for an answer, immediately went into action and after much deliberation her embassy came up with 'Pastuzo', meaning 'slow-moving and solid', which seemed eminently suitable.

Problem number two was solved entirely by chance.

Through Graham I had come to know the Hungarian owner of a small art gallery in Devonshire Street. Like most Hungarians, he was generous with his food and wine, and because he hated eating alone he would often go out into the street and drag complete strangers inside to join him over slices of *saucisson* and a bottle of red wine, or, during the summer months, fresh shrimps with a glass or two of chilled white wine.

I daresay his motives weren't entirely altruistic, for after lunch we would all troop down to his basement, where he had literally hundreds of unpriced paintings stored in racks.

Vin rouge and vin blanc both lend enchantment, and over the years both Graham and I bought quite a few.

One day a young American couple, who obviously didn't know what had hit them, joined us in the back room. Over lunch the man let fall the fact that he was a geologist, lately returned from South America where he had been investigating the presence of various rare minerals.

It was his opinion that the people who made money in Darkest Peru were not the natives who slaved away all day up in the mountains doing the digging, but the few who imported Coca-Cola and followed on behind selling it at vastly inflated prices.

It seemed an ideal occupation for Paddington's uncle, who I had always pictured as a kind of Walter Huston character; a lovable rogue.

But those were the lighter moments. In the mail there were a growing number of letters clearly written by professionals.

Autograph dealers were easy to spot; their letters, usually over-full of praise, were neatly laid out and always enclosed a stamped addressed envelope along with cardboard packing so that any reply wouldn't get bent in the post, but others were more demanding.

One or two resorted to a mild form of blackmail. They usually began: 'You probably won't remember this, but . . .' Ronald Searle told of one such letter from a woman who said she had nursed him back to health after his time as a Japanese prisoner of war. 'You probably won't remember me because you were delirious at the time . . .' I once heard from a man who said that years before he had met me in a public house in Praed Street. I had just written a book about a bear and was looking for a name. He had suggested Paddington . . . He even gave me the exact date. Unfortunately it was some time after the first book was published.

Some letters came straight out with it. Assuming I was now rich beyond measure, they would ask for specific sums of money, painting a dismal picture of what life would be like for their six starving children if I didn't cough up a couple of hundred pounds or so. Occasionally the letters were photostats with only the name of the addressee changed.

In fact, although for a time a lot of money was being generated, the films had yet to be paid for, after which all the other interested parties received their share, and since it was also a time when the rate of income tax had reached its highest level there wasn't that much left at the end of the day.

Hard on the heels of the merchandising came the inevitable pirates. Petticoat Lane on a Sunday morning began to see more and more badly made copies of the toy bear. Even Mrs Thatcher appeared in the press clutching one. T-shirts provided another rich area for rip-offs. All the cases had to be followed up, to protect the manufacturers and the general public, but also the integrity of Paddington himself. One case alone, involving copyright infringement on a T-shirt in America, resulted in damages of $10,000, but cost $100,000 to pursue. For a while, until the rip-off merchants saw the red light, it seemed as though the only people making money out of Paddington were the lawyers.

Graham's office was no longer a haven of peace. The telephone hardly stopped ringing and intelligent unbroken conversation became impossible. During one such interruption I happened to glance idly at the picture of the MGM party and realized it had undergone a skilful operation, rather in the manner of the doctored pictures one sometimes sees taken in Russia during Stalin's regime. Edward Arnold, who had been sitting in the front row between Fred Astaire and Lassie, had been replaced by Graham, clutching a Paddington Bear.

The publishers wanted to bring out a series of books based on the stories in the films and, like everyone else, they needed them yesterday if not before.

Sandwiched in between there would be visits to factories: to Glasgow to see greeting cards being made, to the Potteries for chinaware, somewhere else again I came across a giant machine being fed raw tin-plate at one end and spewing out wastepaper bins adorned with Paddington's likeness at the other. Picturing a world flooded with them, I longed to press the stop button, but the strange thing was that in many cases once the goods left the factory they disappeared into a gaping void. I don't think I have ever seen a Paddington wastepaper bin in anyone's home, although at the time thousands must have been sold.

Ignoring the fact that characters who enjoy longevity are almost always created by someone for no better reason than that they *wanted* to write about them, I began receiving scripts from people anxious to jump on what they fondly imagined was the bandwagon: usually a mediocre story line clearly tossed off as quickly as possible, with a note saying, 'Please see attached list of merchandising possibilities.'

In spring and autumn there would be the trade fairs; for gifts, for stationery, for books, for practically everything one could put a name to; all looking exactly the same, wherever the venue. Endless rows of stands swarming with the buyers and the sellers, distinguishable from each other only by the intensity of their fixed smiles and the number of pamphlets they were carrying, for the most part fair-weather friends.

Being a writer cum many other things, I at least had the advantage of being hard to categorize.

By then, having grown tired of wandering the streets killing time between meetings, I had formed my own company with an office in Soho. I was still commuting from Haslemere, which meant leaving home at some unearthly hour to get up to London ahead of the rush. After a quick whisky to wake me up and set my mind working, it was a case of writing the first draft of a script before the phone started ringing. After nine o'clock there would be a constant stream of people knocking on the door. At night, having waited for the evening rush hour to die down, there would be the drive home in time for a late supper, a sleeping pill and bed.

It was the kind of schedule you can keep up for only so long.

Secretaries came and went. Nice girls all, most of them rendered starry-eyed by magic words like 'Paddington' and 'films' and 'scripts' and 'Soho' – not realizing that it meant endless typing, filing, and all the other chores which go with working in an office.

An exception was Deborah, a distant relative of Maureen O'Sullivan, the Hollywood actress. She had the same lovely blue eyes and brought a feeling of calm and Irish serendipity to the office.

Maureen O'Sullivan's photograph adorns the front cover of an old *Film Pictorial* of mine dated 27 July 1936. The advertisements inside are reminiscent of those which used to appear in the *Magnet* of my boyhood, except that they are aimed at girls and interestingly have headings like 'Why Be Thin?' and 'Who's Skinny Now! – 5 More Pounds Last Week – Thanks to Vikelp Tablets!'

Deborah used to ride to work on an old bicycle which she immobilized during the day with a combination padlock. Given the fact that numbers weren't her strong point, I asked her one day how she remembered the combination.

'Ah, 'tis no problem. I've written them on the outside!'

Some of her predecessors arrived wreathed in smiles and left after a week sobbing their hearts out, leaving me with half-completed VAT returns and the washing-up. Many of them couldn't type properly anyway, and certainly couldn't spell, and there is nothing more embarrassing than presenting a badly typed, misspelled, and above all badly copied script at a recording session.

Sir Michael Hordern once read an entire page on which the last words on the right-hand side had been cut off by the copying machine and still managed to make sense out of it, although seen from the control room he did have a wonderfully puzzled expression on his face.

One day while having an early breakfast at the Regent Palace Hotel before starting work, I found myself sitting at the counter next to an American who very politely asked the waiter if he could possibly have his order as quickly as possible as he had a plane to catch.

The waiter looked him straight in the eye and said very slowly and clearly, 'You'll get your breakfast, Sir, the same as everyone else in this establishment. *Slowly!*' He meant it, and we all suffered as well.

I used to love Soho at that time of the day, before the tourists arrived. It was like a small village, full of familiar faces. To have an office of my own there was in a way the fulfilment of a dream; on a par with having an apartment off Broadway or a studio in Montmartre. By dawn's early light even Carnaby Street possesses a certain charm.

But as I said goodbye to my fellow diner that morning and set off towards my office, I felt the beginnings of disenchantment setting in.

Everything was going well. The television series had been completed and was starting to sell around the world. I was just about managing to keep my head above water with all the work, but somehow at the end of three years there seemed to be even less hours in the day than there had been when I left the BBC. I had my fingers in too many pies.

It's nice to have done different things in life, to have had sudden changes of direction. Not so much at the time perhaps, but afterwards to be able to say: 'Yes, I did that for a while.' However, I felt the need to get back to writing and I no longer had 'thinking time'. Apart from a yearly Paddington story for the *Blue Peter Annual*, which was getting progressively more difficult to write as new presenters came and went, and a strip cartoon in the London *Evening News*, writing had come to mean creating slogans for the backs of packets, for which there was a constant demand by manufacturers. Worse still, my personal life was in tatters.

It would be totally wrong to blame the hectic life I had been leading for the break-up of my first marriage, but it hadn't helped. In some ways it provided a convenient excuse for moving away from home, but in the end I did so with enormous sadness and a deep sense of failure at having let others down. It still surfaces from time to time when something happens to remind me. The fact that years later Brenda and I are still the best of friends – perhaps more so than if we had stayed together – is something of a minor miracle.

One lunchtime I found myself jog-trotting down Beak Street in search of a sandwich because I didn't have time to walk.

Later that day I jokingly told Harvey Unna about it over the telephone. There was a moment's silence. 'That's not right. We can't have that.'

He rang back a day or so later. 'I've been thinking about your problem. Now, what you must do is . . .'

One of Harvey's more illustrious clients was the playwright Francis Durbridge, creator of *Paul Temple*, *The World of Tim Fraser*, and other long-running radio and television series. He had two sons, both in the business; Stephen, a film and television agent, later to go into partnership with Harvey, and Nicholas, a lawyer who specialized in copyright matters and had in fact been handling many of the infringements against Paddington.

Nicholas, it seemed, had itchy feet and was looking for new horizons. 'Take him out to lunch and make him an offer he can't refuse.'

Harvey was right, and to borrow Paddington's phrase yet again, 'He needed no second bidding.'

Suddenly there was a new managing director sitting in *my* chair at *my* desk, answering *my* telephone.

It was one of the best pieces of advice I ever had.

Emotionally drained, I retired into my shell in a flat at the Barbican, that concrete jungle erected over a period of some twenty-six years on a barren bombsite in the City of London; an architect's dream gone sadly wrong. Although there must be people living there happily, I never encountered any of them during my three-year stay. It was before the arts centre had opened up and potential visitors who braved the journey by road tended to get lost on the way, finding themselves heading towards Southend or worse, as indeed I did on several occasions when I first moved in. More often than not those who finally made it fell victim to vandals who had great sport moving the adhesive YOU ARE HERE arrows attached to various maps dotted about the vast area.

There was a fortnightly free magazine – or it may have been weekly or monthly, after a while time ceased to have any meaning at the Barbican – and in it there was a column written by someone who called himself 'The Stroller'. It never ceased to amaze me that come rain or come shine he always discovered things to write about during his rambles.

My own nightly explorations were nowhere near as rewarding as his and in the end I gave them up for fear of being accused of persistent voyeurism. It was hard not to look in other people's windows, although I can't say I ever saw anything exciting going on when I did.

All the flats were provided with balconies. In Italy during the summer months they would have been alive with people – and laundry too, I dare say, although that would have been contrary to the tenancy agreement – but one never saw anyone making use of them. A lone figure on a balcony would have prompted the thought that perhaps they were about to end it all.

There was a scattering of small shops, including a delicatessen run by an Indian lady who had a perpetual cold, and a photographer where I used to get my films processed. One of the assistants had an annoying habit of opening the packet when you went to collect it.

'Just to make sure it's the right one, Sir.'

He would then proceed to go through the prints very slowly, one by one, passing comments as he went, ignoring the queue which was beginning to form behind you.

'Oh, dear me, Sir. What happened here?' When all you had done was take a few shots of your right foot in order to use up the film.

'Ah, I see you've been to the South of France, Sir.'

Followed by: 'Would this be your daughter, Sir? The young lady in the bikini?'

On one such occasion, rather than respond with the usual snarl between clenched teeth as I made an abortive grab for the rest of the pile, the truthful answer would have been: 'No, it happens to be the mother of my child to be.' I doubt if it would have stopped him in his tracks, but at least it would have kept the rest of the queue quiet.

Eve and I had a long and at times very happy relationship in the late sixties when I was writing the Thursday books and she was my editor. What began with casual encounters over such mundane matters as word counts and book promotions gradually blossomed into extra-curricular activities of a strictly non-publishable kind.

Statistically, for example, there can't be many girls who, finding themselves ensconced in a four-poster bed, are so laid-back they use the time to catch up on their reading of a book on car maintenance. But such was the sight which greeted me as I emerged from a bathroom at Broadway's famed Lygon Arms Hotel late one night, freshly pomaded and wearing my Noël Coward-type dressing-gown.

Even less likely is the possibility that on that very same night the local branch of the National Farmers' Union would be holding their annual get-together, and that she would have standing in the back of her Morris Minor a life-size model of Beatrix Potter's Pigling Bland; a sitting target for bucolic revelry when the party eventually broke up and everyone staggered out to collect their cars.

As we crept out to the car park in order to cover P. Bland, Esq. with a blanket, I told myself that it was the kind of situation which ought to be grist to a writer's mill and that one day I would use it, which I suppose is why I mention it now.

Although in the end Eve and I were too opposite in our outlook on life for our relationship to become permanent, out of it came Anthony, of whom we are both very proud. He has successfully surmounted the problem of growing up with a part-time father, and although there have been times when I'm sure both of us would have wished things were otherwise, who can ever say for sure what is right? The best that one can do is always keep one's promises and to be on hand when needed, which I have always tried to do, and to offer advice when needed – bearing in mind Oscar Wilde's famous dictum: 'All advice is bad. Good advice is fatal.'

Anthony was born while I was living at the Barbican and, although he won't remember it, before they moved out of London, he and his mother occasionally came to stay.

Lying in his carry-cot, he would have looked out on a vast rectangular stretch of water which, when I first went there, was well stocked with a variety of mature, not to say expensive, fish.

Sometimes Eve and I took Anthony to see them. Then one day a man who professed to be an expert on the subject reported that they were suffering from a rare disease. His offer to treat them for what seemed like a not unreasonable sum, payable in advance, was accepted. Shortly afterwards he took them all away in a van and was never seen again.

On the day I finally left the Barbican I bumped into a nodding acquaintance in the lift who summed it up admirably.

'Ah, I see you've served your sentence!'

The thought seemed to cheer him up, holding out some kind of hope for the future. If I could do it, perhaps he could too.

The Barbican was a soulless place, but I shouldn't be too hard on it. Even during my most gloomy moments, the times when I went to bed at night not caring overmuch whether or not I woke in the morning, I was always aware that compared with millions of others I was living in luxury. At least my time there had given me the chance to readjust and to start writing again. I became more adventurous with my cooking and the results couldn't have been too bad because one summer Karen came to stay, prefacing her visit with: 'Don't worry, Daddy, there's no need to do anything special – I shall be out every evening!'

And she didn't go out at all, which was lovely. It was one of the nicest summers I'd had for a long time.

CHAPTER 13

Travels With Graham

To travel hopefully is a better thing than to arrive.

Robert Louis Stevenson (1850–94)

During the seventies Graham and I travelled hopefully across France many times, and never once did we meet with disappointment on the way. Our ultimate destination was Cannes and the Marché International Programmes-Télévision, the annual television festival known as MIP.

The majority of British companies taking part either flew there or drove like maniacs all the way down in one day, only to arrive red-eyed and worn out before they started work, having seen little or nothing of the countryside en route. We did that once, before the great Autoroute du Sud was completed, and decided that once was enough.

Driving was not something Graham was best at. He was much too interested in all that was going on around him to concentrate on the job in hand for very long at a time. He had a distressing tendency to go through lights when they were at red, dismissing cries of alarm from the passenger seat with remarks like: 'I know, but just look at that glorious sunset.' It didn't go down too well in English, let alone in French.

Nor was his car, an elderly Bentley known as 'Dud', ideal for the journey. Dud was built with places like Glyndebourne in mind. Although the name was derived from the number plate, it was very apt, for it spent most of its days in one garage or another having its front bumper replaced or dents removed, often because Graham had been too busy conducting to watch the road ahead and had failed to stop in time at a roundabout.

One of the costliest presents he was ever given was a Sony portable CD player, which resulted in both Dud's front wings ending up being almost entirely made of fibreglass.

When Dud *was* road-worthy, setting out in it was not so much a matter of going for a spin as of embarking on a voyage of discovery in a stately ocean liner. Other hazards, apart from Graham at the wheel, were semaphore-type trafficators which stuck open and had to be returned manually or, to put it another way, by means of a sharp clout through an open window; and a button which, according to Graham, oiled all the vital parts when pressed. But on the one occasion when he demonstrated it during a heavy snowstorm on the way to Paris, the engine seized up completely and that was that for a while.

There was also a lever he could pull if he didn't like the look of the car behind, or if the driver started flashing him at night to indicate disapproval. It lowered a venetian blind over the rear window and thus temporarily solved the problem – at least as far as Graham was concerned – out of sight being out of mind.

Once, when for some reason we were returning from Cannes separately, I was on the docks at Calais, one in a long line of cars all waiting patiently for the signal to begin boarding the ferry, when all of a sudden the afternoon peace was shattered by a loud crash from somewhere several cars behind me.

It was followed by a familiar voice. 'I'm terribly sorry, dear boy. Entirely my fault. I'll give you a telephone number. Ring my secretary first thing in the morning.' It wasn't Mahler on that occasion, he had been looking for his passport.

Graham's secretaries spent a lot of their time dealing with such mundane matters and became expert at knowing how to get Dud shipped back home from far-flung places in the shortest possible time.

By mutual consent, we decided early on that the best arrangement was for me to drive my car while Graham settled himself down in the passenger seat, planning the route and looking for suitable places to stay overnight.

I enjoy driving in France, especially when I have a target to aim for, and Graham was not only a very good navigator, but the *Michelin Guide* ranked as one of his favourite reads. He would go to endless trouble searching out the red rocking chair symbol for peace and quiet, and then issue an estimated time of arrival.

'We should get there by seven – just in time for a bath before dinner.'

That, of course, was reckoning without stops en route. After a hearty breakfast followed by a quick stroll to take in the surroundings, we invariably decided to go without lunch, but somehow it never worked out that way. Around one o'clock good resolutions fell by the wayside when Graham caught sight of some little hotel situated on a river bank miles from anywhere, its tiny car park full of cars and long-distance lorries; always a good sign, for it meant people had gone out of their way to eat there.

We took the Route de Cidre in Normandy and numerous routes des grands crus or routes des fruits elsewhere, and sometimes followed the Route Napoleon, long and winding and tiring unless you have power steering. But in springtime, when the fruit trees are in blossom and each turn reveals a new valley awash with blossom, a joy to behold.

And everywhere we went we ate the food of the region. We discovered mussels with almonds in the Basque country, preceded by *pousse rapière* – made with orange, Armagnac and sparkling wine. There was cassoulet in the Languedoc, and there were *quennelles* in Lyons – made from puréed pike and served with Nantua sauce (white wine and crayfish). In Perigord I tasted my first truffles and decided that, like Moselet, when my time came 'I would like to be buried *aux truffes*'. In Provence there were great platters of *fruits de mer*, for if it moves on the ocean bed the French will surely eat it. And afterwards, Graham, who freely admitted to being a bit of a pig at times, would tuck into a *tarte St Honoré*, then wipe his mouth and say: 'I feel sick.' Luckily he was able to keep fit by playing tennis regularly.

In Annecy there was freshly caught *omble* from the lake, and in Orléans we toyed with *pain d'épices*, made with hazelnuts, almonds and honey, and Graham felt sick all over again.

Then there would be churches to visit. Although I was educated by Brothers, I never became a Roman as my mother would have said, but that doesn't stop me getting a feeling of belonging whenever I enter a Catholic church; an honorary member because of my schooling, so to speak, or so I tell myself.

To me, they always have a 'lived in' feel about them. Worshippers come and go and have a kind of air, as though they know something which other people don't. It doesn't necessarily make them any happier, and certainly no better, but by comparison the Church of England seems very sterile. You need to be pretty secure in your beliefs to be able to wander in and out of a church service. But then real Catholics quite unashamedly pray for all manner of things, like divine guidance when filling in their pools coupons, or a good win on the lottery.

Although I very rarely pray for things for myself, believing that the Lord helps those who help themselves, my Catholic education left its mark in other ways. Lighting candles for others gives me great satisfaction and solace, and I still find myself occasionally doing things the hard way as a kind of penance and because I think it will be good for my soul.

I'm also grateful because my upbringing gave me a belief in God, and I can't picture being without that. Prayer focuses your thoughts on others and helps make your own problems seem trivial by comparison.

France is a large country. One tends to forget quite how large, and many of the places we stayed at are lost beyond recall, but on other occasions a whole train of events would be set in motion.

At the Hôtel Pernollet in Belley, in the foothills of the Jura Mountains east of Lyon, where Gertrude Stein and Alice B. Toklas often spent their summers in the twenties, we were served a local cheese – Tomme de Belley. The madame watched over us solicitously while we ate it, for 'it wasn't exactly the correct season – a little early'. From her we learned that Brillat-Savarin had been born there on 1 April 1755, which led me to read M. F. K. Fisher's translation of his great work *Physiologie du Goût*.

Over the years that led me to collect all her many delightful books about life in France and elsewhere, and her exquisitely written essays on food and cooking. Through them I paid the first of many visits to Dijon, where she went to university. Then her *Two Towns in Provence* introduced me to Aix-en-Provence, a city I had by-passed many times on the autoroute to the sun. And I sat, as she had sat, in the Cours Mirabeau, seeing through her eyes the beautiful main street with its four fountains and its seventeenth- and eighteenth-century town houses shaded by the natural arch made by a double row of plane trees on either side.

Driving through France with Graham was a fruitful experience, both in widening my knowledge of the country and in collecting a storehouse of material which I'm still able to draw on.

He always kept a meticulous account of our expenses down to the very last franc, and at the end of the trip we divided it exactly in two. On the other hand, being a born salesman, he couldn't resist any opportunity that presented itself for a little free publicity.

Occasionally, when we had been staying somewhere rather more grand than usual, he would emerge from the hotel having paid the bill, saying: 'Charming girl behind the desk. I thought it would be a nice gesture if *you* were to send her a Paddington Bear when we get back. Don't forget to sign the label. You never know who might stay there in future!'

Having travelled hopefully and never been disappointed, our arrival at MIP, usually late in the afternoon, just in time for the opening reception, was another matter.

Cannes is at its best in the early morning. Private beaches belonging to the great hotels lining the Croisette are being raked and rolled, the mattresses and the parasols laid out with exactitude in serried rows. Locals are exercising their dogs or simply out for a stroll, and everywhere shopkeepers and restaurateurs are preparing for the onslaught later in the day. It's even possible to find somewhere to park, and the air smells fresh and clean.

From ten o'clock onwards things begin to deteriorate, although even then the sun, the palm trees, the yachts moored in the old harbour, the sheer unashamed opulence of it all, give Cannes a certain something which you find nowhere else in the world.

The first time I went there it was with Brenda and Karen. We were actually staying in Nice, having memorably journeyed down on the *Mistral*, one of the last of the great named trains of that era and the pride of French Rail.

It so happened that a few weeks previously I'd been invited to appear on a radio programme called *Desert Island Discs*. During the course of the recording its creator and longest-playing radio host, Roy Plomley, and I discovered not only a mutual love for France and for things French but that we both planned to be dipping our toes in the Mediterranean on the very day when the programme was scheduled to go out.

Roy generously invited us all along to his rented apartment in Cannes to join himself and his wife, the actress Diana Wong, for a celebratory drink. One glass of champagne led to another and eventually to a res- taurant in the old part of the town behind the harbour. There, we outstayed our welcome to such an extent the patron eventually handed us the keys, asking us to lock up when we had finished and put them through the letter box. If we wanted any more wine perhaps we could leave the money on the counter. Given the amount of liquor behind the bar, it was a remarkable display of faith. I can't picture it happening today; certainly not when any of the festivals are in full swing.

MIP being all to do with the buying and selling of television programmes, there is a certain pecking order in the positioning of stands and in where you stay. The very rich charter a yacht, kept at anchor in the bay; which puts them in a class apart. But if you belong to a large company and don't book in at the Carlton Inter-Continental or the Martinez, tongues begin to wag. Smaller companies have a wider choice, but wherever they end up one can sense an immediate pigeonholing on the part of their rivals. If you don't like being valued, another solution to the problem is to stay outside Cannes, preferably somewhere up in the hills.

Early on we opted for the Hôtel France in the hilltop village of Mougins. In the sixties and seventies Mougins had only just been discovered. It had always been popular with artists, and the locals were very proud of the fact that, after years spent in nearby Vallauris, Picasso had at last moved to a large house on the outskirts of the village which he had first visited before the war.

Opening the hotel shutters in the morning revealed a picture-postcard scene: the view across the valley to the Massif de Tapperall, and in the immediate foreground the tiny square with its fountain. There would be the soft swish of hoses, the postman doing his rounds, local dogs going on a tour of inspection to make sure that all was well in the best of possible worlds, and overall there would be a feeling of warmth coupled with all the sounds and smells which herald the start of another Provençal day.

On the tiny patio below the window, Madame would be hard at work preparing the vegetables for lunch and supervising the cleaning of the restaurant, the polishing of the glasses and the laying of tables; the staff, as always, barely recognizable in their mufti.

The drive down to Cannes after fresh croissants with home-made *confiture* and coffee in thick bowls, was literally downhill all the way.

We were staying in Mougins in 1973 on the day that Picasso died and the whole village was plunged into gloom. And we happened to be there again three years later when news came through that the restaurant had

won its first Michelin star. The phone never stopped ringing. Flowers
and messages of congratulation kept arriving. There was champagne from
Roger Vergé at the nearby three-star Moulin de Mougins. Madame was
almost in tears, and one got an inkling of what it meant to be a restaurateur and have a dream come true, for, despite all the arguments, recognition by Michelin is still what matters most.

 We both took extra trouble over dressing for dinner that night, arriving
downstairs by chance at almost exactly the same moment, wearing virtu-
ally identical new brown corduroy jackets. An elderly waiter gave a
double take, put two and two together and having made rather more
than five, fussed over us like a mother hen for the rest of the evening.
We ate extremely well and the service was impeccable, but until that
moment it had never occurred to either of us that we might be thought
of as anything other than just good friends.

 Both of us were of the opinion that the existence of two different
sexes creates problems enough. Adding a third or even a fourth possibility
is asking for trouble.

 Graham was a born communicator. As far as he was concerned, most
problems in this world were caused by lack of communication, and in
Cannes one morning he gave a convincing demonstration that given
goodwill on both sides all things are possible.

 Armed with a pair of trousers he wanted cleaned, he first of all stopped
a French woman and asked her in Italian the way to the nearest *lavasecco*.
Was it to be recommended?

 Having received her assurance that it was, he then had her opinion
confirmed a few yards further on by an Italian lady to whom he spoke
entirely in French.

 When we eventually reached the shop, he announced in English that
he had a pair of flannel bags which needed cleaning and could he have
them back by four o'clock at the latest. Such was his charm that all
three ladies looked as though their day had been made by the encounter.

 In fact, the French like nothing better than being asked their opinion
about something.

 Ask a French waiter a simple question like how is a particular dish of
lamb cooked, and as likely as not he will begin by telling you that first
the lamb was grazed at a minimum height of 300 metres, where the grass
is fresh and free from contamination by exhaust fumes . . .

In Grasse one evening I stopped the car to ask a pedestrian the way to a particular restaurant. Rather grudgingly, I thought, he gave the directions, but clearly he didn't approve of our choice. There was a much better one, he suggested, in the opposite direction. Regardless of a growing queue of other cars behind, he then sought the opinion of other passers-by, who each in turn offered their opinion. We went on our way in total confusion, but he was right about our first choice. The restaurant had changed hands.

Prices along the Côte d'Azur tend to shoot up alarmingly during the season, but while the money lasts out Cannes has to be one of the better venues for a trade fair. Only in France could you dine so splendidly at a beach hut. A lot of business is done over lunch, and it was after lunch one day that Graham had one of his finest moments.

In much the same way that ship's officers change into their tropical uniform when arriving in a foreign port, he often donned an off-white suite and co-respondent shoes for special occasions. One day, having entertained a large party at one of the beach restaurants, he left early for another meeting. Dutifully kissing the eagerly raised hands of all the ladies present, he backed away from the table waving *au revoir* to the rest of the gathering and stepped straight into a children's paddling pool. Most people, in similar circumstances, would have died of mortification and slunk off with their shirt tails between their legs. Without so much as a flicker of an eyelid or a downward glance, Graham simply carried on walking backwards, still waving as the water got deeper and deeper, until eventually he reached the other side.

He did admit afterwards that his biggest fear was not knowing what lay behind him and wondering if he would eventually become totally submerged.

'I'm not sure what I would have done then.' For a moment or two the actor struggled with the salesman. 'The thing is, of course, they'll probably remember the occasion much longer than if I'd kicked up a fuss.'

Style meant everything to Graham.

One year we made a larger than usual diversion in order to visit Robert Florin, our French agent; ex-member of the Resistance, Legion d'Honneur, anglophile *extraordinaire*, who lived in Tourcoing near the Belgian border.

Over dinner the wine flowed, tongues were loosened, and late that night conversation got around to what particular thing in life one would most like to have were it possible to wave a magic wand.

One by one we indulged in our flights of fancy.

My dream was for a small apartment in Paris, where I could escape the telephone and relax and catch up on my writing.

Robert's ears pricked up. One of his daughters, Rita, who rented an apartment in Montmartre, was expecting a baby and she and her husband were looking for something larger. Perhaps while they were searching they could look for me too?

Both Robert and his daughter had a mental picture of the kind of apartment which would befit an English writer. It would be old and rather grand and situated somewhere near the Bois de Boulogne.

What I had in mind was something much simpler, requiring the minimum of attention – one bedroom, a living-room, kitchen and bathroom, on the seventh floor of a modern block overlooking the rooftops of the eighteenth *arrondissement*. Near two late-night bus routes and a métro station, possibly in the rue Marcadet?

Identical, in fact, to the one Rita and her husband were about to vacate.

Some weeks later I found myself sitting at a pavement table outside a café in the rue de Rivoli. Hardly able to believe my good fortune, I sipped my coffee and went through a long and complicated agreement which, as is the custom under French law, only an hour earlier I had had read out to me word for word by a Paris notary.

The sun was shining, and there wasn't a cloud in the sky.

Somehow, one is always much more aware of the sky in Paris. Perhaps the vastness of the squares and the Grandes Boulevards make it that much more visible, but even when you wander the narrow streets, you still catch little glimpses of the Eiffel Tower, or Sacré-Coeur, perched like a wedding cake on top of the *Butte* Montmartre; suddenly, there they are, nudging you to look up.

Afterwards I went for a leisurely stroll in the Tuileries wondering what to do next. Go looking for furniture? Open a bank account?

There are certain things in life which you assume must follow a basic pattern wherever you are in the world. For me, the world of finance was one of them.

Having set in motion all the necessary arrangements with my English bank, and been assured by them that there was absolutely no problem, I eventually made my way to the address I had been given; a bank of such splendour it could well have passed as a miniature version of the Ritz Hotel on the opposite side of the Place Vendôme.

After we had exchanged a few pleasantries, the manager, whose empty desk, although not actually made of marble, was of a size compatible with its surroundings, cast a desultory glance over the papers I had brought with me. He flicked an imaginary speck of dust from the sleeve of his jacket, made a steeple with the tips of his fingers, looked at me over the top of his glasses and asked if I had permission from Le Ministre.

'*Excusez-moi* . . .' I could feel my smile becoming fixed. 'Do you mean the Ministère?'

'Non.' The steeple grew both taller and narrower at the base, the tone of his voice slightly world-weary. 'Not the Ministry . . . the *Minister*.'

It was the first mention I had heard of a Minister.

Heaving a deep sigh, the manager reached for his telephone. Within seconds his room was full of subordinates, all arguing with each other. I began to feel like an intruder and was just wondering if I should creep quietly away and pretend it had never happened, when I heard an English voice say: 'Leave it to me.'

I followed my saviour down a corridor. It was, he explained, Monsieur's last week in office and he wanted no problems.

'Er . . . I hope you don't mind my asking,' he continued, 'but are you the Michael Bond who writes the Paddington books? My small son . . .'

Once again, it was Paddington to the rescue, triumphing this time over French bureaucracy.

I could have done with his help when I tried to use my new cash card. On the first occasion the machine kept it because it was unsigned – or so I learned several weeks later when I got it back.

I tried again. Due to a misunderstanding on my part I had asked for 1,800 hundred-franc notes (£18,000) rather than the 1,800 francs (£180) which was the maximum allowed at any one time. Having asked me twice if I meant what I said and received my *oui*, it not unnaturally *ferméed* its *porte*. I think I would have too, if I'd been the machine, but it took me rather longer to get my card returned that time.

On the third occasion it threw me by asking what kind of account I had. Since neither the words 'current' nor 'deposit' nor anything remotely like them appeared on the long list of alternatives it displayed, I gave up and maintained a low profile for several months. On the fourth attempt the machine didn't even ask me what I wanted. It simply swallowed the card.

Feeling aggrieved, I went inside and complained to a cashier. With a certain amount of ill grace and French cluckings – enough to make me appreciate the enormity of the favour I was asking, and how very fortunate I was that she was prepared to grant it – the back of the machine was finally opened and my card retrieved. She then produced an enormous pair of scissors from under her counter, held them aloft, and before my very eyes cut it in two.

'It is', she announced triumphantly, 'out of date and therefore must be destroyed!'

Paddington would have given her a very hard stare indeed, and he would certainly have asked for his pieces back. I simply retired hurt.

Such moments, annoying though they are at the time, usually go into storage. All is grist to a writer's mill.

Humorous writing is a serious business: often a matter of endless searching for just the right word or phrase. But sometimes, just when things are at their most difficult, Paddington can make me laugh out loud: as when he went in for a competition and won a bookmark rather than a weekend for two in Paris – something that has probably happened to many of us at one time or another.

The idea of a bear who is so self-confident that when he seeks anonymity he simply puts on a false beard and a pair of dark glasses from his disguise outfit, convinced in his own mind that no one will recognize him, also makes me laugh, although at the time of writing it I found myself taking the situation totally seriously.

For a long while Graham, Ivor and I continued working happily together, respecting each other's territory, each of us getting on with our own job. It would have been good to have carried on that way, but nothing is for ever.

Ivor made a second series of *The Wombles* and shortly after that the BBC commissioned another twenty-six episodes of Paddington.

With a less onerous deadline to meet, there was time to be more ambitious and we began tackling episodes from the books which for one reason or another had been rejected the first time round. Paddington was now able to go on the river and visit the seaside and even have a go at mending a burst waterpipe for Mr Curry.

The series was eventually screened by the BBC in 1979 and that same year won a silver medal at the New York Film and Television Festival, the first British animated series ever to win a major award.

Although Ivor carried on supervising the production for a time, other animators came in to ease the load and in time he formed his own company, Woodland Animations, going on to create the hugely success-ful *Postman Pat* and many other programmes.

But before that I was going through a gloomy period at the Barbican, and in a roundabout way it was Paddington who came to my rescue again, although the absence of his 'stand-in' nearly made it a non-starter.

In 1976 Nicholas's brother, Stephen, a successful film agent in his own right, joined forces with Harvey Unna, bringing with him his assistant. Gradually, over a period of time, I became aware of a new and particularly friendly voice whenever I telephoned their office, and I found myself trying to think up reasons for ringing more often.

It wasn't long before I put plan A into operation.

The Paddington play was being staged at a theatre on the outskirts of London. If it was time I caught up with it again, then it was certainly high time that someone in Harvey Unna's office did so too.

Harvey agreed with my suggestion that Sue could be the ideal person to accompany me.

Plan A involved a picnic lunch on the way, possibly on Barnes Common, followed by a leisurely drive to the theatre to take in the play, say another two and a half hours or so, by which time there would be no point in Sue going back to the office . . .

I could see it all. 'How about a quiet drink?' I would say. 'Then, if you're not doing anything, perhaps we could have dinner together?'

Short of actually carrying out a dress rehearsal with someone from the female equivalent of Dial-a-Beau, it all seemed pretty foolproof. I even bought a half-bottle of champagne for the picnic, which I left lying casually on the back seat of the car, suitably chilled of course. A full bottle in an ice-bucket might have looked a mite too calculated.

In the event, there was rather less of Barnes Common than I remembered, and nowhere to park other than a singularly unattractive lane near a public convenience which seemed blessed with a constant stream of seedy-looking characters in raincoats pretending they had been taken short. The picnic was over in no time at all.

One of the problems with children's plays is that they often occupy a theatre just for the afternoon, making use as far as possible of sets designed for a different production in the evening. On the day in question, the evening show was clearly meant for adults only. All the publicity photographs had been carefully covered over to stop tiny patrons asking awkward questions like: 'Mummy, what are those two people doing?' Or even: 'Mummy, what are those *three* people doing?'

The play was over half an hour late starting, and it being term-time the audience was sparse and growing more restive by the minute.

Eventually the curtains parted and a distraught-looking theatre manager came out in front to announce that Paddington was indisposed and his part was being played by someone else. A quick glance at the programme before the lights went down revealed that the 'someone else' was the girl who should have been playing the Browns' daughter Judy, which was why, during the opening scene on Paddington Station, her brother Jonathan came running on shouting: 'Judy can't be here because she's missed the train!'

Quick, not to say desperate thinking on someone's part, but as the play progressed and Judy's absence was felt, it became clear that a chain reaction had set in amongst the cast, all of whom were trying manfully to cope with unrehearsed entrances and exits by people they clearly expected would be playing other roles.

We crept away as soon as we decently could, and it being the middle of the afternoon, Sue returned to her office completely unaware of what I'd had in mind, while I went back to the Barbican to think again.

Graham would have called it a classic example of lack of communication.

Afterwards we learned that the cast had thrown a party the night before during which Paddington had got 'over excited' and fallen into the orchestra pit.

'Some party!' as Winston Churchill would have said. 'Some pit!'

Fortunately, plans B and C met with more success, and it wasn't long before the Barbican flat shows signs of the feminine touch: little things like tights hanging over the wash-basin to dry.

Soon after Sue moved in, I was asked by Collins if I would undertake a three-week promotional tour of Australia and New Zealand.

An additional carrot was the offer of a week's stay anywhere in the southern hemisphere I cared to name once it was over, all expenses paid. It seemed an ideal opportunity for a complete change of scene in a part of the world I had never been to, so I agreed, provided Sue could come with me.

I then had to break the news to Harvey Unna that he was likely to be minus one of his staff for at least a month.

Taking Harvey to lunch was a bit like taking my bank manager out with a view to obtaining an overdraft. I was very unsure of what the reaction would be and it wasn't until we reached the coffee stage that I broached the subject.

Before I had a chance to finish, Harvey posed the obvious question. 'Which particular member of the staff do you have in mind?'

I told him and he carried on eating for a while. Then he said: 'We must do this more often!'

When he got back to work nothing was immediately said, but later that afternoon he called Sue into his office, looked at her over the top of his glasses and remarked: 'Still waters run deep!'

Graham, who had a brother and a host of other relatives in Australia, also wanted to explore the territory with a view to opening up the market, so he asked if he might come too, and on 23 August 1979 we all set off.

It was to be the last big trip involving Graham, and once again we managed a slight diversion on the way; staying two nights at Raffles Hotel in Singapore, drinking gin slings by the pool and pretending we were living in the days of Somerset Maugham. And before the second leg of the journey we ate at a wonderful restaurant called Fatty's, near the street of a thousand transvestites, which had been recommended to us by one of the stewards on the flight from London.

The first thing you want to do when you arrive somewhere after a long flight is get off the plane. Given half a chance, most people are at the luggage racks before it has come to a complete stop. But in Australia you have to sit tight while officials from the health department go round the aircraft fumigating it, which makes you feel a bit of a pariah.

I was still in my pariah mode after we had checked in at the hotel, so Sue and I went out for an early evening stroll to cool off. We had barely covered a quarter of a mile when a car drew up. There were four men inside and one of them opened a window, leaned out and shouted: 'Go home you Pommie bastard!'

It wasn't as if I had even been carrying a rolled umbrella!

I managed to get some mileage out of the incident later that night when I looked out of our hotel room and saw placed outside one of the other doors in a vast corridor a solitary pair of co-respondent shoes.

Early next morning there was a knock on our door. 'You won't believe this,' said Graham, as he entered clutching his shoes in one hand and a piece of paper in the other. 'Someone put this note under my door last night. Look what it says: "Clean them yourself, you Pommie bastard!"'

For our time in Australia we were in the hands of Jan Garvan, a delightful and extraordinarily efficient lady, whose address book included the names of everyone in the media world who might conceivably be of use. As an exercise in how to get the most mileage out of a promotion it was copybook material and once the tour was underway there was no stopping it.

The first morning in Sydney, before an invited audience, the television show's resident host asked me the usual question:

'How did you get the idea of Paddington?'

He then left me to it while he went off to have a row with the studio manager. In retrospect, if I'd been more confident I would have got my own back by asking him to repeat the question.

It was the nearest I got to BBC standards. By the time we reached Perth the chat-show host was doing the make-up as well!

Signings mostly took place in vast shopping malls which people entered in the morning and where they stayed until it was time to go home at night – or so it seemed. All of them had huge recreation areas, where there were nonstop hour-long diversions of one kind or another to keep the little ones amused while parents did their own thing.

My initial encounter, the first of many, was in a suburb of Sydney. As I climbed, totally unprepared, on to the stage someone handed me a black object with a wire attached and said: 'OK, it's all yours!'

Fortunately, I was accompanied by someone dressed up as Paddington, which the audience found much more interesting. Little ones were never quite sure if it was real or not, older members found out by the simple expedient of stamping on its paws whenever they got the chance.

Drawing on memories of warm-up artists doing their patter, I gradually settled into the role of straight man to a bear.

In each of the towns and cities we visited – Sydney, Melbourne, Adelaide, Brisbane and Perth – having been waved on our way by weary reps, we were greeted at the next stop by a fresh batch ready for the fray.

And at every stage, from television interviewers, and from radio and newspaper reporters alike, there would be the same inevitable opening question: 'Tell me, Mike, how did you first get the idea of Paddington?'

In between there were photograph sessions in zoos and wildlife parks, when a scar-faced keeper would hand me the inevitable koala bear on a high from eucalyptus leaves. Usually they seemed quite pleased to get rid of it. But not half as pleased as I was to give it back.

Much to my relief the costumed bear didn't fly with us. The suit itself was rushed on ahead so that Paddington could be waiting to greet our plane on its arrival. Sometimes, depending on which member of the Collins staff had drawn the short straw, the lone figure on the tarmac looked tall and gangling, at other times short and fat and covered in folds like the Michelin man. It was very hot inside the costume and I grew to recognize the danger signs: when the paw went limp it was time to take emergency action and rush for the nearest dark corner in order to remove the head and let in some fresh air. By the time two weeks had passed the skin practically had a life of its own.

Every time we flew anywhere I was given a Gabrielle bear to carry, and shortly after take-off there would be a message inviting us up to the flight deck. But it was Paddington who was always asked to remain behind. Later, when I went collect him, there he would be – strapped to a spare seat, a fully integrated member of the crew, who were having a high old time.

On one occasion the message said: 'Hope you don't mind if Paddington stays up here. He wants to land the plane!' I looked round at the other passengers and wondered what they would think if they knew.

With the best will in the world, endless queues tend to lose their identity after a while, merging into a sea of look-alikes. But at one signing session, having asked what name the person would like inscribed in his book, I became aware of a certain restiveness.

I looked up to see a teenager standing in front of me, wearing a duffle coat and bush hat and carrying a suitcase, his face covered in brown dye. I felt very bad for not having noticed.

On another occasion, as I automatically held out my hand for an autograph book and met nothing, an elderly voice said: 'Is this the queue for getting your eyes tested, mate?'

And once I overheard two women talking as they pushed their way past.

'Who's that?' asked the first.

'Michael Bond,' said the second, clearly reading from a poster.

'Michael Bond?' said her friend. 'I thought he died years ago.'

I was beginning to feel the same way, and more than ready to shoot the next person who asked me how I thought up the idea for Paddington.

At the end of the two weeks, aching all over, feeling as one feels at the height of a severe bout of 'flu, vowing *never again*, we reached the Indian Ocean and Collins' warehouse in Perth.

The manager invited me into his office, summed up the situation at a glance, and pointed to a chair behind his desk.

'You look', he said, 'like a man who could do with a large glass of whisky.'

Never have words sounded more welcome. I lay back and watched while he opened the bottle. The sound of clinking ice was like Oscar Peterson running his fingers over the ivories, the pouring of the whisky reminded me of a mountain stream.

'You know,' he said, handing me the glass, 'there's something I've been dying to ask you. How did you think up the idea for Paddington?'

Luckily I didn't have a gun with me.

If Australia was all on a high, New Zealand brought me down to earth with a bump. It was probably no bad thing, but it was like going back in time to pre-war England; everything moved at a different pace.

Shortly after we landed in Auckland, having travelled all night without sleep, I found myself being interviewed on a television programme by someone who had no idea who I was or why I was there. By then I wasn't too sure either.

In Christchurch, it was back to signing copies of *A Bear Called Paddington* for stock; the sole customer a small boy who cried when I wrote in his book. He refused to be comforted, having been strictly brought up never to do such a thing himself.

Afterwards the manageress of the department looked at me and said: 'What did you say your name was?'

In Wellington one evening the three of us went out to a Chinese restaurant to eat. The only other customers were two heavyweight characters at the far end of the room who kept looking in our direction. Mindful of the first evening in Sydney, it seemed to me they could be spoiling for a fight, and when one of them rose to his feet and ambled slowly towards me clutching a bottle I was sure of it.

'Are you Michael Bond?'

Other than shaking my head and pointing to Graham, there seemed little point in denying it. I braced myself for the worst, recalling all the films I had seen over the years, when the cornered hero creates a diversion by upending his table. Would the three of us make it through the door, or would Graham and I lose valuable time by being awfully British and insisting on ladies first?

Sue, being Sue, would probably have said: 'No, after you!'

Our would-be assailant plonked the bottle on the table. 'Heard you talking about Paddington on the radio this morning. Great character. Welcome to windy Wellington. My friend and I would like you to have some wine on us.'

I remember it with affection as the high spot of our visit to New Zealand, which suddenly didn't seem such a bad place after all.

The next day we parted company. Graham left us to make his own way to California and the head offices of FilmFair. He was suddenly very downcast at the thought of the long journey ahead of him. You leave in the afternoon, seemingly fly for ever and arrive in Los Angeles several hours before you left. I think he suddenly saw it as a reflection of the occasional emptiness in his own life, but I suspect he also had premonitions about the future.

Sue and I flew back to Sydney, and such is the power of the media there was instant recognition in Immigration and Customs. Officials suddenly melted. Baggage handlers called out, asking after Paddington's well-being, and there were flowers and messages waiting for us at the hotel. It all felt warm and friendly, as though we had arrived back home again; a complete reversal of our first evening.

From Sydney we flew to Jakarta, which I'd picked as our holiday venue for no better reason than the fact that I had once seen the film *Road to Bali*, with Bing Crosby, Bob Hope and Dorothy Lamour.

After half a day on the beach, we spent most of the remaining week in bed, unable to move because of acute sunburn. At least I wasn't on a charge for damaging Queen's property, although having managed to hobble along endless corridors to visit the hotel doctor, who refused to come to us, I got the feeling that he would have been only too happy to oblige.

He had a friend in reception. When we left and I was presented with the bill, I said brightly: 'Collins are paying', and discovered a whole new meaning to the phrase 'impenetrable oriental stare'.

With as many credit cards as I could muster mortgaged to the hilt, we boarded a Garuda Airlines 737, and while reading about a crash in a similar aircraft which had lost its tailplane only the week before, took off into a spectacular tropical thunderstorm.

It had been a short, sharp, concentrated dose of limelight, and it left me with a new respect for pop groups, royalty, politicians, film stars: anyone who is exposed to constant attention from the public. At least, the god Thor permitting, I was about to make good my escape, and the sobering fact is that within a matter of weeks the whole thing might never have happened. I don't think New Zealand ever knew that it did.

After the second *Paddington* series had been completed, Graham and I were celebrating in his office over champagne and Marks & Spencer pork pies, to which he had become gravely addicted, when I idly remarked that stop-start puppet animation had now developed to the point where anything was possible.

'Why,' I said airily, searching for a suitable example, 'one could even have Paddington dance the Gene Kelly routine from *Singin' in the Rain*.'

It must have been the champagne!

'Paddington Goes to the Movies', a half-hour 'special', which included a frame-by-frame remake of the classic sequence, brilliantly animated by Ivor's successor, Barry Leith, took over a year to make and gave rise to innumerable headaches on the way. But in 1982, with Gene Kelly's blessing, it was screened by the BBC. A repeat showing the following year gained an audience of over eight million and the film was eventually nominated for an Emmy award.

The Home Box Office channel in America bought it, and commissioned some more. But I began to grow increasingly restive over the amount of interference. The BBC were always, quite rightly, nervous of showing Paddington doing anything visually dangerous which a small child might innocently try to copy – balancing on top of tall stools, taking saucepans off a kitchen stove, plugging in electrical appliances, all the things one can happily get away with in books – but in every other respect I had been allowed a free hand.

American television is riddled with constrictions. Audience ratings are everything; the difference between success and failure much more marked. Above the line you are a success, below it a failure, and the two are poles apart. One way to ensure high ratings is to upset as few people as possible. For example, Paddington couldn't say things like 'the outlook was black', in case it offended any coloured people watching, or use words like 'headmaster' instead of 'principal' for fear children wouldn't understand what it meant. The list of taboo items grew longer and longer. And there were other problems.

In order to satisfy an audience conditioned to cartoon animation, the cardboard cutouts of the other characters had to have lip-synch when they spoke. Ivor's deliberately muted background colours had to be brightened. And with each change, Paddington became more and more submerged.

What they failed to appreciate was that the original films were successful *because* of the style in which they were made, and once you have something that works you play around with it at your peril.

The catch was that because the half-hour films were costly to make, a sale to America was essential. In the USA the money can be recouped on a first home showing, which means that overseas sales become the jam and cream on the bread and butter. In the UK, unfortunately, the reverse is true. After the third film I had had enough – it was breaking faith with the character and selling the audience short. I think Graham was secretly relieved when I said 'no more'.

After twenty or so years of writing almost exclusively for children I was beginning to feel the need for a change. Inside me there was another writer wanting to get out.

Another major reorganization in my life was long overdue.

Over a period of time, Nicholas had built up the side of Paddington and Company which dealt with merchandise, but it was becoming increasingly clear that to handle just one character was not only a waste of his growing expertise but in terms of profit and loss it wasn't maximizing the company's potential. I was also beginning to find the wheel going the full circle and my involvement was hardly growing any less. That precious commodity 'thinking time' was hard to find.

The obvious answer was for Nicholas to form his own company and take on Paddington as one of his clients.

Meanwhile, having proved her worth with a magazine publishing company, Karen became the victim of internal wrangling. Listening to her pour out her troubles over lunch one day, I took the line that life is too short to argue over such mundane matters as who should keep the keys to the office filing cabinets, and suggested she should look for another job. In the meantime she might like to lend me a hand.

Much to my surprise and pleasure, for it had never been intended as a permanent arrangement, she took to it like a duck to water. As with her visit to the Barbican, she came for a short while and stayed.

She manages with almost unfailing good humour to combine the role of wife and mother of three small children with that of company director, yet still find time to serve on school committees and attend board meetings of Paddington's chosen charity, Action Research.

I know it's not always plain sailing, because Robyn, her eldest, came into the kitchen one morning, did a double take and said to her: 'Mummy, why are you kicking the refrigerator?'

On 8 July 1981 Sue and I were married at the Marylebone Registry Office. It was followed by a ceremony at the Church of St Mary's on Paddington Green.

In saying 'I do' I gained not only a lovely wife but a mother-in-law of great charm, who once trod the boards with Mrs Stella Patrick Campbell and was destined for Hollywood had she not been swept off her feet by Sue's father, who, alas, died before I met her; a brother-in-law, Michael Berkeley, who is a classical composer of not one but many notes, a sister-in-law who is a literary agent of repute, and as many half-sisters, uncles, aunts, nephews, nieces and cousins by marriage as there are days in the year.

Graham was best man and he brought his Bentley out of semi-retirement for the occasion. All spruced up, it transported us in great style from the registry office to the church. And after the ceremony, with Graham at the wheel, it successfully negotiated the few hundred yards to our home in Little Venice.

It was to be the last time we ever rode in Dud.

CHAPTER 14

Enter Monsieur Pamplemousse

The discovery of a new dish does more for the happiness of mankind than the discovery of a star.

Brillat-Savarin (1755–1826)

One of the questions most commonly asked of a writer is 'Where do you get your ideas?', and it's almost impossible to answer. One might just as well ask a chef what leads him to discover a new dish, or a London taxi driver how he manages to remember all the streets in the capital.

'Hard work, guv,' the taxi driver would say. 'Two years' graft learning the "knowledge".'

The fact is, the brain tends to develop according to the use to which it is put. In the case of writing, ideas often come about through sheer chance: overhearing a snatch of conversation, or perhaps seeing an unusual street sign; being in a certain place at a certain time. The moment of inspiration is there one second for all to see or hear, gone the next. It needs to be captured before it disappears for ever. Then comes the hard work. As the proverb has it: 'Writing is 10 per cent inspiration, 90 per cent perspiration.'

France is, for me, a great source of inspiration. Whenever I feel my batteries need recharging, that is where I head for.

If I settle back and let my mind go into free orbit, it almost always alights of its own accord somewhere there, and a whole montage of pictures awaits me.

Paris, which I got to know well the hard way when I wrote a guide to the city, reporting on a few of its ten thousand restaurants, and have grown to love more and more over the years; a score of tiny cobbled streets in towns and villages across the vast and varied countryside, which come to mind for no better reason than the fact that I was happy strolling along them at some time; springtime in the Auvergne, undisturbed except for the buzzing of bees hard at work amongst the myriad wild flowers; a rainy clifftop in Brittany with a gale blowing; a simple plaque let into a wall to mark the spot where someone died for their country.

To say, as some people do, that France would be a wonderful place if it weren't for the French, is to forget the fact that it is the people of a country who make it what it is, and one of the many things I like about France is that even in Paris the little politenesses of life remain; the formalities are observed. That things are done in the correct way matters greatly, for they have a built-in sense of style. You see it in the way they dress their shop windows, or lay out a display of fruit and vegetables in a market. There is a right and a wrong way of going about matters, from parcelling up a single croissant in the *boulangerie* to laying a vast table for a wedding breakfast with exactness and precision, lining up the glasses like soldiers on parade, with not a stem out of place. You see it in the way they go about presenting a dish before serving it at table . . .

It was in France in the autumn of 1981 that I discovered a new dish; or one that was new to me, and that in turn led me back the full circle to where I had begun – writing for adults.

If you drive along the Avenue Victor-Hugo heading south out of the town of Valence in the Rhone Valley, about halfway along on the left-hand side, opposite an Audi showroom, you will see a sign bearing the single word Pic.

It could herald yet another new brand of petrol, but in fact the name Pic has been synonymous with good eating in and around the area for three generations. Of all the restaurants I have been to, it is the most welcoming, the most generous, the most genuine in its desire to please. People from all over the world go there to dine, but no less welcome are the locals who turn up in their droves for Sunday lunch and for weddings and birthdays and other celebrations throughout the year. All are treated as equals. It's that kind of a place; a family restaurant in the truest sense of the word.

One of the specialities in the days of the second generation was

Poularde de Bresse en Vessie 'André Pic'; a large Bresse chicken stuffed with seasoned *foie gras* and with generous slices of truffle slipped beneath the skin, is encased in a pig's bladder, which is then sealed and pricked. Placed in a pot of chicken consommé, it is left to simmer for two and a half hours, no more, and no less. Needless to say, it has to be ordered well in advance, which enhanced our expectations.

Taste buds began to salivate as the *moment critique* drew near, for a certain amount of ceremony is involved. First a serving table was placed in position, then the dish itself was presented. Diners at nearby tables paused over their meal to watch.

As the *maître d'hôtel* took hold of his implements and with a D'Artagnanesque flourish applied the tip of a sharp knife to the outer case, the writer in me wondered what would happen if something other than a *poularde de Bresse* was revealed.

For a long while I had been toying with the idea of writing a detective novel. I had a clear picture in my mind of the main character; a kind of Maigret figure, dogged and determined, always getting there in the end but rather more interested in the reason for a crime than in the crime itself.

I planned to call my detective Monsieur Pamplemousse, and if one accepts the late James Agate's definition that 'comedy is unreal people in real situations, and farce is real people in unreal situations'; then it would lean towards the latter, for he would be accident prone and much giving to landing himself in compromising situations.

For a while I pictured him being the last detective in Paris still riding a bicycle. Several years earlier I had even bought myself a genuine French racing machine in order to get the feel of it: a Vainqueur Galaxis, with dropped handlebars, rat-trap pedals, and a ten-speed derailleur gear.

Setting off downhill on my maiden outing, the first person I narrowly missed bumping into was the local vicar. As I shot past him he raised his hat and called out: 'Ah, saving fuel, I see!' It wasn't at all the effect I'd intended and shortly afterwards the idea was shelved.

The leather saddle was much harder than I remembered their being when I was a boy, and the hills around Haslemere a lot steeper than driving a car had led me to believe.

Another problem was that I didn't want the books to be set entirely in Paris. France is a large country, and it seemed a pity not to make use of the fact. My knowledge of French police procedure was also rather hazy. I just about knew the difference between a *gendarme* and a member of the Garde Nationale and that was it.

Suddenly, that evening at Pic, everything fell into place. Monsieur Pamplemousse would be an inspector working for a food guide, a job which would involve him travelling all over France reporting on hotels and restaurants. As an ex-member of the Paris Sûreté who had blotted his copybook at some point in time and been forced into taking early retirement, his mind would be for ever on the alert for nefarious goings-on. Instead of riding a bicycle, he would be wedded to his Citroen 2CV. And on his travels . . .

As is often the case in France, Madame Pic looked after things out front. She was aided and abetted in her task by Giankin, a large black dog of indeterminate pedigree who took a proprietorial interest in all that was going on, particularly when it came to what the customers were ordering. He never bothered people at table, but simply watched points, making it seem as though his nod of approval was something to be sought, for it clearly wasn't given lightly.

The sight of him eyeing our table that evening triggered off another thought. Monsieur Pamplemousse would need a companion. What better than a dog? Preferably one with gourmet tendencies like Giankin, who would add weight to his master's gastronomic deliberations. Perhaps a bloodhound who had also worked for the Sûreté, but had been made redundant because of a cutback? A leaving present for Monsieur Pamplemousse from his colleagues? Pommes Frites would be a good name.

Nothing untoward happened that evening, and we enjoyed our first taste of *Poularde de Bresse en Vessie 'André Pic'*. It was all I had been led to expect of a dish which for many years had graced their entry in the *Michelin Guide*; one of three recommendations for the restaurant. But I didn't give it my full attention. For most of the meal my mind was on other things.

Lap-tops not having been invented, I had to content myself for the rest of the holiday with jotting down notes on the backs of envelopes.

As soon as we arrived home I sat down and wrote what was to become the middle chapter of the first book. I wanted to establish the relationship have total trust in each other and be able to communicate on one level, yet at other times remain blissfully ignorant of each other's thoughts. The reader would see both sides, aware – even when Monsieur Pamplemousse wasn't – of the important part Pommes Frites was playing.

With that picture in my mind, I set to work, and as is so often the way with the first book in a series, it came together very quickly.

Monsieur Pamplemousse was published in 1983. As a dish it wasn't greatly to Auberon Waugh's taste: '. . . I cannot, off-hand, think of any book which amused me less . . .', but otherwise it enjoyed good reviews – enough to make me want to start work on a second; enough for the publishers not to say no.

One of the nice things about getting back to writing for adults was the lack of constraints and a feeling of freedom. Without being in the slightest bit disloyal to Paddington, caviar and oysters made a welcome change from marmalade sandwiches, although for a while it was inevitable that comparisons would be made by reviewers, and by the odd member of the public who didn't bother to read the blurb or pause to wonder for a moment why the book was on display in the crime section rather than the children's department. (To give them the benefit of the doubt, perhaps it wasn't always. If the *Thursday* books can turn up in the wildlife department at Foyles, anything can happen!)

Among the thank-you letters, I began to receive the occasional broadside from maiden ladies in odd parts of the world taking me to task for offending their susceptibilities – something I never deliberately set out to do.

'Evil', as I tried to point out, 'is often in the eye of the beholder.' But I suspect I was wasting my breath.

The position is reversed in the case of compilers of books on aphrodisiacs, who make no bones about assuming evil intent on the part of the reader. Why else, they might well ask, as they illustrate their point in graphic detail, did he, or she, pick it up in the first place?

Lists beginning with Absinthe wind up with Zodiac and Zulu, for there is a whole alphabet of magic potions aimed at satisfying man's – and woman's – carnal desires.

The ancient Greeks put their money on pomegranates and phallic breads, the Chinese on ginseng – ideally dug up at midnight under the light of a full moon. The Aztecs favoured chocolate, and many Japanese swear by herring roes. In Egypt it was always bottles of Spanish fly the natives peddled. Madame Du Barry, who knew a thing or two, secretly laced Louis XV's bonbons with amber when he wasn't feeling up to the mark.

Is there such a thing as a never-fail aphrodisiac? Probably no one will ever know for sure. It's a bit like hypnotism. It's said to be impossible to make anyone under hypnosis do things that are out of character, but we only have the hypnotist's word for that.

A great many aphrodisiacs rely not so much on any mysterious powers as on auto-suggestion. A fresh oyster lying glistening in its shell has obvious physical associations, as do long-stemmed fungi and peeled bananas. Champagne, soft lights, sweet music, comfortable surroundings; all play a big part. You can spoon mountains of caviar into the mouth of your intended, or reach into your pocket and unwrap a fresh truffle you just happen to have with you, but if the chemistry isn't right or your companion is unwilling it will be to no avail.

Henry Kissinger once said that power is the ultimate aphrodisiac and he must have had many opportunities to put his theory to the test.

But as long as man has wanted to seduce woman – or perhaps, more to the point, as long as woman has wanted to be seduced – there has been a ready market for aphrodisiacs of every shape and kind.

It is just possible, of course, that as with Bernard, one of Monsieur Pamplemousse's colleagues, the user has stumbled on a love potion quite by chance and in so doing has become an innocent victim of circumstances.

In the second book, *Monsieur Pamplemousse and the Secret Mission*, our eponymous hero is sent by the director of *Le Guide*, Monsieur Henri Leclercq, to investigate some strange goings-on at a small hotel in the Loire valley run by a distant aunt of his. The Hôtel du Paradis in the village of St Georges-sur-Lie is suddenly overwhelmed by customers and, much to the Director's consternation, for Tante Louise has never been renowned for her culinary skills, finds itself in line for a Stock Pot – *Le Guide's* equivalent to the Michelin star.

Listening to Bernard stumbling through his tale of woe about what happened to him following a visit to the Hôtel, Monsieur Pamplemousse inwardly hopes that his colleague has retained the services of a good lawyer.

'So what happened then?'

'I parked by the side of the road,' said Bernard, 'and went into a wood meaning to try and sleep it off. I'd put it down to too much to drink. I was in such a state by then I sort of – well, it sounds a bit silly talking about it across a table like this – but I got lost. I must have been going round and round in circles. That was when I heard all these voices.'

'Voices?' Monsieur Pamplemousse reached for the bottle. His throat felt unaccountably dry. 'What sort of voices?'

'Girls' voices. I'd parked near a school. A convent, actually, which makes it sound even worse. You know what convent girls are supposed to be like. They were on some sort of ramble. I bumped into them in a clearing and . . .'

'And?'

'They say I started behaving in a funny kind of way. Like . . . beckoning to them . . .'

'Beckoning?'

Bernard nodded. 'I can actually remember doing it in a hazy kind of way. First of all some big blonde sixth-former came over.' He paused in order to emit another series of whistles. 'I think she must have been in charge. Then the others followed.'

'Beckoning doesn't sound a very major crime,' said Monsieur Pamplemousse thoughtfully. 'I don't see what all the fuss is about.'

'It depends,' said Bernard, slowly and carefully, 'on what you beckon with . . .'

Before the end of the book both Pommes Frites and Monsieur Pamplemousse have need of a good lawyer: Pommes Frites stands accused of mass *chienne* ravishing, and Monsieur Pamplemousse is in hot water with the girls of a local drum-and-fife band led by Miss Sparkling Saumur.

The idea for the story was triggered off in a rather strange way.

One night we were having dinner at a picturesque old mill house in the Dordogne. Everything in the garden was lovely, or it would have been had the rain not been bucketing down outside. In between receiving her guests and taking orders, Madame spent most of the evening gazing anxiously out at the rapidly rising mill stream; not without reason, she let fall afterwards. The last time it had rained that much they'd had to set in motion a mass evacuation of the dining-room.

After dinner we went up to our room and were about to retire when we noticed drips coming from the overhead canopy of the four-poster.

It was a large bed and 50 per cent of us, having searched through the phrase book and come up with things like: 'Our bed has no headboard/ is too hard/too soft/has a broken spring' but drawn a blank on the vital, 'There is a large bulge in the canopy overhead', was all for making the best of things. The other 50 per cent, whose French was more than equal to the occasion, decided otherwise.

Madame wrung her hands in mortification, Monsieur abandoned his stove and arrived post haste with a pair of steps and a bucket, maids appeared from nowhere laden with blankets and pillows and bowls of fruit.

In the morning the sun was shining, the water level in the river outside had gone down, and the owners of the hotel were full of apologies and solicitations for our future well being.

As they waved goodbye they presented us with a tin of tea, and they even telephoned ahead to the next hotel to make sure we were given a glass of champagne when we arrived.

Not being much of a tea drinker myself, it was some weeks before I examined the tin more closely. When I opened it up it seemed to be full of twigs and bits of bark rather than actual leaves. It also had a strange, overpowering smell I couldn't place. Reading the small print on the side of the tin it said it was highly recommended for use on honey-moons! Could it be . . . ? I have yet to find out.

I also shamelessly made use of Madame Terminé. Madame Terminé was an imposing lady of what my mother would have called 'the old school', who worked in a local restaurant we often went to when we were in Paris.

She had a habit of taking charge the moment you entered. Uttering commands of '*Avancez! Avancez!*', she literally swept all before her as she ushered you to your seat.

There was only time for a very quick Kir before she reappeared, flourishing her notebook, ready to take the orders; lips pursed and *drum drum* if you hadn't made up your mind. Once, when I had chosen fish, she refused point blank to accept an order for *pommes frites*, even though

I could see people at other tables happily tucking into them. It was *pommes purées* or nothing. Wine was opened at the table, the cork sniffed, the glass filled. There was no question of tasting it.

I christened her Madame Terminé because as soon as she caught sight of a near empty plate there would be a loud cry of '*Terminé!*' and it would be whisked away before the luckless diner had a chance to say *oui* or *non*.

All the same, to see her deboning a plaice on the vast centre table when the restaurant was in full swing was to witness poetry in motion, and I occasionally fantasized about what it would be like to go to bed with her – not with any intention of ever trying to find out, of course! – for she must have been attractive in her youth, and beneath her black bombazine dress and white apron there undoubtedly lurked a heart of gold. I think she would have been very kind and loving, giving value for money. Her grip would have been vice-like; her patience not inexhaustible. And when she deemed satisfaction had been accorded there would have been a brisk cry of *Terminé!* indicating that it was time to leave.

She would certainly have had no time for aphrodisiacs, and I'm sure she's right. As Anatole France once said: 'Of all the sexual perversions, chastity is the most peculiar.'

But just as there are always people looking for a method of producing truffles all year round, so there will always be people searching for the perfect over-the-counter aphrodisiac. One hopes that neither of them succeeds. There are too few mysteries left in the world.

One evening, not so long ago, we arrived at the restaurant for dinner and the place felt empty; we had missed by one day Madame Terminé's retirement to 'somewhere in the country' – probably the town or village where she was born. It felt as though a light had gone out and that the world was somehow a greyer place.

It was also a reminder that nothing is for ever and that one should always make the most of things while they are there. Nothing is for ever, and everything is relative.

To the owner of another restaurant we have been patronizing regularly for the past fifteen or sixteen years, we are counted as being among his oldest customers, which we probably are, for we went there soon after the establishment first opened.

Over the years we watched as in-house romance blossomed and he married the waitress. Then, after perhaps two years of happiness, she disappeared from the scene and the patron looked shattered. The *Maître'd'* confided that Madame was dying of cancer.

After it was all over Monsieur was devastated and it took him a long time to recover. For a while he scarcely came out of his kitchen, but gradually things returned to normal.

Nowadays our arrival is greeted with Kirs 'on the house'. The patron joins us at the table to discuss our order and I am no longer allowed to see the wine list. According to our choice of food, so a bottle is recommended. Never one of the more expensive wines, but always something 'special' hidden away in a cupboard.

The last time we were there was shortly after the crippling wave of national strikes of '95. We listened to a long tale of woe. *'Une catastrophe! Une Catastrophe!'* And then in hushed tones he related the fact that he'd had it on good authority from the man who supplied him with *foie gras*, who also, the voice become lower still, 'supplied the commandant of an army detachment in the 15th *arrondissement*, that during the troubles they had been on constant alert!'

We felt very honoured to be privy to such information, which, given the impeccable nature of its source, had to be true.

Privilege of a different kind was bestowed on us recently at another local restaurant we have been going to for almost the same length of time.

Monsieur Coillot has been cooking the same dishes year in year out for over thirty-five years. For a while they earned him a star in the *Michelin Guide*, but then he lost it, perhaps for lack of innovation, or possibly because the decor – framed pictures of monks going about their daily tasks – has hardly moved with the times. Because he is French and doing things the right way matters greatly to him, he cooks what he has always cooked to perfection. On nights when trade is slack he leaves the door to his kitchen open and you can hear him singing. On busy nights the door remains firmly closed so as not to disturb his concentration.

Madame is always welcoming and attentive. Doing things the right way matters greatly to her too – 'you must maintain yourself' – but in fifteen or so years Monsieur never uttered a word to us. To him we remained newcomers, objects of suspicion, or perhaps he feared that if he did speak we might say something back to him in English.

Then recently, as we made to leave, Madame beckoned to him and he came out from his kitchen. After rubbing large hands clean on his apron, we both received a beaming smile and a warm, not say bone-cracking handshake as he bid us *bonne journée*. We had arrived!

Roots begin to form. The girls in the *supermarché* along the street probably wouldn't recognize their own mother if they served her, so they certainly don't recognize us, but the plumber has taken to waving from the bar opposite his shop whenever we go past, and Madame in the boulangerie allows herself a glint of recognition from time to time. Her tarts and *brioche au sucre* are the best in the area, so that is a big plus. The local cobbler now has a vested interest in our shoes. He takes pride in his work and the last time I took a pair in he gave me a long lecture on the impossibility of repairing them.

'*Alors!*' With one swift lunge of a Stanley knife, sole and upper parted company. A shrug said it all. But having said what he had to say, he took them in without question and a month later when we went back to enquire how they were getting on he gave us a progress report. Work had been halted because he wanted to obtain my approval for what he had done to date before proceeding further. He showed me a partially assembled shoe with pride. It was a work of art, like a model for an exploded diagram of how a shoe is made.

It is all part of a way of life one fears in the end may be doomed.

But there is hope. The French care passionately about their land, their way of life, and the minutiae of living; they are interested in everything that goes on around them, which immediately becomes a matter for discussion. They embrace technological progress without dispensing with the tried and true. Uniformed men equipped with state-of-the-art cleaning machinery patrol the streets, alongside colleagues who still use lengths of rolled up carpet to divert water swirling down from the heights of Montmartre. They then sweep the gutters clean with brooms made from plastic imitation twigs, because no one has come up with anything better, and that is a practical and sensible compromise.

Although I couldn't believe my eyes at the time, and left the building fuming, vowing never to return, I still remember with muted affection the clerk who cut my credit card in two. It was done with such enormous style and panache, one couldn't feel too aggrieved at the way in which she savoured her moment of triumph.

238 Bears and Forebears

Such moments are to be treasured, for they provide the material which allows for the fleshing out of the bare bones of a story. Collecting them is one of the great pleasures of writing.

Not so long ago we were staying at a small hotel in Arcachon which was *sans restaurant*, but which boasted a small bar where if you wished you could have snacks in the evening. At the bottom of the menu it said: 'This menu has no gastronomic pretensions.' In England the hotel would probably have had a board outside saying 'Good Food' or 'Fine Wines'; a statement which in many cases is taking chances with the Trade Descriptions Act.

They were quite right, of course. They might have had as a customer a man who one evening was sitting at the table next to us at La Coupole. He listened with interest as we ordered our meal and when the first course arrived gave a nod of approval. Clearly, in his opinion we had chosen well.

'It is a good restaurant,' he said, when we passed some comment about the food. 'It does not seek to deceive.' Which struck me as a very French way of putting it.

Such niceties are instilled at an early age.

Outside a junior school near our apartment there is a board displaying the week's menu. Clearly, it has no gastronomic pretensions, but neither does it seek to deceive. I sometimes feel the urge to put on short trousers and eat there myself.

Time spent doing research or checking facts is never wasted, one thing leads to another and one wrong fact or piece of misinformation can undermine everything. However, there are occasions when you begin to wonder if your journey is really necessary.

In 1986 an airship started flying over our house and I immediately had a hankering to go up in it. It was the Flying-Flea syndrome all over again. Whenever I heard the distinctive sound of its two turbo-charged engines I rushed out into the garden, anxious to catch a glimpse. It looked so safe, so stately, so romantic, so *smooth*; and unlike the R101 it was filled with non-combustible helium rather than hydrogen.

Having discovered that the service operated out of a small airfield north of London I reserved a seat for myself some weeks ahead and spent the intervening period thinking about possible plots for a story.

By the time the day arrived I had the basic idea in my mind. It centred around the creation of a luxury air service between England and La Baule, on the west coast of France. It would be seen as a return to a more leisurely age. To celebrate the occasion, the French President has invited the then British Prime Minister, Mrs Thatcher, to travel with him on the inaugural flight.

A dirigible moving through the sky at a speed of less than sixty knots offers a sitting target, and the possibility of sabotage occupies the minds of the authorities to such an extent that, incredible though it may seem in a country so devoted to food, one important factor escapes everybody's notice. No provision has been made for a meal en route.

Quelle horreur! The honour of France is at stake. Heads will roll if nothing is done about it – quickly and secretly – for if news of the omission leaks out they will be the laughing stock of the world.

The advice of *Le Guide* having been sought, Monsieur Pamplemousse is despatched post haste to the Loire-Atlantique.

In the meantime I set off for the wilds of Hertfordshire in order to make sure I had got my facts right.

I was familiar with the basic details of the airship: length 59 metres; diameter 15.2 metres; gondola length 11.7 metres; number of passengers 13; but it was not until I arrived at the airfield in Hertfordshire and saw a dozen or so figures in three groups straining at ropes as they tried, not entirely successfully it seemed to me, to hold it down, that the possibility of a less than smooth flight crossed my mind. I had even been hoping there might be refreshments while we were aloft; a glass of champagne, perhaps, accompanied by smoked salmon sandwiches.

Some people never learn!

My worst fears were confirmed when we were given a brief lecture on how to climb into the gondola without injuring ourselves or upsetting the delicate balance of the whole. Clearly, it wasn't as easy as falling off a log, although parallels could be drawn.

If you are one of those people who, when they are going up in a high-speed lift, sometimes wonder what it would feel like if something went wrong and it failed to stop at the top floor, then you have some idea of the sensation of taking off in a balloon once they let go of the ropes. There can be no comparison with ordinary powered flight, because everything takes place in slow motion. Directional control is both sluggish and over responsive. The pilot constantly has to correct even quite basic manoeuvres – like steering a straight course. Worse still, from time to time he has to put the nose down at an angle of forty-five degrees or so in order to see where he's going.

Three-quarters of an hour later, having taken a few desultory photographs of the River Thames from a variety of angles and offered up a silent plea that we would make it safely back to base, I closed my eyes and sought solace in the thought that at least my prayers had a head start over any that might be emanating from Westminster Cathedral a thousand or so feet below us.

I disgraced myself shortly before we landed, but I was past caring anyway. A girl sitting opposite, who had been quite chatty when we first took off, had long since stopped talking to me. By an odd coincidence, my accountant happened to be on board too, and even he looked the other way. I think he wished he hadn't let on that he knew me.

Perhaps not surprisingly, when I came to write *Monsieur Pamplemousse Aloft*, Monsieur Pamplemousse's first flight was hardly any better than mine, although his powers of endurance were tested still further when he opened an envelope handed to him before he left Paris. It contained a letter from the director of *Le Guide* outlining the kind of meal he had in mind.

Beginning with *foie gras* served with raw oysters, Monsieur le Directeur weaves a gastronomic path through course after course. Poached eggs with mussels, followed by lobster *a là crème* and tartlets made with eggs, almonds and cream . . .

'To round things off, for by that time they should be on the last leg of their epic journey and nearing Londres, in deference to our English guests, I suggest that with the *café* we serve, instead of *petits fours*, one of their own specialities. There is one I am thinking of which they call a "trifle" . . .

'It seems to be a concoction which is made by emptying the contents of a can of tinned fruit over what are known as "sponge-fingers", which have themselves been previously steeped in sherry. The whole thing is then immersed in something they call "bird's custard". I cannot imagine what that is, nor what it must taste like

– I have enquired at Fauchon and they promised to telephone me back, but they have yet to do so – however, it appears to be very popular. The dish is then topped by a layer of thick cream . . .

'I am not sure what would go with it; the combination might prove altogether too rich, but if there is any of the Château d'Yquem left –'

The airship gave a lurch. Monsieur Pamplemousse suddenly felt extremely sick . . .

Regardless of the sign warning him to keep his seatbelt fastened, he released the clip and staggered towards the rear of the airship. He beat the stewardess by a short head, but pretended not to have seen her. Never had the word TOILETTES looked so welcoming, nor a basin coming up to greet him so inviting. Pushing the door shut behind him with his foot, he slid the catch home all in one movement. It was no time for old-fashioned gallantry, more a case of every *homme* for himself. Not the most engaging girl he had ever met. No doubt she was prone to headaches.

I'm glad to say Mrs Thatcher's powers of endurance were never put to the test. The mind boggles at the thought of her racing the French President to the TOILETTE, but at least my mother's recipe for trifle hadn't gone to waste. Neither had my first and last trip in a dirigible.

Another question writers are often asked is: 'How long does it take to write a book?' Once again, it is impossible to answer.

There is a moment in time when, with files full of cuttings and pieces of paper and old envelopes covered with scribbled, barely decipherable notes, your mind awash with scraps of dialogue, you clear the desk and start work in earnest.

At which point it is helpful to have an understanding partner, someone who doesn't talk too much at breakfast, or take umbrage when attempts at conversation during the day are met with an impatient grunt. Gradually over the weeks and months the drawer containing all the debris of your mind is cleared, the scraps of paper consigned to the waste bin, and you start to become a civilized human being again. There is light, as they say, at the end of the tunnel. And as you freewheel towards the end, knowing that you can do it, a corner of your mind even detaches itself from the main part and starts thinking about the next book as a precaution against postnatal depression.

And then there is the day when the book is actually finished and you can go out and celebrate and take in the world around you. All that is measurable in terms of perhaps three months, or four months, or however long it normally takes you in real time.

But if you count the hours your subconscious spends working on an idea it is impossible to give a straight answer. The subconscious operates in mysterious ways, often taking totally unrelated happenings and ideas, mixing them all together and coming up, days, weeks, months, or sometimes years later with an answer which bears little or no relationship to any of the many parts.

One of my earliest ambitions was to write a novel about Hollywood. Directing a major film has to be one of the most demanding jobs there is, which is perhaps why over the years it has attracted so many larger-than-life characters. It needs the qualities of a despot or a masochist to take the job on in the first place. Hitler would probably have made a good film director had his ambitions not lain elsewhere.

My inspiration was Eric Linklater's *Juan in America*, plus all the movies I had seen as a boy. In the early fifties I even began work on a book about the making of a biblical epic; the last and the greatest and possibly the most disastrous film ever made dealing with the coming of Christ and the Crucifixion.

But it was a case of diving in at the deep end without having first learned to swim, and with no very clear idea of where I was heading, or indeed without any first-hand knowledge of the subject.

Writing in longhand, I got about a third the way through the manuscript before finally abandoning it, although out of the attempt came several mini short stories involving the producer, Hirem K. Weisensteiner, and a voluptuous bimbo called Lola la Verne, who was to have played the Virgin Mary. The rest was relegated to my subconscious.

Meanwhile Hollywood itself had changed. The great studios were still there but in name only, given over to making television series or turned into theme parks; and with their passing had gone the whole studio system and the people who had run it. The idea no longer seemed viable.

The idea surfaced again in the seventies when I was visiting FilmFair and watched the making of a commercial in the desert behind Hollywood.

It then lay fallow for a few more years, until we were on holiday in Provence and spent a night near Les Baux, that strange rocky excrescence rising out of the flat and often barren countryside to the north of the Camargue.

West of Les Baux lies the Val d'Enfer – Hell Valley – bare and forbidding. The old town itself is the subject of many legends; of the ancient courts which once held sway there, lurid tales of the sadistic Raymond de Turonne, whose favourite after-dinner sport was watching prisoners being thrown to their death from the highest point.

It struck me – as it must have struck many others – that it would be an ideal setting for a biblical extravaganza.

The whole area is steeped in religion. Legend has it that Mary Magdalene, having been cast adrift in a boat, came ashore on the coast of France at Les Saintes-Maries-de-la-Mer. She then took refuge in a cave high up on the northern face of La Sainte-Baume Massif, where she spent the remaining thirty years of her life.

And there were other places nearby, like Fontvieille, where the writer Alphonse Daudet once lived and wrote his immortal *Letters from a Windmill*. There was no shortage of locations.

Ideas began to flow and take shape.

The story would be about the making of a series of perfume commercials. The whole of the Bible – the story of the Ark, the coming of Christ, the parting of the Red Sea – all compressed into a few minutes; arguably the most expensive project ever. More expensive even than the Chanel commercial for 'Egoist' when, at a cost of untold millions, the director ordered a reconstruction in Brazil of Cannes' Hotel Carlton simply because the light was better.

The product would be called XS – a name which would echo the cost of the whole operation. Monsieur Pamplemousse would be seconded to the unit as an adviser on the food of the time. Pommes Frites might even have a role in the film. Von Strudel, a German director renowned for his biblical epics in the thirties, but not noted for his ability to stick either to a script or a budget, would be brought out of retirement. Playing the part of Jesus would be a pop star called Brother Angelo – real name Ron Pickles – by nature unbelievably lecherous and profane, but with the looks of an angel. Not a million miles from the person I had once shared a Nissen hut with in Manchester during the war.

Books about the area began to pile up on my office floor, brochures on Hollywood-style trailer accommodation arrived from America. Apicius' writings on Roman food became required bedtime reading, along with books about the perfume industry and yet more on the world of advertising.

One of the problems with research is that at times it can become overwhelming, leading you off on a dozen false trails. You wade through piles of material on a subject for the sake of a single sentence.

Fortunately I returned to the area to check on various things and to take reference photographs before I got too far, for none of the places mentioned in the guide books turned out to be as I had pictured them. Rule number one is always make sure your sources are up to date.

Far from standing in splendid isolation on a tiny hill just outside Fontvieille, Daudet's windmill was a seething mass of tourists and clicking cameras; the vast car park behind it engulfed in a permanent dust storm as coach tours came and went.

The queues shuffling round the little church in the Place de l'Église in Les Saintes-Maries-de-la-Mer were worse than those for the Royal Academy on the opening day of a new exhibition. Michelin's advice to have one franc at the ready to feed a coin-operated light switch just inside the door simply did not apply in July.

Outside the cave in La Sainte-Baume Massif, where Mary Magdalene spent her remaining years, there were notices saying NO FLASH and CHIENS INTERDIT. Neither seemed to be having much effect.

And for the 'Last Supper' I'm pleased to say Monsieur Pamplemousse opted, not for roast guinea-pig, as depicted in a painting which hangs in a church in Cuzco, Peru, but lamb with bitter herbs and other condiments.

According to my notebook I began writing *Monsieur Pamplemousse On Location*, the ninth in the series, on 26 February 1991 and finished it on 18 December. So, to answer the second question, the writing of it took just under ten months, or nearly forty years – which ever way you care to look at it.

Coincidentally, some time after the book was published, Paco Rabanne launched a perfume called XS, but as far as I know they never made a commercial starring Ron Pickles and I can't say I blame them.

CHAPTER 15

Ashes to Ashes

Let us be grateful to our parents: had they
not been tempted we should not be here.

Talmud (Jewish Law)

Harvey Unna always maintains, and I think he is right, that people never recognize themselves in books.

Writers use anything and everything that comes their way, including people, in a quite shameless manner. In most cases by the time they appear in print they are almost always so changed to meet the needs of the story there is very little of the original left to recognize.

My parents live on in the Paddington books, for they are in essence the Mr and Mrs Brown who found Paddington on the station and took him home to live with them, although I doubt if they ever recognized themselves. Unlike Mrs Brown, there were times when my mother was so right wing she stopped just short of being a fascist, although she wouldn't have recognized that either.

While I was away in the army she got a job in a small nursing home as part of her war work. I'm not sure what she did, for she hated the sight of blood and hospitals were anathema to her.

All her life she remained faithful to tried and tested home remedies. The smell of camphorated oil and Wintergreen was never far away.

It was camphor that very nearly did for my father. One spring morning he changed into some old togs and settled down with his pipe and the morning paper before starting work in the garden. Gradually a change came over him and he literally began to go green.

It turned out that when my mother put his jacket away for the winter she placed some camphor balls in the pockets to keep away the moths.

She forgot to take them out and one had rolled into my father's pipe before he filled it.

'I thought it hadn't taken much tobacco,' was all he said afterwards.

My mother's spell at the nursing home didn't last very long. She was asked to leave when they discovered she had been putting all the clocks on when it was getting near time to go home. When I suggested that must have meant she'd had to get there next day to put them right, she said: 'Oh, no. They did that. The first thing I did was put them all on again.'

She didn't tell my father for he would have been scandalized.

Soon after I was demobolized he developed a bad attack of sciatica, the fashionable treatment for which at the time was to be encased in a plaster jacket.

It's almost impossible to convey to those who didn't experience it what six years of war was like. In the beginning it crept up on people gradually and so they got used to it, but it took its toll. What with one thing and another – fire-watching duties, the Home Guard, 'digging for victory', bombings, and in the latter part of the war travelling up and down to London in blacked-out trains which took for ever and occasionally didn't arrive at all – my father had had a tiring six years and he was noticeably quieter than I remembered him.

He seldom complained, but he found the plaster jacket claustrophobic and it was obviously playing on his mind. He couldn't wait for the day of his appointment to have it removed.

An encounter with a prima donna surgeon who waved him aside like an errant fly, telling him to come back in two weeks' time, resulted almost immediately in a nervous breakdown.

I asked our family doctor where he would send *his* father if he had the same problem and he mentioned a hospital at Moulsford, outside Reading.

When I was small the name 'Moulsford' had entered the local language as a synonym for 'looney bin', but he said the name had been changed and it was quite different now.

He was right about the first, but not the second. A new name, a fresh coat of paint and a visitors' car park, gave no indication of what was to come.

I left my father, minus his braces, his shoelaces and his dignity, holding up his trousers in bewilderment, a forlorn figure amongst hundreds of others, many of them clearly abandoned by their families, with no one left to 'sign' for them, and I wondered what I had done.

As the weeks went by and there was no visible change it dawned on me that nothing would happen without some table-thumping. The overworked and probably, like all the staff, underpaid mid-European psychiatrist I saw was like something out of a film, but he was kind and sympathetic and promised to do what he could.

Several doses of shock treatment later I collected my father and took him home.

He never talked about it; I'm not sure if he even remembered or knew what had gone on, for which one can only be grateful. Although he gradually recovered and became his normal self again, it had slowed him down and it was clear that the promotion he could normally have expected at work was not going to happen, so he took early retirement.

After a spell of living by the sea on the outskirts of Worthing, which didn't work out because they found themselves surrounded by much older people whose first waking act was to look out of their windows to see who hadn't drawn their curtains that morning, my parents finally settled down in a village near Hindhead.

It was a place where no eyebrows were ever raised by the fact that the local newsagents called itself 'Gay News' (although there must have been a few disappointed tourists seeking a little light relief after the Devil's Punchbowl), and where the fashion house of Augusta Rolph reigned supreme, which suited my mother down to the ground.

In later life, whenever I took my parents out for lunch, I had to conceal the menu from my mother for fear she would lie awake that night worrying about it. She always equated the bill with what it would have cost to cook the same dishes at home.

I tried taking her to places where guests weren't permitted to see the prices, and then I discovered in the *Good Food Guide* an inn at Itchen Abbas where the owner, who was rather cantankerous, didn't even *have* a menu. He simply recited the bill of fare twice – once forward and once backward. If you didn't remember what he'd said, which we rarely did, it was too bad; he totally refused to repeat it. So we tended to order the same thing every time. But since it was trout, freshly caught from the

River Itchen, made famous by Isaac Walton in *The Compleat Angler*, it hardly mattered.

She never lost the habit of coming out with statements which brooked no argument. Towards the end of her life we used to drive down from London and take them for rides in the country; my father sitting in the front of the car smoking the inevitable pipe, so that it was often difficult to see where we were going, my mother sitting in the back armed with a bag of boiled sweets which she sucked rather noisily in between commenting on the passing scene, or closing her eyes when we went down a steep hill.

'Don't like flowers much,' she announced one day as we were passing through a particularly beautiful stretch of countryside. 'The blessed petals fall off and make the place untidy.'

On another occasion, thinking it would be a treat, I took them to the site of an old Roman villa. I parked the car near a group of houses and as my mother climbed out she looked around and said: 'What a funny place to build a Roman villa – right next door to a housing estate!'

Harvest time and its attendant traffic jams brought out the worst. 'Blessed farmers – holding up the traffic. Why they always have to do their haymaking at this time of the year I don't know!'

'I was lying awake last night thinking of these drives,' she remarked on another occasion, when we were heading down the Portsmouth road towards the sea, 'and I suddenly thought of all the murderers we must pass on the way. I hope you never give any of them a lift.'

One day she read in a newspaper that putting a few corks under the bedclothes was a good cure for cramp. She acquired several and when they didn't achieve the hoped-for result, she invested in a whole bagful. It was around that time that my father began sleeping in the spare room, complaining that it was uncomfortable when he tried to turn over.

It must have been the last time they slept together, for in the autumn of 1981 my mother fell ill. At first it was just a case of her rheumatism being worse than usual, but then she stopped going out in the car. Boiled sweets remained uneaten, books were left unread.

One day I was summoned because she had turned over rather sharply in bed during the night and was now in pain. I arrived just as the doctor was leaving and, in a manner I couldn't quite put my finger on, he suggested I take her into Guildford Hospital for a check.

An X-ray revealed a broken collar-bone and at one point during the proceedings I overheard a doctor mention six weeks to the sister. Nothing more was said and I took her home again, assuming he had been talking about the time it would take for the bone to mend.

But it soon became clear there was something seriously wrong.

Shortly before my mother died, when she was still living at home, I went to see her and, having made the coffee, commented on the fact that there was some milk in the refrigerator which had 'gone off'.

A look of alarm came over her face. 'I hope you haven't thrown it out. I always keep sour milk for the pastry!' It was magic ingredient X and I pass on the tip for what it's worth, although I dare say there is more to it than that.

The end, when it came, was mercifully swift. Her worst fears were realized. She went into a hospice and never came out again.

I took my father in to see her and he, always seeing the best in things, emerged puffing his pipe saying: 'I thought your mother was looking a little better today.'

But she wasn't. Until that moment I had never seen anyone look so ill or change so much in such a short space of time. Three days later she was dead, riddled with bone cancer.

It would have been good to have known the truth in the beginning, but, then again, perhaps not.

The hospice where she died was staffed by nuns and they were wonderfully kind and reassuring. Just before the end, when I went with Karen to see her for the last time, she tried to form words with her lips, but nothing happened. I sometimes wonder what she wanted to say. With her dying went the answers to many questions I would now like to ask, but it's too late.

One should never put off these things.

I placed an announcement of her death in the *Daily Telegraph* and it would undoubtedly have confirmed her views of that otherwise excellent newspaper which she had long since cancelled on account of the large number of misprints it contained at that time. They got her first name wrong: they put *Francess* instead of Frances!

She had led a good and simple life. My father never went to work looking anything other than immaculate: shirts ironed, buttons firmly sewn on, glasses washed in soapy water (when he wasn't looking, of course). She began to trust banks less and less, so cash was always kept under the bed. It exercised her considerably when bills arrived late.

'The electricity came on April the twelfth last year,' she would say indignantly, 'and here it is the fifteenth! I can't think what's gone wrong.' When it did arrive she would be up to the showrooms at Hindhead in a flash, and it was the company's turn to be exercised, for they weren't expecting anyone quite so soon and were not really geared to taking cash.

After she had been cremated I was offered her ashes. They were in a large brown plastic pot with a screw top and I didn't like to say no, although it seemed a strange end to a life and I had no clear idea of what to do with them. It was the start of a series of mishaps that would have tried her patience sorely.

To begin with I had the romantic notion of scattering them on the mill stream at Newbury, near to where both she and I had been born, and where she had once taken her pony upstairs, and before that had been tossed by a mad bull which had escaped from the market and was being chased along the tow path. Fortunately it had been a southpaw and she had landed in her own front garden rather than in the canal, but it had put her off cows and their like for the rest of her life.

Emotionally, although she had not lived there for well over fifty years, she had never really left the scene of her childhood.

My plan got off to a bad start. The day before I intended putting it into action I was having lunch with an old girlfriend and for some reason or other the conversation turned to the strange things people keep in their car boot. When it came to guessing what was in mine she failed miserably and was quite put out when I told her about my mother's ashes. It cast a gloom over the rest of the meal.

The following day it began to snow and the urn stayed where it was for several weeks. When I did eventually find myself in the West Country, planning to drive back to London via Newbury, the car wouldn't start and I had to return by train. In desperation I decided to put plan B into action and scatter the ashes over the railway line as we went through Newbury. At what I judged to be the appropriate moment I went along to the toilet, only to discover the window wouldn't open. By then it was far too late.

It was another week or so before I was able to collect my car. Determined to do the deed come what may, I returned to Newbury for the first time in some forty years and made my way to West Mills in the centre of the town.

It wasn't quite as I remembered it. The mill was still there and so was the lock-keeper's cottage. There were no mad bulls on the tow path; instead it was crowded with people and obviously in regular use as a short cut from the main street to another part of town. Ignoring curious glances from passers-by, I hung around for a while furtively clutching a carrier bag containing the plastic pot, pretending I was admiring the view rather than about to jump in the canal. Eventually there was a lull and I seized my opportunity. Undoing the screw top, I began emptying the contents of the jar into the fast-flowing stream.

Even allowing for the fact that my mother's figure had come under the heading of generous rather than sylph-like, there were rather more ashes than I had expected. A large black cloud rose from the water, then disappeared round the corner at a rate of knots. Fearing I was probably breaking all sorts of by-laws to do with pollution and that any second I might be reported to Greenpeace, I hastily replaced the cap and made my way back into town, where I wandered around for a while pondering whether or not to deposit the rest of the ashes into a waste bin. I'm sure that's what my mother would have done – I sensed how impatient she would have been by then, but it didn't seem right.

In the end I drove a few miles out of town to Savernake Forest, a place she had often spoken of fondly, for it was a favourite picnic spot when she was a child. There I scattered the remaining ashes in a secluded glade. I hope she was as relieved as I was to find peace at last.

Graham Clutterbuck fared even worse when he tried to deposit his brother's ashes on top of a hill they had both known when they were small. Having parked his car at the bottom and climbed all the way to the top, he opened the container only to discover they were in a sealed tin – and not a tin-opener in miles!

It had always been assumed, most of all by my mother, that if statistics were anything to go by, my father would die before she did. I think she always nursed plans of what she would do when that happened. She had devoted her life to looking after him. He never went outside the door without being given what she called 'a square meal'. I doubt if he ever had to boil a kettle, let alone manage anything involving a saucepan.

Whenever he came to stay with us I always gave him a boiled egg for breakfast and every morning he would smack his lips and remark: 'I say, Mike, lovely boiled egg this.' It got to be so predictable I began to wish he'd find something wrong with it; a foreign body inside, a tiny feather, a piece of broken beak – *anything*!

One day, having been particularly fulsome in his praise, he asked how long I gave them. I went into a long discourse about all the many variables: size, age, temperature, whether or not you put them into cold water and brought them to the boil, but since I usually put mine into boiling water I made sure they were at room temperature first and pricked the shell to prevent it cracking. All in all, on average and knowing his taste, to answer the question, about four and half minutes.

'Ah,' he said. 'That's interesting. I usually give mine twenty.'

In short, at the age of eighty-three he was ill-equipped to fend for himself.

Since we were away a lot and not in a position to have him live with us permanently, the first assumption led to a second on the part of those who knew him. He would have to go into a home where he would be well looked after.

But he would have none of it. He dug his heels in, and when my father dug his heels in there was no shifting him.

It was his decision, and although there were times when we wondered if it was the right one, it made him happy so we respected his wishes, fetching him up to London as often as we could, and keeping him well supplied with food.

He developed a great liking for biscuits, chomping his way through pounds at a time until even the check-out girl at the local Tesco store knew when he was coming to stay.

'Your mother never knew I like biscuits,' he announced one day.

It struck me as a sobering thought that two people can live together in apparent happiness for around sixty years and still lack communication over such a basic matter, although thinking about it later she probably didn't like all the crumbs.

For the rest of his days my father enjoyed a new lease of life, timing the journeys up and down the A3, much as he would have done when he was checking postmen's rounds. Nodding his approval when we were on schedule, casting dark glances at what he called 'those blessed jugger-nauts' when we weren't. ('They shouldn't be allowed on the roads!') Meeting what he referred to as my 'colleagues'; people who until then had only been names he'd heard me talk about.

It was hard to tell how much he missed my mother. I think in some ways the treatment he received when he had his nervous breakdown anaesthetized him to major shocks, but I also suspect he treated her absence as being of a temporary nature.

A story he was fond of telling about her concerned a pair of slippers he had been given shortly before she died. He had been looking forward to wearing them, but when the time came to try them out, they were nowhere to be found.

All through her life my mother had been prone to making spur of the moment gestures and it transpired that having seen pictures on television about a major earthquake in Italy she had gone straight out and given them to a relief organization.

The strong probability that being brand new they had ended up on the feet of the local Mafia boss was of less concern to my father than the fact that she hadn't donated her own slippers.

In any case, as people grow older their horizons shrink and they become more concerned with how things are going to affect them. If ever we said we were going away it was never a case of asking where, which at one time would have been his first question, but always: 'When will you be back?'

Graham usually joined us for supper on a Sunday evening and my father would watch with increasing concern as the remains of the joint grew steadily smaller, knowing that each extra slice for Graham – and there were usually a good many – meant one less for him during the rest of the week.

He remained a civil servant until he died; always reading the small print and a stickler for abiding by the rules and regulations.

He was at his most infuriating when he donned his official hat. One day during the war, as a member of the Post Office Home Guard he was doing sentry duty outside the telephone exchange when some enemy aircraft were sighted and the building was put on red alert. His orders were clear. No one was allowed in without a pass. He refused entry to a female colleague who had left her pass at home; a girl who not only shared the same room with him every day but who lived in the same road.

'Funny thing,' he used to say, wearing his slightly aggrieved expression, 'she didn't speak to me for about six weeks afterwards.'

After one weekend in London there was a muddle over which day he was going back. Thinking it was Tuesday, he cancelled his Monday delivery of meals on wheels.

In the event, I took him back home on the Monday morning and to my relief we arrived at his front door at the same time as the wagon.

Helping my father out of the car, I told him the good news.

He gave the lady at the wheel a Paddington-type hard stare. 'If, when you return to headquarters,' he said severely, 'you care to consult your superior officer, you will ascertain that I made arrangements to cancel today's meal. I am afraid, therefore, that I am unable to accept delivery.'

It was reminiscent of my solo party piece at school and it had a similar effect on his audience; it stopped the lady from meals on wheels dead in her tracks. She couldn't believe her ears, and neither could I.

We both protested, pointing out that since she was there with the meal he might just as well have it, but we were wasting our breath. It was returned uneaten.

Despite his normally gentle ways and impeccable manners, he had a hard core of toughness and nothing daunted him.

Taking a short cut one evening across some wasteland between his club in Haslemere and the bus stop for home, he was waylaid by a gang of youths and sent them packing with his walking stick.

It was probably just as well they didn't know what was in his wallet. One day, after he had been to collect his pension, Sue discovered him trying to force some money into it. Like my mother, he had given up on banks, and there was over £800 inside.

Once, when we arrived to collect him, he appeared at the front door with his head in bandages, pointing with great glee to some bloodstains on the wall where he had fallen down the stairs.

On another occasion I found him in the kitchen in his shirtsleeves surrounded by tools – hammer, pliers, chisels – in a state of nervous exhaustion. He had been trying to open a 'child-proof' plastic pillbox and was getting desperate because it was way past the time when he was meant to take them.

Although for most of my father's life snooker was the only game in which he took an active part – it suited his temperament and he was actually a very good player – he was a great follower of sport in general. He could recite cricket scores and football league positions until the cows came home, and often did whether or not anyone was prepared to listen; usually beginning with: 'I know you're not interested, but . . .'

Had he been a newspaper editor he would undoubtedly have reversed the order of things and printed the results on the front page.

On one occasion he was introduced to the Duke of Somerset, who came forward, hand outstretched, saying: 'Somerset, you know.'

'Oh, really?' said my father. 'That's interesting. I usually follow Middlesex myself.'

He couldn't believe his eyes the day he was watching a snooker match on the BBC and they interrupted play in order to show a live transmission of the siege of the Iranian Embassy. He talked about it in aggrieved tones for a long time afterwards.

But towards the end of his life he became much more concerned with falling attendances and began to quote the number of people who had gone to see a game, rather than the final score.

One day I was doing-it-myself in an upstairs room, installing a new fire back. It involved a good deal of work with a club hammer and a cold chisel. The moment came when a large and rather heavy cut-glass ashtray fell off the mantelpiece and landed on my head. As I staggered round the room clutching it, I realized that blood was pouring from the wound, so I dashed downstairs and through the living-room, heading for the kitchen sink.

My father was reading the daily paper and as I went past he said: 'I know you're not interested, but there were only just over two thousand watching Brighton last Saturday.'

One Christmas, knowing his liking for facts and figures, I bought him a copy of *The Guinness Book of World Records*, thinking it might be something he could refer to from time to time. I showed him the entry for the *Magnet* and left it with him. The next time he came up to stay he said he had got to page twenty-three and he was enjoying it very much indeed.

In his remaining years my father often quoted a mysterious 'they'. '*They* say it's all going to happen in 1984.' It was useless trying to explain that 1984 was the title of a book by George Orwell. 'Ah!' was all he would say, adding darkly: 'That's not far away, you know.'

He enjoyed Karen's and Tony's wedding, marvelling at the cosmopolitan atmosphere of the Edgware Road as we returned home late that night. It was one way of putting it, and for a while it made me see it in a new light. And he took great pleasure in 'apprising' Anthony at an early age of the rules of draughts. It must have left a deep impression because when Eve asked Anthony who had won, the response was: 'Nobody beats Pop at draughts!'

He would have adored his great-grandchildren, Robyn, Harry – who was recently heard describing me to a friend as having 'white hair with a hole in the middle' – and India, and they would have adored him. Children are often so much more understanding of old age.

They would probably have called him 'Gumboil' as Karen always did; an affectionate nickname which began as a childhood mispronunciation of his name and somehow stuck because we all laughed at the time, and which in later years often gave rise to odd glances from passers-by if they happened to hear it being used.

My father didn't quite make 1984. One evening, some two years after my mother died, he folded his napkin after dinner. It took him an agonizingly long time, for he was determined to get it right, but we knew we mustn't interfere. Then, after shaking hands with Sue and myself as he always did, and thanking us for a lovely day, he tottered off into the adjoining room.

The following morning, when he didn't appear for breakfast, I went to wake him and found him lying across the bed, still fully dressed. It must have happened within minutes of saying goodnight.

Although he had died of a heart attack, an autopsy revealed that the principal cause had been cancer. At least he had been spared all the pain and the indignities of a long illness.

A few days later, going through his belongings I came across a cardboard box. His whole life was done up in small piles, all neatly tied with ribbon: receipts, letters, official documents, certificates of birth and marriage, and last but not least, a list of addresses and telephone numbers of those who would need to be informed of his passing.

Diaries listing all his visits to London, a half-used block of blue chalk from his snooker days, a little silver case in which he kept his supply of

Swan Vesta matches and his beloved pipe are among my souvenirs.

Latterly, although he had always kept his pipe filled, he never managed to light it. Going through the motions of striking a match and applying it to the bowl, he seemed perfectly happy with the result, saying: 'Very good tobacco, this Gold Block.' Puff. Puff. 'I bought a two-ounce tin over a year ago and I still haven't got through it.'

The particular smell of a newly opened box of Swan Vestas always reminds me of my father and the pleasure he got from his pipe, just as for a long while the smell of bay rum reminded me of my grandfather.

CHAPTER 16

Reflections From a Café Terrace

If you sit outside the Café de la Paix in Paris long enough eventually someone you know will pass by.

Legend

I have taken coffee on the terrace of the Café de la Paix on a number of occasions, but I have never actually seen anyone I know go past.

Perhaps I'm too impatient; once I've finished my coffee I want to be on my way. I used to be in trouble with Karen when she was small because on holiday no sooner had we unpacked than I would start saying 'Where shall we go next year?' And Anthony despairs of my ever reading an instruction manual all the way through, particularly the kind that comes in six different languages all inextricably woven together, with one's own language appearing on every sixth or seventh page due to the fact that some nations have difficulty in translating even quite simple phrases like 'camera back release pin', which in French becomes *'goupille de retenue du dos de l'appareil'* and in Spanish *'pasador de Retención de la Tapa Trasera'* all of which take up extra space.

Be that as it may, as you grow older the wheel tends to go the full circle; paths cross, strands come together, and you begin to bump into people at odd times and in odd places – or not, as the case may be.

There are those who will never go past the Café de la Paix and there's no point in waiting around in case they do.

Tim, my earliest 'best friend' and one day younger than me – a matter of considerable importance when we were small – was the first to remind me that life is finite. Together, we shared many of the problems of growing up and he was also best-man when Brenda and I were married. A few years later I returned the compliment, then somehow or other we drifted apart and went our separate ways.

In the nature of things there are numerous uncles and aunts, and in some cases their children, who will never go past: I didn't ever get to meet my cousin, Pat Langford, the only son of my Auntie Dolly in Canada, for in 1944 he was shot in cold blood by the Gestapo, one of fifty selected at random from the seventy-three who were caught after they made the Great Escape from Stalag Luft III.

I was barely aware of Patsy's father at the time, but I'm sure he registered me that day in the early thirties when his daughter did her 'big jobs' behind my back. Called up for the Navy, he drowned in the Irish Sea after his ship was torpedoed.

Graham Clutterbuck would almost certainly have put in an appearance, probably pausing for a moment or two while on his way to the opera, which was one of his great loves in life.

He couldn't resist studying menus outside restaurants, and occasionally went inside to discuss them with the owner.

Once, when we were out for a morning stroll along the banks of the Seine, he stopped by an establishment on the Quai de St Augustine. It so happened the patron and his wife were standing in the doorway watching the passing scene and an animated conversation ensued during which a table for three was reserved for that evening and the entire meal ordered, including the wine and Graham's preferred type of mineral water. He held strong views on mineral water and its effect on the liver.

Going on our way he fell strangely silent. I suspect that even he realized he had gone a little too far, or perhaps he was totting up the bill, for he hadn't stinted himself. Sure enough, after a particularly heavy lunch *chez nous* – heavy because Graham had done the shopping, remarking on his return: 'I don't know how you two do it every day', which we certainly didn't – doubts crystallized and by popular vote Sue was deputed to phone and cancel the booking.

'Say I've been taken ill.'

Nor did he ever go back to a newly opened restaurant he spotted one evening having driven over Hammersmith Bridge. Stopping to investigate, he went inside and spent some time advising the owner on what was wrong with his menu. Rabbit was the main thing it lacked. It was one of Graham's favourites, and there would have been a long dissertation on the many ways it could be cooked.

Pleading an urgent appointment, and promising to call back another day, he went on his way.

Whether it was because the owner took advantage of the freely offered advice and nobody else in Hammersmith shared Graham's passion for *oryctolagus cuniculus* in any shape or form, we never knew, but a few weeks later the restaurant closed down.

Sadly, on 30 April 1988 Graham died of cancer of the liver.

He fought the disease for long time and even gave it a name. (Not 'Rupert', as did Dennis Potter.) For a while it seemed as though he was winning, but then he began to complain that things didn't taste as they once did.

One day he rang me after a routine visit to the hospital where he was having chemotherapy treatment. One his way back to the office he had called in at a restaurant in Marylebone High Street where he had partaken of bacon, sausage, eggs, baked beans, tomato and chips.

'And do you know,' he said rather plaintively, 'I feel sick!'

He derived a certain amount of comfort when I said that after listening to him describing the meal I did too, but it was the beginning of the end. He gave up walking to work, which must have been a blow to his morale, for he was a great believer in his morning constitutional through Regent's Park, come rain or shine.

He once told me that on the way he always asked himself the simple question: 'What happens if it all stops right now? How much am I worth? And how much do I owe?' It was sound advice given by one who'd had the rug pulled out from under him once in his life and didn't intend to let it happen again if he could help it. But the final reckoning wasn't far away.

After Graham died, and indeed long after I had taken part in his memorial service, it occurred to me that although, as he himself would have been the first to admit, he'd had his share of faults, I never once heard him speak ill of anyone, even those who had done him an injustice. He always found an excuse for their behaviour. One can't say that about many people.

If Kaye Webb had stopped by it would have been for champagne rather than coffee, and after that goodness knows what would have happened, for she was a mistress of the unexpected.

One Friday evening when I was living at the Barbican I had a sudden attack of guilt at not having seen her for a while, so I telephoned and suggested she might like to have lunch the following day, in which case I would pick her up.

'What a lovely idea, darling.' There was a slight pause. 'Could you make it early?'

'Of course.' Thoughts of 12.30 or even midday flitted innocently through my mind.

'How about 8.30?' It so happened Kaye had an appointment with an osteopath somewhere in the wilds of Oxfordshire the next morning.

At around two o'clock that afternoon, having shopped for a picnic and read all the papers, I found myself sitting under a tree in a field miles from anywhere, sipping champagne and wondering how on earth I'd allowed myself to be talked into it. But Kaye could talk anyone into anything, if you allowed your guard to slip for a moment, largely because she had an uncanny knack of leaving the salient bits of information until it was too late to turn back.

Once, when I had a manuscript to deliver, she suggested I dropped it off at her house. 'And could you bring a shovel with you?' were her parting words.

Since I was wearing my best suit, I conveniently forgot to follow her instructions and I was glad I had. When I got to her house I discovered she had a lamp-post she wanted moved.

Years later I was having lunch with a lawyer and for some reason the conversation came around to Kaye, as it so often did. 'Funny thing,' he said. 'I once had to move a lamp-post for her!'

She and Graham did not get on well together.

At heart Graham was a frustrated variety act. Two other people constituted an audience. For Kaye two other people constituted rivals for her affections. On the one occasion when they met, Graham won hands down in the performance stakes, reducing Kaye to silence.

But she had the last word. For some reason best known to himself he had been wearing an incredibly threadbare overcoat, the herringbone pattern of which looked as though it had been run over by a car at some point. Knowing Graham's driving, it was probably a self-inflicted wound.

'I didn't think much of your seedy friend, darling,' said Kaye after he left.

If Dick Miller went past he would almost certainly be rushing to catch a plane. He is the original 'If it's Monday, it must be Paris, France, because Tuesday it's Tokyo'. Except he would probably say 'Are you talking a.m. or p.m.?'

One evening I was sitting quietly at home when the telephone rang and a girl's voice asked if I would accept a reverse-charge call from China.

Being in the middle of dinner I said firmly: 'No, I don't know anyone in China,' and hung up.

A few minutes later the phone rang again.

Would I, asked a plaintive voice, accept a reverse-charge call from a Mr Miller in China?

Fearing the worst – a signing at W. H. Wong in Chungking at the very least – I hesitated for a second or two, then resisted the temptation to say, 'In that case, certainly not!' A joke is a joke is a joke. The simple explanation was that Dick had mislaid his credit card and had run out of local currency. Indefatigable as ever, he was on his way back to the States and wondered if he came via London, would I be free for lunch?

We meet in that way from time to time; unexpectedly and always rewardingly and the intervening months roll away as if by magic.

Miss Bryant, the belle of my first job in a solicitor's office, went past one day when I was signing books, not at the Café de la Paix, but at a fête near Farnham. She was looking as immaculate as ever. The passing years since we had shared an office in Reading had not only been kind to her but had put us on more equal terms. I no longer felt in awe – I'm not sure that I didn't detect a certain degree of it on her part for a change, but that may have been wishful thinking. She was married by then, although I didn't like to ask if it was to her man of bygone days.

Then, a few years ago I was in the basement of Fortnum & Mason looking at some tablemats, when I felt someone materialize alongside me. A woman's voice passed some comment or other about how hard it was to find the right pattern these days. I responded with some equally innocuous remark and after a slight pause she moved away.

In the short time she was there I had hardly looked at her and yet the encounter had left me feeling strangely disturbed, almost as though

I had seen a ghost. I turned round quickly and whoever it was had gone, so I rushed out of the department, up the stairs and into Piccadilly, but there was no one I recognized.

Had it been N.K., my first great, unspoken love? Something told me that was who it had been. And if so, what then? Would it have been like a scene from *Brief Encounter*, sharing a table over coffee in a crowded room, unable to say all the things one wanted to say? Would I have told her that I still carry in my wallet a tiny piece of parchment bearing a picture of a shepherd, hand drawn in black ink, followed by the inscription 'Christmas/New Year card from N.K.' and the date, 1945/46?

Once again, I shall never know.

Given the opportunity, Uncle Jack might well have appeared outside the Café de la Paix, and that would have been worth waiting for. Like P. G. Wodehouse's Uncle Fred, he had a way of popping in and out of people's lives and leaving them feeling, if not richer or poorer, at least different.

Whenever there was news of his impending arrival in England, a frisson of alarm would run through the family as everyone wondered when and on whom he would bestow his favours. It wasn't that he was unwelcome; simply that he was so much larger than the sort of life most people were used to leading they were understandably nervous if he announced he was thinking of coming to stay. Alarm bells would sound, much as in olden times drawbridges would have been raised.

Everyone was very fond of Uncle Jack; but at a distance. They enjoyed hearing of his adventures involving other members of the family: like the time when he was staying with Auntie Ethel, by now living in Oxford to be near her family. He went out one evening to buy a packet of cigarettes – and no doubt to smoke them one after the other before he returned, for Auntie Ethel didn't allow them in her house. He didn't arrive back until about three o'clock in the morning some three days later, having been at a party given by, so he maintained, the Duchess of Argyll. Since it was a very long road and all the houses looked exactly alike, and since he had totally forgotten the number of Auntie Ethel's, he started at the beginning of the road and worked his way along, knocking on all the doors.

'Ho! Ho! Ho!' we all went as we related the story, falling about as we pictured all the bedroom lights coming on one by one, for distance lent enchantment. But when it came to having him to stay we all began clutching at straws in case something similar happened to us.

He never lost his wanderlust, but after he retired he began hankering after his roots and went to live in Brighton, where he was born, and where the racecourse and the sea was not too far apart.

A story he never tired of repeating, I think because it emphasized the fact that you should never trust anyone, not even little white-haired old ladies, concerned a time when he was staying at a hotel in San Francisco and happened to notice one such little old lady feeding some pigeons on the window ledge of an apartment opposite.

For a while he basked in the pleasure of it, deciding that perhaps, after all, the world wasn't such a bad place.

'And then, you know what? As soon as one of the pigeons got inside the room she slammed the goddam window shut on it!'

He, who had seen it all, was reduced to silence by the thought of her living on pigeon pie for the rest of the week.

Pommes Frites would have had no such qualms. As far as pigeons are concerned, finer feelings go by the board. Although I never had the good fortune to meet him, Sue tells me her father felt much the same way. Both would have agreed with the Club des Pigeons Citadins' policy of mixing contraceptive grain in with their feeding stuff.

But on a sunny spring morning, if his master happened to be between cases, Pommes Frites might well pass by the Café de la Paix, perhaps on his way to the gardens of the Palais Royal. If it so happens that there is an empty table, Monsieur Pamplemousse might even pause for a while to combine business with pleasure. Monsieur le Directeur encourages snap visits to well-known establishments.

And since it is Paris and the French are much more welcoming to their domestic pets than are the inhabitants of most capital cities, while Monsieur Pamplemousse sips his *café* the waiter will bring a bowl of water for Pommes Frites so that he can slake his thirst after the long walk down from Montmartre.

Monsieur Pamplemousse will note that the Café de la Paix is no longer quite the centre of the world as it was once thought to be – or the centre of the *French* world, which amounts to much the same thing – and that nowadays it is mostly patronized by tourists rather than the likes of Salvador Dali and Maurice Chevalier.

From time to time he will glance at his watch to make sure they arrive at the Palais Royal in time to watch the midday firing of a miniature cannon – a practice which has recently been revived by another of Paris's many caring societies. And if it happens to be a hot day and the cannon is set off automatically by the sun's rays, taking everybody including the pigeons by surprise, then Pommes Frites will think it well worth a detour.

I would never be surprised to see Paddington coming up the Avenue de l'Opera, especially now the Channel tunnel is open. He would be looking forward to his elevenses, but whether or not he would be allowed in is another matter.

The Ritz Hotel in London certainly had cold feet.

HarperCollins came up with the idea of running a competition in which the prize for the two winners and their families would be a trip to London, followed by afternoon tea with the author and Paddington Bear, or to be pedantic, someone dressed up to play the part of the latter.

It seemed like a good idea and all went well until they tried to book a table.

As soon as the Ritz heard that Paddington was to be one of the nine guests they went cold on the idea, and I can't say I blame them. I was beginning to feel a trifle unenthusiastic myself. All the same, there was more than a hint of desperation when they said they couldn't allow him in because he wouldn't be wearing a tie. It more or less duplicated a story I'd written many years before called 'Paddington Dines Out' in which he was refused admission to the Porchester because he wasn't wearing evening dress.

'Bears don't have evening dress,' said Judy, squeezing his paw. 'They have evening fur – and Paddington's has been washed specially.' Which solved the problem.

In the end, perhaps fearing they would be blacklisted by Animal Rights, the Ritz relented sufficiently to let him take part in a photo call in a side passage off the main foyer. Thankfully, more by luck than judgement, he didn't get stuck in the revolving doors, and the staff accorded him due respect.

Sir Michael Hordern had a lot in common with Paddington, which is probably why he brought so much warmth and understanding to his readings of the scripts.

If he were still with us and in Paris then it's more than likely he would be found, not at the Café de la Paix but sitting on the bank of the Seine clutching one of his beloved fishing rods, waiting patiently for a tug on the line and wearing that faintly quizzical expression one came to know so well.

Eddie Clarkson will never go past, and that is sad too, because in life he was the most convivial of companions, full of unstinting Yorkshire hospitality, yet stubborn as a mule, and like Paddington rather accident-prone – not many people can say they had to struggle down the aisle on crutches the day they got married. He was always the best of friends and Paddington has lost a great champion.

Some while ago I received a letter from my old school telling me that Brother Ambrose was retiring and asking if I would be prepared to make a presentation marking his many years of devotion to children.

But I could still clearly hear the rustle of his gown as he leapt from the platform, his white face towering above me, and feel his clenched fists with their nicotine-stained fingers as they battered me to the floor.

In declining the invitation I was tempted to explain why, but in the end I took the coward's way out and made other excuses. Times change, and I doubt if the person who wrote to me would have understood. Nor, I suspect, would Brother Ambrose, who must have forgotten the incident by then.

If I were a schoolmaster I'm sure I would be sorely tempted to wallop my charges all the time, and some of us must have tried his patience beyond measure. Quite possibly I was being punished for the many, just as there are moments when I lose my temper and all the wrongs and injustices of the world are added to my wrath. At such moments I often give the nearest inanimate object a good thump and get more than I bargained for. Animate objects are much more vulnerable.

I wasn't a very good pupil. I was disinclined to work hard at things which didn't interest me. Not that I didn't have a thirst for knowledge. In some ways it was insatiable. At home I worked nonstop on my amplifiers, and my marionette theatre, and read everything I could on the subjects. I was bored stiff with *Quentin Durward*, but of my own free will I waded through the *Admiralty Handbook of Wireless Telegraphy*, which to most people would have been dull reading indeed, and I knew all there was to know about bicycles. And as with the *Magnet*, I read catalogues from cover to cover and could have recited the cast list from a hundred films. But when it came to things like history and geography, nobody actually set my mind alight.

Brother Ambrose will never darken the doorway of the Café de la Paix. I'm sure he was very well thought of, but I didn't think much of him at the time.

Nor, I imagine, did he think very much of me. He must have considered me one of his failures. And yet, I suppose I do owe him a debt of gratitude, for he was instrumental in shaping my life. He helped make me want to leave school at the earliest possible moment and he instilled in me a desire to prove myself in other ways.

In 1990 the BBC invited me to a party being held at the Lime Grove studios to mark their final closing.

The old scene dock, now empty of flats, had been turned into a buffet and was packed with familiar faces. Some came bounding up, hardly changed after almost twenty-five years; others hobbled around on crutches looking hard done by, and there were some noticeable gaps in the ranks.

It was a strange occasion; a step back into the past. But the memory of the happy times I had spent in television was still fresh in my mind and I felt sad as I said goodbye for the last time. Sad that in more ways than one the party was over. Sad as I left the building at saying goodbye to studio H, where Percy Thrower nailed his onions to the floor and where, one memorable evening, all three cameras broke down in quick succession and we went off the air and nearly went home as well. Except we didn't. We waited around until one by one they were mended and we carried on again, wondering if anyone was still watching.

The Lime Grove studios have been knocked down. There was no last-minute reprieve, and where they once stood there are now blocks of flats. The piles of rubble must have been full of memories, but they have been carted away and disposed of. I was lucky to have worked there when I did, for it had been a period of great creativity. In many ways the viewing public never had it so good, and probably never will again. There was a spirit of adventure, of pushing things to their limit, and there was something for everyone.

In twenty-five years the world has changed and television has changed with it. Technically, anything is possible nowadays, but maximizing viewing figures within fixed time slots at minimum cost is all too often the order of the day. It needs a dedicated person with the rare talent of Dennis Potter and the will to 'fight and kick and bite' to triumph over such constrictions. There is a lot to be said for the days when programmes occasionally finished early and there was time to relax for a few minutes, watching the hands of a potter at work on his wheel, or the endlessly viewable speeded-up film of the London to Brighton train journey. At least with the latter you knew you had six minutes in which to relax. There was even a time when the BBC rang a bell during the interval of a play to warn viewers to take their seats again. Nowadays they are hardly allowed to draw breath in case they switch channels.

The public's attention span has become minimal. Increasingly the cry is 'What's new?', and the sad truth is that the more channels there are, the less chance there is of finding anything new. A short spell of 'channel surfing' in America effectively demonstrates that more is seldom better. Now digital television has opened up the possibility of five hundred channels or more, and one's heart sinks.

In twenty-five years the BBC itself has changed. Standards have slipped. Once upon a time it led by example; a guardian, not just of speech but of the nation's good manners and behaviour. Now, like a vicar coming down from his pulpit, adopting a matey approach with his flock to show that at heart he is really just like the rest of us, it has lost its mystique and the respect it once enjoyed.

The great ship of broadcasting has been decimated. Much of it has been dismantled, often in the very areas which made it the envy of the world. The days when anything needed was provided 'in-house' at the turn of a tap have gone for ever. In many respects it is a remake of the demise of Hollywood.

That many good things manage to survive is a tribute to those who are prepared to do battle for what they believe in, come what may.

Over the years the world of children's books has changed enormously too. Picture books for the very young still thrive, albeit often packaged along with a toy or some other desirable object, but nowadays they have to do battle with CD-ROMs and all manner of other distractions which can be worked at the touch of a button. Demand for books in the middle age range has suffered accordingly. Many more children now grow up without ever having discovered the joy of reading to themselves, and that in turn is beginning to be reflected in the sales of adult books where the law of supply and demand prevails.

But one lives in hope. Fashions come and go; in food, in clothes, in all the many things which are part and parcel of our daily lives. In the long term they tend to go the full circle, not once but many times.

People who read books have always been in a minority and books are like truffles, the 'black diamond' of the culinary world; highly prized by those who are prepared to seek them out.

At the turn of the century it was estimated that some 2,000 tons of truffles annually found their way into the Paris markets. Then came the First World War and they all but disappeared. France had only just begun to recover when the Second World War dealt the country another devastating blow. When peace was finally restored there came the great electronic revolution and the pace of life accelerated. Few had the patience to plant acorns and wait ten or fifteen years in the hope that they would eventually find *tuber melanosporum* beneath the roots of oak trees; understandably they wanted to catch up on all the things they had missed out on.

However, in the end you get out of life what you are prepared to put into it, no more and often a great deal less, and there are refreshing signs of the wheel beginning to turn. A new generation, suffering a surfeit of life in the fast lane with all its attendant problems, their palates jaded by an increasingly industrialized food industry, is gradually returning to its roots.

They are starting to read the small print on the packets, and there is a growing demand for pesticide-free, organically grown vegetables, farmhouse cheese, meat from humanely reared animals and for produce which is free of chemical additives. Truffle-oak saplings are being planted and the search for the 'black diamond' is once again on. Perhaps, as people grow tired of pressing buttons and staring at screens, the same thing will happen with books, the food of the mind.

On the whole, one has to be patient and accept the world as it is, not as one would like it to be; there is no future in living in the past, and there is no turning back the clock.

I doubt, for example, if I would ever have returned to the house in Reading where I spent the first nine years or so of my life had it not been for another invitation. It arrived out of the blue from a national newspaper asking me if I would contribute to a series they were running about childhood memories.

I viewed the occasion with a certain amount of trepidation, wondering who might open the door. A Chinaman? A man from outer space? A Chinaman from outer space? The reality was a bit of a let-down; there was nobody at home. So I explored the immediate neighbourhood instead.

The primary school where I pretended to be asleep during the afternoon's compulsory rest period is still there, but the playground now has a high wire-mesh fence around it, rather like a zoo. Whether it's to protect the children from the outside world or vice versa is hard to say.

The narrow passageway leading to the back of our old house, along which I used to hurry on my way home, has been snipped off at some time, taking with it part of the back garden, in order to make room for a row of lock-up garages.

Prospect Park, where I used to play endless games of cricket with my father, is still intact. Olga would make a meal of the grass and Paddington might well have a go at batting, provided Pommes Frites fetched the ball, which I'm sure he would. One of the nice things about being an author is that you are never alone.

Old Mrs Robins' corner shop where we bought our groceries has gone back to being a house again, which is what it must have been originally. But the newsagent where my father introduced me to the *Magnet* has survived, although its new owners are rather duskier than I remember.

The streets where I once played as a child, and which hardly ever saw a car, are now mostly one-way, with signs saying RESIDENTS PARKING. And when you reach the Oxford Road other signs indicate LEFT TURN ONLY, forcing drivers to head out of town rather than enter Reading.

Having invented the automobile and made a near-necessity of it by closing railway lines and bus routes, we now wish we hadn't and do everything possible to make the ownership of a car seem anti-social; towing it away, clamping its wheels, slapping tickets on the windscreen, or sending it packing so that it becomes someone else's problem.

When I eventually returned to Gloucester Road, having first made an appointment, it was by train and I walked the three-quarters of a mile or so from Reading station, making little excursions on the way: past the building in Friar Street where I had my first job in a solicitor's office, and after a year joined the BBC, then only a few doors away. The damage caused by the bombs, which at the time nearly tore my world apart, was only a pin-prick compared to all the changes that have taken place since at the hands of developers.

Of the nine cinemas I knew as a boy, only two are left; the Odeon, and what was the Central, now the MGM, both subdivided into three small units.

Their place in the world of entertainment has been largely usurped by video stores, offering up copies of films made to be seen on a large screen in the dark by an audience of several hundred, and paced accordingly. Viewed at home by two or three people behaving as they never would in a theatre or a cinema – getting up and walking around from time to time to pour another drink, make a cup of tea or answer the phone; arguing about what they saw him or her in last, or isn't he or she like so and so and hasn't she aged – the effect is often a pale shadow of the original, only one degree better than watching it on the back of someone else's aircraft seat, which has to be the worst fate of all to befall a film-maker.

Next door to the Odeon, where the Palace Theatre once stood, there is now a row of nondescript shops, but by closing my eyes I could still hear the orchestra tuning up and the sound of the applause and feel the tingle of excited anticipation as the curtain went up.

Castle Hill, where as a child I learned to fly a Reading Corporation bus, is now more suited to landing a jumbo jet, being part of a vast inner circulatory system. Its coming has meant the demise of many old shops, including the one belonging to Tim's parents, where I used to pick up a parcel of 'the usual' for one of the school Brothers, but the traffic wouldn't be allowed to park anyway.

Another casualty is the old pub where N.K. and I spent our last evening together before I went into the Air Force, and where shyness prevented my giving a simple answer to a simple question.

Missing, too, are the smells I remember looking forward to when I was out doing my deliveries around the town: roasting coffee beans as I passed the Cadena Café on a Monday morning, the bitter-sweet smell of yeast on days when Simonds were brewing their beer, freshly baked bread.

Huntley & Palmers, Suttons Seeds and Simonds Brewery, once the mainstays of the town and its *raison d'être*, are all gone; Suttons uprooted to Cornwall, the other two swallowed up by larger combines.

The town is dotted with monuments to its past benefactors; statues and parks, streets and houses, but somehow it seems to lack a soul, and one doesn't need to walk far to find the reason.

Like other towns of its size, Reading evolved slowly over the years. The men who helped create it during the Industrial Revolution were also the driving force behind the building of new roads and the transport systems and the housing of the population. And when they had made their fortunes, more often than not they repaid the town in full by devoting their energies to serving the community, helping to found the university, becoming the mayors and the aldermen and Members of Parliament; planning for future generations. Many of their names are enshrined on the street signs.

Now they are all gone and in the space of a few years much of what they achieved has been pulled down. Whole areas have been razed and the gaps filled with anonymous-looking tower blocks occupied for the most part by the outposts of vast conglomerates with a remote hierarchy, who have no interest in the town other than the ease of communication and a readily available labour force, and who would wash their hands of it without a second thought if it suited them. Power is increasingly shifting away from government into the hands of the few. Labour has been casualized and there is an abdication of responsibility. In the process people have lost their respect for authority, but then more often than not authority does very little to earn it.

It reminded me of *Drayneflete Revealed*, Osbert Lancaster's classic postwar book about the rise and fall of an English country town.

All the same, at various points along the way I came across little pockets of memories which remain more or less intact.

The café in the Harris Arcade where over endless cups of coffee I fell in love with N.K., and where years later love blossomed yet again with Brenda, survives – albeit under another name and nowhere near as romantic as I remember it.

The Lloyds Bank where one day I was called in by the manager and made to feel a criminal because of a relatively modest overdraft is still there, a monument to the folly of investing in 'futures'; in my case a landlady who, until she suddenly decided her own future lay in married life, had been extremely tardy in paying in my cheques. Nowadays overdrafts have become respectable and I would probably be welcomed with open arms.

At the time I didn't dare tell my father. Besides, although he never told me, I knew he'd had to sell his precious gold watch when I married Brenda, and I didn't want to embarrass him. I went to a money lender instead and for something like 100 per cent interest endured the washing of the oily hands in invisible soap and the invitation to come and see him again should I ever feel the need. Fortunately I never did.

In the Forbury Gardens, where one dark night Mrs Chambers' hot breath had set my pulse racing, if nothing else, old men sat enjoying the autumn sunshine as they read their newspapers, or perhaps they too were dreaming of days gone by and their own youthful adventures.

And there, beyond the railway bridge in the Oxford Road, was the little lane leading up to Reading West station, where I used to wait impatiently with my bucket and spade for the first puff of steam heralding the train which would take us all on holiday.

It being a small world, when I finally reached my old home the girl who opened the door revealed that she worked in publishing, so there was an immediate rapport.

Memories came flooding back. There, in front of me, was the flight of stairs down which I used to run at top speed after pulling the lavatory chain, intent on reaching the bottom before the cistern stopped filling. In my mind's eye the world always stopped for a moment, its inhabitants watching my progress with bated breath.

The house felt warm and friendly. It wasn't just the central heating, or the wall-to-wall carpeting in place of varnished floorboards and rugs. The changes that had taken place were things that I would have done too had I still been living there; turning the two downstairs rooms into one, filling the alcoves with books, replacing doors with archways.

The kitchen was full of gadgets; refrigerator, washing machine, central-heating boiler; things undreamed of in my mother's day. Gone was the old copper boiler which from the 'crack of dawn' on wash days was always full of 'scalding hot' water, and along with it the wooden table with its covering of chequered American oil-cloth and memories of breakfasts past.

Where the back door used to be there is now a picture window, through which there is a view of the garden with its tiny lawn where I pitched my first tent and for a treat was allowed to sleep out one night with Binkie. Afterwards we both pretended we had enjoyed the experience, although I think Binkie was as glad as I was to get back to his own bed.

I found myself wishing my parents could have been there to see it all, for I'm sure they would have felt at home too, and I could have thanked them for my childhood, which I never did. It is the kind of thing one always leaves until it's too late.

Most of all I could have thanked them for giving me a love of books and the gift of being able to read them at an early age, for it brought me not only immeasurable pleasure but my livelihood too.

But there is no going back. Besides, the bathroom has been modernized. I'm not sure that I would trust the sleek new toilet to keep on flushing until I reached the bottom of the stairs, and who knows what might happen if I didn't make it?

Muggeridge

Richard Ingrams

With calm authority Ingrams has managed to contain wonder-
ully well the outrageously unquiet spirit of a great journalist'
PENELOPE FITZGERALD, *Independent*

A Fabian idealist who was the first journalist to expose the
horrors of Stalinism; a hard-drinking philanderer who was
transformed into 'St Mugg', evangelical Catholic and
conscience of the nation; the controversial editor of *Punch* who
became the voice of orthodoxy, Malcolm Muggeridge was a
man of endless contradictions.

Richard Ingrams, long-time friend and admirer of Muggeridge,
penetrates the restless and troubled private life of a man who,
despite his seeming inconsistencies, remained constant in his
unerring sense of the absurd and pretentious, his fierce indepen-
dence of opinion and his deep suspicion of political messiahs.
His engrossing narrative incorporates many fascinating aspects
of Britain's post-war culture and society, encountering along the
way some of this century's most celebrated figures: Gandhi,
Khrushchev, Montgomery, Beatrice Webb, Graham Greene,
George Orwell, P.G. Wodehouse, Mother Teresa, and the
Beatles.

Drawing on private papers, including intimate correspondence,
Muggeridge is an unflinchingly honest portrait of an extraordinary and complex man.

'This accomplished and perceptive book makes such compul-
sive reading that I missed lunch and dinner to finish it at a
sitting'   RAYMOND CARR, *Literary Review*

Madam Speaker

A Biography

Paul Routledge

The first biography of the queen of parliament who, as Speaker of the House of Commons, has captured the hearts and minds of the British people.

From her humble beginnings as the only child of an impoverished textile-working couple in the Pennine town of Dewsbury, Betty Boothroyd rose through the Labour ranks to become a figure almost as well-recognised around the world as Lady Thatcher or Princess Margaret, and has carved a unique place for herself in the nation's affections. She has brought to the hurly-burly of the House particular qualities of charm, dignity, firm diplomacy and – most importantly – a sense of humour, rising above the pettiness of inter-party rivalry to wield quiet authority.

Madam Speaker is a thoughtful and revealing account of her life by one of Britain's leading political commentators. From her early desire 'to change society', through her adventurous career as a dancer, to the political foothills of the Labour party and to the Speakership itself, Routledge shows how Boothroyd fought for recognition in the man's world of Westminster and, as Speaker, has impressed the stamp of her own unusual personality on this most demanding of roles.

'Routledge begins in a spirit of tribute but is too good a journalist to leave stones unturned'

MALCOLM RUTHERFORD, *Financial Times*

'An exhaustive investigation'

CHARLES POWELL, *Sunday Telegraph*